The Gourmet Chinese Regional Cookbook

by CALVIN B.T. LEE
and AUDREY EVANS LEE

The Gourmet Chinese Regional Cookbook

CASTLE

To
Audrey Wilcke Evans
and
Hugh Bean Evans

Drawings by Honi Werner
The map of China on pages 14 and 15 is by Patrick Leeson.
It is from *Living in China* by Andrew Watson,
published by B. T. Batsford Limited, London, and reproduced
by permission of the publisher.

Arrangement has been made to publish this edition by Castle Books,
a division of Book Sales Inc. of Secaucus, New Jersey

PRINTED IN THE UNITED STATES OF AMERICA

ISBN NO.: 0-89009-384-9

JUNE – 1982

The CASTLE trademark is registered in
the U.S. Patent and Trademark Office.

Contents

INTRODUCTION

CHINA is a vast country of great diversity. Bordered on the west by the soaring Himalayas, on the north by the harsh Gobi desert, and on the south and east by the Pacific, China encompasses an extraordinary range of climates and landscapes. The north of China, separated from the rest of the country by the Tsinling Mountains, whose highest peak reaches eleven thousand feet, is arid, windy, and dusty, with Arctic winters and scorching summers. The semitropical south, on the other hand, is blessed with a constant year-round temperature that supports abundant yields of bananas, oranges, and lychees. In the southeast are found the fantastic karst hills of Kwangsi and Kweichow that inspired Chinese landscape artists. In the west the fjordlike gorges of the Yangtze River give way to large, placid lakes and gently rolling hills on its lower course.

China is also a land of 700 million people who throughout their long history have demonstrated an almost obsessive interest in matters gastronomic. It is a land where people greet each other not with a "Good morning—how are you?" but rather with "Have you eaten?" From earliest times, a respect, even a reverence, for food has permeated all levels of society from the peasant working his tiny plot of land patiently, diligently, for his family's survival to the scholars, princes, and even emperors who unashamedly wrote treatises and lyrical poems on the subject. Gastronomy, in short, was placed alongside philosophy, literature, and the fine arts as a suitable concern for the wealthy, powerful, and wise.

Legends, rituals, and festivals are intimately intertwined with food. In China a man has at least three banquets given in his honor during his life time. The first takes place one month after his birth. Red-colored eggs are served at the end of the meal to symbolize good luck and fertility. The second is held at his wedding. The third is after his funeral. This is the only banquet at which fresh fish is served. The meal is eaten on the floor and traditionally bean curd is served to the guests.

Reflecting an adventuresome spirit, Chinese culinary history is full of such curious delicacies as bear's paw, camel's hump, shark's fin, fish lips, and a soup featuring the flesh of a poisonous snake which, for whatever reason, may be eaten only in the winter. On a more prosaic level, one reads that menus in the Sung Dynasty (c. A.D. 1000) featured such items as "brushwood eels" (grasshoppers) and even "household deer," a felicitous label for the ubiquitous rat. We will not discuss the proverbial "two-

11

legged mutton" of that same period whose origin is best left to the imagination, although it should be mentioned that it came in various grades, each admired for its special qualities.

Some have suggested that this preoccupation with food was the result of chronic food scarcity. This may well be so, but one is led to comment that few societies have been so inventive with so little. The cooking of China ranges from delicate wine sauces to rich stews and burning curries. The Chinese relish every taste sensation: hot, bitter, salty, sweet, and sour, frequently combining two or more in a single dish and delighting in the contrast. Texture, too, has been treasured to a much greater extent than in Western cooking, as in the rich glutinous quality of shark's fin, the fresh crispness of bean sprouts, the delicate smoothness of Chicken Velvet, the crunchiness of cloud ear fungus.

A degree of whimsey indicative of more than routine interest in food can be found in the names of such dishes as Squirrel Fish, Drunken Chicken, and Peking Dust. There is a legend about Emperor Chien Lung of the Manchu dynasty who was touring through Hangchow when he stopped at a peasant's food stand and asked the peasant to serve him lunch. The poor frightened peasant put together the few meager ingredients which he had and served the dish to the emperor, who enjoyed it so much that he asked what it was called. The peasant, not wanting the lord to know what was actually in the dish, called it "red-beaked green parrot with jade cake." After the emperor executed several palace chefs because they could not reproduce this dish by cooking a parrot with a piece of valuable jade, the peasant was finally summoned to the palace where he confessed that the dish he had served to the emperor was actually spinach with red roots and fried bean curd.

When taken as a whole, Chinese cuisine is perhaps the richest and most varied in the world. But to understand this variety—its why and wherefore—one must look to its roots: the many regional cooking styles of China. Each region has its own distinctive style of cooking which, as we shall see, is based on the climate, the topography, the crops that can be grown, the availability of fuel, the history and traditions of the people who live there.

For this reason, we are embarking on a gastronomic grand tour of China. We will start with the eastern coast, centering on Shanghai which has perhaps the most representative cuisine of China. From there we shall proceed to the north, the birthplace of the civilization and traditional center of government with its own very distinct gastronomic traditions deeply influenced by constant contact with the nomadic people to the north of China. Then we will explore the west of China, an isolated region whose food is redolent of spices and peppers. Finally, we will look at the south, where natural bounty has made possible perhaps the greatest variety of tastes and dishes. But first, a bit of history to set the stage.

The Food and Cooking
of China: *A Historic Overview*

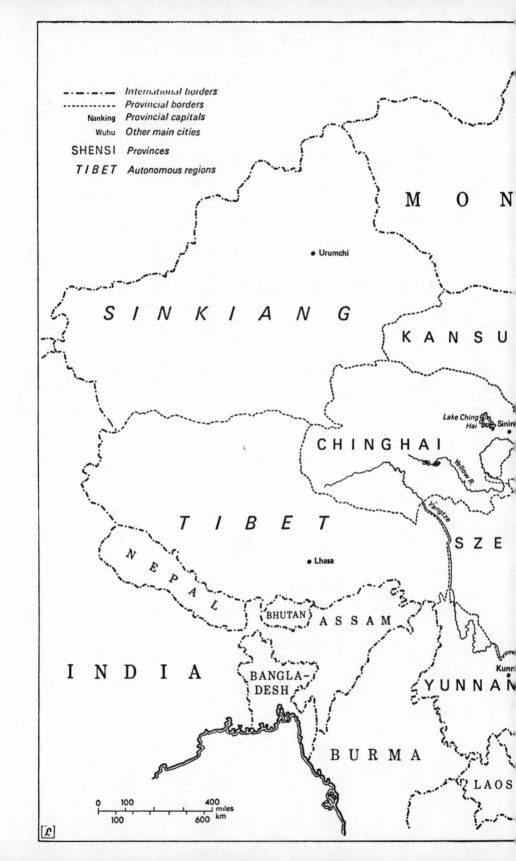

M O N

• Urumchi

S I N K I A N G

K A N S U

Lake Ching Hai • Sinin

C H I N G H A I

Yellow R.

Yangtze

S Z E

T I B E T

N E P A L

• Lhasa

BHUTAN

A S S A M

I N D I A

BANGLA-
DESH

Y U N N A N

Kunn

B U R M A

LAOS

0   100   400 miles
   100   600 km

MOST of China's early history is veiled in myth and legend. Historians have been hard put to explain the beginnings of this society which, by the first millennium B.C., had evolved a brilliant and sophisticated culture. What is presently known is that Chinese civilization emerged first in north central China near the point where the Yellow and Wei rivers converge. There, the treeless, naturally terraced loess gives way to the great North China plain that stretches eastward for hundreds of miles to the mountains of Shantung and the sea. From earliest times the Chinese led an agricultural existence that set them apart from the nomadic herdsmen to the north and west and the hunters of the forests to the south and east. Their crops included millet and wheat, and a number of animals were domesticated and raised for food, among them sheep, goats, pigs, and dogs. In most primitive cultures, the domesticated dog was valued primarily as a companion and aid to the hunter. In China, however, where agriculture rather than hunting was always the principal means of obtaining food, the dog himself was raised for food.

Viewing themselves from a very early period as a civilized people surrounded by barbarians, they called their land the Central Country, later translated as the Middle Kingdom, which is still the Chinese name for China.

By 1000 B.C. distinctively Chinese communities could be found throughout the Great Plain. There was also the beginning of expansion toward the forests of the south and the Yangtze River Valley. The barbarians of these regions were either assimilated or pushed back before the advancing Chinese who cleared the land and planted their crops. Typically, these farmers lived inside walled villages for protection against brigands and barbarians, going out to the fields during the day to farm their crops. To protect their land from encroachment by the nomads from the north, construction of what was to be the Great Wall was begun along the border between the arid lands of the nomads, and the cultivable lands of the Chinese. Such large scale public works coincided with the development of an intricate class structure. Elaborate planned cities were built usually as local centers of government. The primitive pictographic system of writing rapidly evolved into the sophisticated abstract system we know today. Artistic mastery may be seen in the magnificent bronze vessels that have survived from this period. Here clearly was a distinctive and highly sophisticated society.

By the middle of the first millennium B.C silk had become an important product, lacquer work had been developed, and copper coins very much like those used today had replaced shells as common currency. Iron smelting was by then widespread and iron was readily available to the common man, unlike bronze which was limited to the elite. Iron tools replaced wooden ones and as a result agricultural productivity increased. Major flood control projects were undertaken along the Wei and Yellow rivers. It was the beginning of the age of the philosophers and the classics dominated by such figures as Confucius and Mencius.

An elaborate cuisine was available at least for the upper classes. The staple food animals were pig, duck, goat, and chicken. Fish was also favored. For the rich, there was such game as boar, bear, wolf, hare, deer, quail, and pheasants as well as the more exotic edibles such as turtles and snails.

As the Chinese moved into the Yangtze River basin they learned to cultivate rice from the indigenous tribes of that region. Rice began to replace wheat as the staff of life in all but the north of China. Salt curing and pickling were developed to preserve food. Dishes were steamed, grilled, roasted, and deep-fried, although the typical Chinese technique of stir-frying had not as yet evolved. Food was seasoned with ginger, garlic, scallions, cassia which resembles cinnamon, a form of artemisia related to the French tarragon, a variety of cardamom, and vinegar. Peaches, quince, and plums were widely raised in the north. Chopsticks replaced fingers and knives as utensils by the third century. The concept of the five flavors (salty, sour, bitter, sweet, and hot) were well established.

Portions of two poems from the *Ch'u Tz'u*, written in the late Chou dynasty, provide a vivid picture of the best Chinese cooking during this early period:

> O soul, come back. Why should you go far away?
> All your household have come to do you honor; all kinds of good
>   food are ready:
> Rice, broom-corn, early wheat, mixed all with yellow millet;
> Bitter, salt, sour, hot and sweet: there are dishes of all flavours,
> Ribs of the fatted ox cooked tender and succulent;
> Sour and bitter blended in the soup of Wu;
> Stewed turtle and roast kid, served up with yam sauce;
> Geese cooked in sour sauce, casseroled duck, fried flesh of the
>   great crane;
> Braised chicken, seethed tortoise, high-seasoned, but not to
>   spoil the taste;
> Fried honey-cakes of rice flour and malt-sugar sweetmeats;

Jadelike wine, honey-flavored, fills with winged cups;
Ice-cooled liquor, strained of impurities, clear wine, cool and
refreshing;
Here are laid out the patterned ladles, and here is sparkling wine.

The five grains are heaped up six ells high, and corn of zizania
set out;
The cauldrons seethe to their brims; their blended savours yield
fragrance;
Plump orioles, pigeons, and geese, flavoured with broth of jack-
als' meat;
O soul, come back! Indulge your appetite!
Fresh turtle, succulent chicken, dressed with a sauce of Ch'u;
Pickled pork, dog cooked in bitter herbs, and zingiber-flavoured
mince,
And sour Wu salad of artemisia, not too wet or tasteless,
O soul, come back! Indulge in your own choice!
Roast crane is served up, and steamed duck and boiled quails,
Fried bream, stewed magpies, and green goose, broiled.
O soul, come back! Choice things are spread before you.
The four kinds of wine are all matured, not rasping to the throat;
Clear, fragrant, ice-cooled liquor, not for base men to drink;
And white yeast is mixed with must of Wu to make the clear
Ch'u wine.
O soul, come back and do not be afraid!*

Imperial food preparation had become an important and highly specialized process. Records show that fully 60 percent of the 4,000 people re-
sponsible for running the various imperial palaces dealt in food and wine.
These included 162 dieticians, 70 meat specialists, 128 chefs for the imperial family's food, 128 chefs for food served to guests, 62 assistant
chefs, 335 specialists in grains, vegetables, and fruit, 62 specialists in
game, 342 specialists in fish, 24 specialists in turtle and shellfish, 28 meat
dryers, 110 wine officers, 340 wine servers, 94 icemen, 31 bamboo-tray
servers, 61 meat-platter servers, 62 pickle and sauce specialists, 62 salt-
men, and even 170 who specialized in a mystery called the "six drinks."
Although a common culture and a strong sense of Chinese identity were
to be found extraordinarily early in Chinese history, political unity was
elusive until the third century B.C. when the kings of the tiny kingdom of

*From David Hawkes, *Ch'u Tz'u: The Songs of the South*, © Oxford University
Press 1959. Reprinted by permission of the Oxford University Press, Oxford.

Ch'in unified the Chinese. The brief Ch'in dynasty, perhaps best remembered for its infamous book burning, also effected the standardization of measurement, language, currency, and gauge of cartwheels.

It was during the four hundred years of the Han dynasty from 206 B.C. to A.D. 220 that China reached a peak of social and cultural greatness. In recognition of this achievement the Chinese still refer to themselves as the Han people. The conquered lands of the Ch'in were consolidated, and the native states in the area of Yunnan and Kweichow were brought under Chinese suzerainty for the first time. The lands around Kwangtung, though conquered, were not colonized but ruled by the Chinese through local tribes.

Perhaps more important for our concerns was the establishment of Chinese domination of the Kansu corridor in the northwest and beyond to central Asia. Quasi-agricultural, quasi-military outposts were set up in the Kansu corridor to maintain order, and irrigated patches of green appeared in the desert. Through the corridor came caravans traveling west along the Silk Road, marking the first significant trade with western Asia and even the Roman Empire. Silk, ginger, and cassia flowed westward. Rome became so enamored of Chinese silk that the Emperor Tiberius forbade men to wear silken garments in order to keep enough for the women. Not surprisingly, the Romans gave China the name "Seres," a word derived from the word for silk. Returning caravans brought precious stones, ivory, wool, linen, and other luxury items. They also brought grapes and new grains from India and horses from central Asia to enrich the local stock. Even so, China exported a great deal more than she imported, a source of concern for Roman emperors who saw their gold and silver vanishing forever into the East. Although trade was not direct during this period, some knowledge of the ways of other civilizations did creep across the thousands of miles that separated them.

It was toward the end of the Han dynasty that tea became known as a refreshing beverage, particularly along the Yangtze where the evergreen shrub *Thea sinensis* grew. Many legends surround its discovery. One of the oldest attributes its discovery to Emperor Chu-ming. During a cholera epidemic this philosopher-king discovered that if water was boiled before drinking, the disease would not be contracted. He therefore ordered all his subjects, on penalty of death, to boil their water. One day a leaf from a nearby tea bush fell into the emperor's cup of unpalatable boiled water. He tasted it, liked it, and a delicious new drink was found.

After the Han Empire crumbled as a result of internal dissension, China entered a politically chaotic period for the next four hundred years in which she reverted to her feudal past. In A.D. 304 a flood of invasion from the north began. Large numbers of Chinese fled to the relative safety of Szechwan and the Kansu corridor, but most of all to the Yangtze River basin to escape these marauding invaders who eventually gained control of the north in 316. Han society was reestablished in the south with Nanking as the capital for a series of short-lived and ineffectual dynasties. Politically it was a period of constant revolts alternating with unsuccessful attempts by the Chinese to reconquer their northern homelands. Even so, this turbulent period marked a major development of China beyond the purview of the North China Plain. Hard-earned knowledge was transferred from the marginal agricultural regions of the north to the fertile regions beyond with the result that thousands were able to live off land which in the past had supported hundreds. With the court in Nanking, eastern and south China began to rival the north in sophistication. Sericulture and porcelain industries flourished and became major components of the southern economy. Technological advances increased productivity throughout China. The invention of the watermill made more effective irrigation possible and led to a greater output of refined flours. The efficient wheelbarrow was invented centuries before it appeared in Europe. Coal was discovered and its long-burning qualities helped offset the need for firewood in the treeless north. Buddhism arrived in China and its establishment as a major philosophical system, as a matter of culinary interest, led to the development of a very elaborate vegetarian school of cooking.

About A.D. 300, Arab traders arrived in Canton and established a colony which was to endure for generations. The Arabs were to provide a steady commerce between China, India, Africa, and even Europe. It was through the route used by the Arabs, for example, that the noodle found its way from China through the Middle East to Europe perhaps by as early as the eleventh century. With the Silk Road closed by the northern tribes, the sea route to India and beyond was of considerable importance. Through this route the chair was introduced to China from India and over the centuries gradually replaced sitting pads and mats.

Meanwhile, in the north, the northern invaders were discovering that there were simply too many Chinese to have foreign ways imposed upon them. Gradually Chinese again became the language of state, and the Chinese administrators ran the state in their Han manner. The barbarians came to admire and adopt Chinese ways and customs, and began to intermarry with the Chinese. After a few generations the barbarians found themselves so assimilated that it was impossible for them to view themselves as anything other than Chinese. Thus, when the south was brought under the control of the north at the beginning of the brief Sui dynasty in 589, the cultural clash of this union was negligible.

The great T'ang and Sung dynasties ruled almost without interruption for the next seven centuries until 1279, and this period represents another high point in Chinese history. The Chinese Empire was restored. Great palaces were built and the Grand Canal was constructed to transport rice from the Yangtze Valley rice-growing area to the imperial tables at Sian and Loyang on the Yellow River. Trade resumed along the Silk Road and increased by sea as naval technology improved through the invention of the compass and other discoveries. This increase in maritime trade stimulated the development of the southeast coast and its ultimate integration into the Chinese empire.

From the Indians the Chinese learned how to make sugar out of sugarcane and wine out of grapes, although grape wine was to remain something of an expensive curiosity. Kohlrabi was introduced from Europe, pistachio nuts from Persia, spinach and perhaps a form of celery from Nepal. Students arrived from Korea and Japan for a thorough indoctrination in Chinese civilization. The main demand from the West was still for silk and art objects, but the tea trade was beginning as well. Fragments of Chinese porcelain from the Sung dynasty have been found as far afield as Zanzibar and Egypt. The arts flourished with exquisite figure and animal paintings and lovely porcelain.

In 1125 the Jurched tribes from the northern steppes invaded China and so, for the latter half of the Sung Empire, the capital of China was again moved to the Yangtze River, this time to Hangchow. In 1234 the Mongols under Genghis Khan routed the Jurcheds from northern China and proceeded to conquer the rest of China. The Mongols were among the most primitive of the Asian peoples and were not at all well received by the Chinese who viewed them as uncouth, immoral, brutish, superstitious, and given to great excesses.

In the face of native hostility, the Mongols in China as elsewhere employed many foreigners, particularly Moslems from central and western Asia, as administrators. Descendants of these administrators may still be found in Kansu and southwestern China. Islam has remained an important faith particularly in those areas. The control of the Mongols over the whole sweep of central Asian trade routes permitted for the first time the travel of a number of Europeans to the court of China. Some of these travelers were Franciscan monks sent by the papacy for diplomatic and evangelical purposes. Some were merchants like Marco Polo. Through these travelers word of China drifted back to Europe, accounts of China's black stones that burn, of bound feet, of long fingernails, and of the cormorant—that strange breed of birds trained to fish for its master. Chinese inventions such as gunpowder, paper money, printing, paper, and playing cards were introduced to Europe and were incorporated into European life. Some of the tales of Marco Polo and others sounded so incredible to European ears that they were not believed for several centuries.

The Mongols were followed in 1368 by the Ming and later the Manchu dynasties which ruled through the beginning of the twentieth century. Although the Manchus were another alien people, they, like their predecessors, were rapidly assimilated into Chinese culture and failed to make any significant social changes save for imposing their curious custom of shaving men's heads and wearing a queue. This span of more than five hundred years was one of remarkable peace and prosperity. Yet it was not a period of dynamic growth or of scientific and cultural breakthroughs. Instead of building for a new and different future, the Chinese chose to recreate earlier periods of Chinese greatness, namely the Han and T'ang dynasties. Originality in the arts declined. Perfection and refinement of old art forms was held in higher esteem than possibly coarse originality. All things new were viewed with suspicion and mistrust, although science and technology progressed. However, as the Western world was emerging from its medieval trance into the Renaissance and the rapid development that followed, the Chinese chose to stand still. The most advanced civilization of its time was quickly surpassed by Western upstarts.

Although China may well have preferred to shun all contact with the rest of the world, the rest of the world would not leave her alone. China silk and tea was in great demand as was Chinese porcelain. Unfortunately, the Chinese responded to this great demand for her porcelain by making certain items particularly for export in line with what they thought foreigners would like. The result, however, was almost universally inferior.

Like the other arts, Chinese cooking during this period became increasingly refined, almost precious. Fortunately, as trade increased with the rest of the world new foods were introduced. When the Portuguese started to arrive in Canton in 1516, they brought with them plants from the New World across the Pacific. Among them were the potato, tobacco, and the capsicum pepper that was to make such a dramatic change in Chinese as well as Indian cooking. Later came the Spanish, Dutch, British, French, and American ships. Other imports were the tomato, peanuts, pineapple, papaya, and maize. More recently, even a few processed foods found their way into Chinese cooking, among them ketchup and Worcestershire sauce. Curiously enough the word "ketchup" is derived from the Chinese words meaning "brine of pickled fish," although the tomato-based condiment is strictly a Western invention. Worcestershire sauce was introduced to China by its British concocters. It is not surprising that it has found a role in Chinese cooking since its two main ingredients are soy sauce and vinegar.

Despite barbarian invasions, the rise and fall of dynasties, many intercultural contacts, and political upheaval, day-to-day Chinese life has remained for the most part unchanged for more than three thousand years of recorded history.

Fully 80 percent of the Chinese still live in the countryside or in villages of less than twenty-five thousand. Their particularly intensive form of agriculture from prehistory onward has led one observer to describe China as a nation of gardeners.

In terms of the geography of China, only about 10 percent of the land is cultivable. The rest is too dry, too hilly or mountainous, or the climate permits only a short growing season. Thus the population of the most populous country in the world has crowded into those few places where crops can be grown, namely the Yellow River basin in the north, the Lower Yangtze plain in the east, the southern coastal area around Canton, and the Red Basin of Szechwan in the west. Most of these areas have a rural population density in excess of two thousand people per square mile. Statistics from the first half of this century suggest an average of 3.7 crop acres per farm household with an average of 6.2 persons. This is in contrast to an average of 40 acres in Denmark and 155 acres in the United States during the same period.

Even when China still had areas of underdeveloped farmland, migration to these areas was slow. It took famine, barbarian invasions, wars, and other catastrophes to spur the Chinese farmer into moving from an overcrowded area where only a marginal existence was possible to an area that promised abundance. One reason was the great distances and geographical barriers between cultivable areas such as the rapids of the Yangtze gorge and the rugged hills of the south.

Perhaps a more important deterrent to migration was the extraordinary strength of the Chinese family structure which tended to keep a young man home rather than encouraging him to seek his fortune farther afield. From earliest times the family rather than the individual, the church, or the state has been the basic unit of society. It was the source of all physical, economic, and social security and one did not stray far from it. If the family was wealthy, a man and his wife would ideally live in the family compound along with other brothers, sisters, and more distant relatives. If the family was poor, they nonetheless tried to remain in the same general area. Reverence for one's ancestors and ancestor worship was and is an important precept of the Chinese people. In the north of China the burial mounds dot many fields. They significantly decrease the crop yield, but to destroy them or even move the bodies to a more convenient spot would be sacrilegious. The strength of this tie to family can be seen even in overseas Chinese communities, where numerous family societies serve as benevolent societies for all people with the same last name. Second only to the family societies are the village societies which minister to the immigrants from a particular village in China even to descendants of the second and third generation. So strong are the ties to one's extended family and one's native village that few willingly moved away. This tendency to stay put for generations when combined with a virtually nonexistent communications system encouraged the development of the many different dialects and a strong provincialism that is reflected in the various traditions, customs, even eating patterns to be found. Only the existence of a uniform writing system and a mysterious sense of Chinese history and identity seems to have held China together for these many centuries. And as people have stayed put the population has increased, creating the need for a more and more intensive use of the land.

No effort has been spared to create cultivable land. Hills have been terraced even if only enough land could be reclaimed to plant a single row. Dikes protecting flood plains have been built and rebuilt to allow for safe planting. Fertilizer is made from compost, animal, and even human wastes. China has also been systematically deforested. At one time a forest animal, the black bear, roamed over most of China. Unfortunately, this compulsive hacking down of forests has created serious soil erosion in certain parts of China. It has also led to a scarcity of lumber for buildings and easily accessible fuel for cooking.

Food is raised almost exclusively for human consumption. Grazing land is considered wasted land if wheat can be grown there. Cattle and water buffalo are cared for only because they till the fields. Indeed it is said that the Chinese take better care of their cattle than they do of themselves. If a draft animal is used for turning the irrigation wheel, the Chinese build a shed to protect the beast from the sun, but if manpower is used, no shelter of any sort is considered necessary. To eat one's faithful servant amounts to heresy in many parts of China. Because goats and sheep need pastureland they are not particularly common in China. Meat is synonymous with pork, for the small Chinese pig feeds happily on table scraps or just about anything that can be found in the farmyard. The pig matures in a year and then goes on to produce two litters of up to a dozen piglets every year thereafter. Chicken and ducks are similarly prolific and consequently popular. Of course, fish and seafood are free for the catching.

In addition to the ordinary methods of catching fish using a baited line or nets, the Chinese employ an ingenious fish-catcher—the cormorant. Cormorants are fish-eating birds. A ring is placed around their necks so they cannot swallow the fish. Sometimes they are attached to the boat by string but most are so well trained that they return to the boat voluntarily, knowing that at the end of the day the ring will be removed so they can share in the catch.

This scarcity of food, land, and timber has very much affected the way in which food is prepared and served throughout China. First of all the general scarcity of food and the ever-present potential for starvation has led to a cuisine that utilizes whatever is available and edible. Waste could not be tolerated. Some native-born Chinese in this country—even though they have lived in a land of plenty most or all of their lives—experience a twinge of conscience when they discard so much as a grain of rice. There is a standing joke that the reason no one has found any trace of dinosaurs in China is that the Chinese ate them all. Actually, the famous carved oracle bones that were to give so much insight into early Chinese history were discovered on the market in Peking in the 1930's where they were being ground up for medicinal use. One may also speculate that the Chinese tradition of adding extra dishes to the family menu when guests dropped by rather than increasing the quantity of existing dishes was a product of poverty—of not having much of any one ingredient—rather than a search for gustatory variety. Because meat was scarce, vegetables were routinely used as a filler along with rice or noodles. Traditionally, the mean has been one part meat to three or four parts vegetable. It is significant, though, that while Confucius austerely recommended that one's breath should smell of rice rather than meat, Chinese banquets given to mark the passing of life's milestones feature a disproportionate number of meat dishes for they conspicuously convey a sense of wealth and status.

A second important factor in the development of a distinctively Chinese form of cooking has been scarcity of fuel. The Western notion of keeping a stockpot simmering away on a back burner with the consequent need to keep feeding the fire would be incongruous to most Chinese. The traditional source of cooking heat has been the brazier. It is fed with anything that will burn: charcoal and coal are preferred for their intense heat and long-lasting flame, but wood, straw, twigs, or even cakes of dried manure have served. Once the fire is going, the heat is intense and must be utilized immediately and efficiently. It was early discovered that if the ingredients were cut into smaller pieces they would cook more rapidly. If they were cut into pieces of the same size they would cook at approximately the same rate and be done at the same time. If one were going to bother to cut ingredients into the same size, it was probably rather quickly discovered that if you slice your meat across the grain it will be more tender and that if you cut stringy vegetables thinly and diagonally they will not only be more tender but will cook more evenly and quickly because more of the surface is exposed to the hot pan.

The uniquely Chinese technique of stir-frying arrived on the scene rather late, but it is a very efficient cooking technique in terms of the maximum utilization of heat. In stir-frying, small amounts of food are rapidly cooked in a small amount of fat over a very hot flame. The hot oil immediately and effectively seals in the flavor and nutritional value of the ingredients, which are kept from burning by rapid tossing. The temperature of the pan is modified by the addition of liquid and other ingredients. To keep the cooking from stopping altogether, however, the cook warms liquids by pouring them onto the hot metal of the inside of the pan before stirring them into the food. The whole process rarely takes more than five minutes.

Other cooking methods favored by the Chinese also tend to conserve fuel. Poaching is common, but instead of simmering the chicken or fish until it is done, the Chinese bring the water to a slow boil, toss in the meat, cover the pot, and remove it from the heat. The food is cooked by the retained heat in the pot. This method of poaching takes longer than the Western method of steady simmering, but it does conserve fuel.

Deep-frying is also common, for the oil heats up faster and reaches a much higher temperature than water. Steaming is popular in part because several steamers can be stacked one on top of the other over a single pot of boiling water, enabling one to cook a great deal of food over a single heat source. Pastries and breads are prepared in this manner rather than in an oven which is notoriously wasteful of fuel. Indeed, it is unusual in most Chinese houses to find an oven. Roast meats are traditionally bought ready-cooked at the market along with the few baked goods that exist.

The traditional Chinese kitchen when compared to Western kitchens is a very simple one indeed. Its implements are few, but they are capable of great versatility. It is as though the Chinese, rather than inventing a total-ly new gadget in the Western mode, preferred to modify existing tools to meet the new demands. This attitude would appear to be in keeping with the essentially conservative genius of the Chinese people.

The Chinese tile stove is a direct descendant of a simple brazier. The fire is lit below. There are no burners, merely holes in the top of the stove where the spherically shaped wok rests suspended only by its flaring sides. The flames leap up from below to touch and heat the bottom of the wok.

The wok is the basic cooking vessel. It is made of thin iron which dis-tributes the heat evenly and rapidly. Its spherical shape allows for the efficient cooking of both large and small amounts of food. It conserves cooking oil because of the small area at the bottom of the pan and readily allows tossing because of its flaring sides. In it one can cook rice, deep-fry, poach, and sauté.

Other utensils are the *siou hok* and the *wok chu* which are used together in stir-frying. The siou hok is really a ladle that also serves as a handy measuring cup as well as an instrument for stirring the food and adding liquids. The wok chu resembles a flat spoon and a pancake turner. It is also used for stirring food; its slight curve corresponds to the shape of the wok and the upturned edges hold the gravy as food is removed from the pan. In addition there are wire strainers for draining food, a pair of wood-en chopsticks for stirring liquids and tasting the food, and a porcelain soup spoon for tasting the sauce without burned lips.

To prepare the food to be cooked the Chinese need only a chopping block and a cleaver (called a *choy doh*) or two. The chopping block or *jum bahn* is simply the cross section of a tree trunk about a foot wide and half a foot thick.

Perhaps the most versatile tools of all are the Chinese cleavers that come in a variety of weights. The heavier ones are used exclusively to cut through bones. The lighter ones are used for all other cutting from slicing vegetables to boning a duck. The side of the blade is used for mashing garlic, ginger root, or flattening meats. The blunt top of the cleaver is used to tenderize meats and mince garlic and ginger root. The handle is used as a pestle to grind spices and to bruise such ingredients as brown and black beans to release their flavor. The side of the blade is used to transport ingredients from the chopping block to the wok. It can also be used to smooth out the almost transluscent pastry used to make filled dumplings.

For mincing large amounts of meat, for instance, a second cleaver of the same weight would be used to speed up the process—one cleaver for each hand. As for a honing stone, the unglazed bottom of a rice bowl or some other vessel serves quite adequately for minor sharpening.

The twentieth century has brought many changes to China. Land productivity has been increased by large-scale irrigation projects which in the northwest, for instance, have enabled fruit trees to grow where once there was only grass. Water control projects on the major rivers have reduced the frequency of major flooding and famine. Reforestation efforts followed by scientific husbandry has reduced soil erosion in many areas and provided much needed lumber for building and fuel. The stepped-up mining of coal has also led to a greater abundance of fuel for cooking.

Improved transportation and communications systems have made the greatest difference to Chinese life. With better roads and the development of rail and air transportation, the traditional provincialism of China has begun to break down. Now, new knowledge and technological advances pass rapidly from one part of China to another over substantial distances and physical barriers. Disaster relief in the form of food and medicine is possible on a much greater scale than a century ago.

Improved communications and an energetic program to make Mandarin the universal spoken language of China has also done much to mold one nation out of a people who were previously united only by a sense of common history and tradition.

In culinary terms, one can envision the almost inevitable breaking down of regional cooking styles as Chinese society becomes increasingly homogeneous. But such changes come slowly, for people are notoriously conservative when it comes to food patterns and thus one can hope that these traditions will not be entirely lost. On the other hand, the greater availability of food and the development of means of transporting it from one area to another may very well enrich the daily diet of the Chinese people both nutritionally and in terms of greater variety.

1

EAST CHINA

Kiangsu, Anhwei, Chekiang,
Fukien, Kiangsi

IF one region could typify China, it would be the eastern section along the lower course of the Yangtze River. Here where north and south China meet and occasional snow may fall on palm trees and wheat, the staple of the cold, dry north, gives way to rice, which requires the milder climate and abundant water to be found in the rest of China. In addition, the great Yangtze River connects the isolated western region with the rest of China so that, except for those who fly, all travelers from north to south and from east to west must pass through this area.

It is a region of hills and water. The Yangtze River, often called the main street of China, dominates most of east China. It and an extensive network of streams and canals provide the main means of transporting goods and people, for the swampy lowlands and the often steep hills make travel other than by foot extremely difficult. Genghis Khan ruefully faced this problem when he found his mounted warriors, who had so quickly swept through the flat, dry northern plains, slowed to a crawl by the alternately hilly and swampy terrain along the Yangtze.

Another gift of the Yangtze is the hundreds of shallow lakes around which much of China's rice is grown. Rice was probably first cultivated in Thailand over 5,000 years ago. By 1650 B.C. the original non-Chinese tribes along the Yangtze were raising it and they passed their skills on to the recently arrived Chinese immigrants from the north.

While rice and water dominate the lowlands, the hills are a source of fine silk and tea, Hangchow silk being the finest. The province of Kiangsi has rich deposits of kaolin, the clay used to make the finest Chinese porcelains.

Historically this area developed rather late. Large-scale Chinese migration to this area began only as the Yellow River plain became overcrowded and famine increasingly common. When the north fell to nomadic invaders in the fourth century A.D., the capital was moved to Nanking for the next two centuries. The presence of the imperial court led to rapid physical, economic, and cultural growth for this city and the surrounding area which at that time was the frontier of the Chinese Empire. Later, nearby Hangchow became the capital-in-exile during the Mongol conquest of the thirteenth century and it too took on a new glitter. Marco Polo, a visitor to Hangchow during that period, was so taken by it that he described it as "beyond dispute, the finest and noblest city in the world"

31

and "where so many pleasures may be found that one fancies himself to be in paradise." Hangchow's setting on the beautiful West Lake certainly must have recommended itself to the Venetian. He described the hundreds of pleasure boats always to be found on the lake. There were also boats carrying singing girls, others on which one could play various games, and still others provided all manner of food and drink.

His description of the markets gives us us some clue of the gastronomic riches of Hangchow during the period:

> [There] are ten principal markets, though besides these there are a vast number of others in the different parts of the town. . . . In each of the squares is held a market three days in the week, frequented by 40,000 or 50,000 persons, who bring thither for sale every possible necessary of life, so that there is always an ample supply of every kind of meat and game, as of roebuck, red-deer, fallow-deer, hares, rabbits, partridges, pheasants, francolins, quails, fowls, capons, and of duck and geese an infinite quantity; for so many are bred on the Lake that for a Venice groat of silver you can have a couple of geese and two couple of ducks. Then there are the shambles where the larger animals are slaughtered, such as calves, beeves, kids, and lambs, the flesh of which is eaten by the rich and great dignitaries.
>
> These markets make a daily display of every kind of vegetables and fruits; and among the latter there besides peaches in their season both yellow and white, of every delicate flavour.
>
> . . . From the Ocean Sea also come daily supplies of fish in great quantity, brought twenty-five miles up the river, and there is also a great store of fish from the lake, which is the constant resort of fishermen, who have no other business. Their fish is of sundry kinds, changing with the seasons. . . .
>
> All the ten market places are encompassed by lofty houses and below these are shops where all sorts of crafts are carried on, and all sorts of wares are on sale, including spices and jewels and pearls. Some of these shops are entirely devoted to the sale of wine made from rice and spices, which is constantly made fresh, and is sold very cheap.

The food of this region reflects many different styles. There are delicate pastries that can be consumed in one bite, perhaps descendants of those served to an emperor centuries ago, and some subtle soft-fried dishes from Soochow, a city also famed for its beautiful women. There is also shrimp toast and Yangchow fried rice, a true banquet dish only distantly related to some of its coarser and more common cousins. The rice wines produced in this area are by far the best in China and are as varied as the grape wines of Europe.

Home-style cooking is quite different, however, and perhaps the best word for it would be robust. Slowly simmered casseroles are favored, perhaps the best known being Lion's Head, a combination of meatballs and leafy green vegetables simmered in a stock. Longer cooking even of basically stir-fry dishes is common. Instead of adding liquids only at the very end of the cooking process, a Shanghai chef is more likely to lower the heat after the addition of liquids and allow the dish to simmer gently an additional fifteen or twenty minutes to blend the flavors. This technique is more akin to braising than sautéing, to use Western terms. Soy sauces are widely used and form the basis for the red sauce in which everything from fish to pork is simmered. These sauces are used over and over again, gaining in character from each dish cooked in them. To counteract the saltiness of the soy a relatively large amount of sugar is used in many recipes and this, too, is a hallmark of the cuisine. Pickled and salted greens are a traditional specialty of Ningpo and preserved foods of all kinds are a specialty throughout the region, for example, salted fish, shrimp and shrimp eggs, dried bamboo shoots, and mushrooms.

To the south of the Yangtze River plain along the coast are the provinces of Chekiang and Fukien. While the northern part of Chekiang along the Yangtze is very densely populated, as one travels southward toward Fukien the land becomes increasingly mountainous and at points even impassable. This is a land of beautiful scenery with sheer rock cliffs, broad-leaf evergreen forests, and wherever possible tiny fields clinging to a mountainside. The coastline is also rugged and dotted with hundreds of rocky islands.

The terrain has made travel and communications extremely difficult. Living in almost complete isolation from each other, many communities have over the centuries developed their own traditions. Even along the coast where the communications are somewhat easier, it is not uncommon to find one fishing area with a quite different style of junk than the next area down the coast. Furthermore, not all the people are true Chinese. In the hills live a variety of non-Chinese tribes, descendants of the first inhabitants of the region. There are also the Hakkas, or "guest people," who migrated to Fukien centuries ago from Honan in the north and provide a relatively unchanged example of the early Chinese.

Not surprisingly, more than one hundred different languages and dialects may be found in Fukien alone. Most of the Chinese in Fukien and southern Chekiang live along the coast and rely heavily upon the sea for their livelihood. Because of the lack of flat land even along the coast, all the cities have a sizable boat population made up of families who spend their entire life on water and have no home on land.

The major cities are Amoy and Foochow, famous for its fine lacquer. Until recent centuries the major port was Chuan-chou. Marco Polo was impressed: "Here is the harbour whither all the ships of India come. . . . It is also the port whither go the merchants of (South) Manji, which is the region stretching all around. In a word, in this port there is such traffic of merchandise, precious stones, and pearls, that it is truly a wondrous sight. From the harbour of this city all this is distributed over the whole of the province of Manji. And I assure you that for one shipload of pepper that goes to Alexandria or elsewhere to be taken to Christian lands, there comes a hundred to this port of Zaitun.''

Fukien was for centuries the center of the world tea market. Tea is the one crop suited to the mountainous, well-drained terrain. The belief is that the higher the elevation, the more tender the tea leaf. The moist, cool atmosphere is also thought to be good for the tea. Women have traditionally been used to pluck the leaves from this small tree that is carefully pruned to keep it a shrub, but there are stories of trees plucked by monkeys trained by Buddhist monks near Amoy who can navigate the steepest slopes.

Although Fukienese cooking is not well known outside China, it has been held in high esteem by Chinese gourmets. Some have even included Fukien among the five classic schools of cooking along with Shantung, Honan, Szechwan, and Kwangtung. They praise the simplicity of the cuisine and the respect shown for the natural sweetness of the freshest ingredients. Seafood is, as one might suspect, quite important and the Fukienese handle seafood dishes masterfully. Although Fukien is noted for its fine soy sauces, very little is used in any one dish. Vinegar and scallions are also used, but with the utmost discretion. Perhaps the most distinctively Fukienese flavoring is red wine sediment paste, a rather fruity sauce made from the lees of rice wine. This paste is almost impossible to find even in large Chinatowns and for that reason we have included at the end of this section a recipe that approximates its flavor.

RED-COOKED CHICKEN

The people of the lower Yangtze are fond of cooking their food in large quantities of soy sauce and other spices. This sauce is used again and again, and gains in character with each use.

1 chicken, about 4 pounds
1 clove garlic
1 star anise (8 sections)
1¼ cups light soy sauce
1 cup dark soy sauce

1 cup chicken stock
4 tablespoons rock sugar
1 tablespoon dry sherry
2 slices gingerroot, the size of a
  quarter

Preparation and cooking
Wash the chicken and dry thoroughly with paper towels. In a pot bring all of the remaining ingredients to a boil. Add the chicken. Simmer for 45 minutes, turning the chicken over every 10 minutes and basting often. Remove the chicken and cool. Chop into bite-size pieces. Reheat ¼ cup of the sauce and pour over the chicken just before serving.

Yield: 3–8 servings.

The following variations are very good for buffets or as appetizers.

RED-COOKED EGGS

1 dozen eggs

Boil the eggs for 15 minutes and rinse with cold water. Peel the eggs and soak overnight in sauce for Red-Cooked Chicken (see previous recipe). Slice the eggs in quarters. Serve on a bed of lettuce leaves.

Yield: 12 servings.

RED-COOKED CHICKEN WINGS

2 pounds chicken wings

Clean the chicken wings and dry thoroughly with paper towels. Simmer in sauce for Red-Cooked Chicken for 20 minutes.

Yield: 3–8 servings.

RED-COOKED CHICKEN LIVERS

½ pound chicken livers

Wash the livers and simmer in sauce for Red-Cooked Chicken for 10 minutes.

Yield: 2–4 servings.

ROCK-SUGAR CHICKEN

The people in and around Shanghai have a fondness for sugar in their cooking. Rock sugar gives the dish more body than granulated sugar and also imparts a slight glaze to the meat.

1 chicken, about 4 pounds
2 tablespoons dark soy sauce
1 tablespoon dry sherry
1 teaspoon salt
4 Chinese black mushrooms
½ cup sliced bamboo shoots
1 tablespoon rock sugar or
   light brown sugar

½ cup chicken stock
2 tablespoons peanut oil
2 slices gingerroot, the size of a
   quarter
2 teaspoons cornstarch mixed
   with 1 tablespoon water

Preparation
Chop the chicken into bite-size pieces. In a large bowl combine the soy sauce, sherry, and ½ teaspoon of the salt. Place the chicken in the bowl and marinate for 30 minutes.

Soak the mushrooms in water until they are soft, or about 30 minutes, cut off and discard the tough stems, then drain. Slice the mushrooms thinly and set them aside with the bamboo shoots, sugar, and chicken stock which will be added later all at the same time.

Cooking
Heat a wok or skillet over high heat until a drop of water immediately sizzles into steam. Add the oil, the remaining salt, and the gingerroot. Stir for 30 seconds. Add the chicken and stir-fry for 2 minutes.

Add the chicken stock, sugar, mushrooms, and bamboo shoots. Stir until the sugar has dissolved. Lower heat to medium. Cover and simmer for 15 minutes. Thicken sauce slightly with the cornstarch mixture.

Yield: 4–10 servings.

STEWED SHANGHAI CHICKEN

Although the ingredients are similar to the preceding recipe, the proportions are quite different and so is the flavor. Here the wine, instead of the sugar, balances the saltiness of the soy sauce.

1 chicken, about 4 pounds	1 tablespoon dark brown sugar
8 Chinese black mushrooms	½ cup sliced bamboo shoots
½ cup chicken stock	2 scallions, cut into pieces
¼ cup dark soy sauce	2 slices gingerroot, the size of a
¼ cup dry sherry	quarter

Preparation
Chop the chicken into 1-inch pieces. Soak the mushrooms in water until they are soft or about 30 minutes. Drain the mushrooms. Cut off and discard the tough stems. Slice the mushrooms thinly.

Cooking
In a skillet or wok combine the chicken stock, soy sauce, and sherry. Bring to a boil. Add the remaining ingredients, cover, and simmer for 20 minutes.

Yield: 4–10 servings.

STEAMED CHICKEN WITH ASPARAGUS

The Chinese are fond of steamed dishes which preserve the natural color and freshness of the ingredients. It is in the east and south, however, that steaming is raised to a true art. Cooked in this manner the tender young asparagus is incredibly good.

1 chicken, about 3 pounds	1½ tablespoons dry sherry
1 tablespoon light soy sauce	¼ cup rice flour
1½ teaspoons sugar	1 bunch young asparagus
1 teaspoon minced gingerroot	½ teaspoon salt

Preparation
Chop the chicken into bite-size pieces. Mix with the soy sauce, sugar, gingerroot, and sherry. Marinate for 1 hour. Roll the chicken in the rice flour.
Remove tough parts of the asparagus. Slice diagonally into long strips.

Arrange evenly in a heat proof dish and sprinkle with the salt. Place the chicken pieces on top of the asparagus.

Cooking

Put in a steamer over rapidly boiling water for 20 minutes or until done.

Yield: 4–10 servings.

BRAISED CHICKEN WINGS

1½ pounds chicken wings
 4 Chinese black mushrooms
 3 scallions
 2 tablespoons peanut oil
 ½ teaspoon salt
 2 slices gingerroot, the size of a
     quarter
 1 cup coarsely chopped celery
     cabbage

1½ teaspoons light brown sugar
 2 teaspoons light soy sauce
 2 teaspoons dark soy sauce
 ¾ cup chicken stock
 2 teaspoons sesame oil
 2 teaspoons dry sherry
 2 teaspoons cornstarch mixed
     with 1 tablespoon water

Preparation

Cut each chicken wing into 2 pieces at the joint. Soak the mushrooms in water for 30 minutes or until they are soft, and cut off and discard the tough stems. Slice the mushrooms into thin strips. Slice the scallions into matchstick strips.

Cooking

Heat a wok or skillet over high heat until a drop of water immediately sizzles into steam. Add the peanut oil, salt, and gingerroot. Just before the oil begins to smoke, add the chicken wings. Stir-fry for 4 minutes until they are browned.

Add the cabbage, mushrooms, sugar, both soy sauces, and chicken stock. Lower heat, cover, and simmer for 20 minutes.

In a small frying pan heat the sesame oil over medium heat. Add the scallions and stir-fry for 15 seconds. Add the scallions to the chicken wings along with the sherry. Simmer for another 10 minutes. Remove the chicken wings to a serving dish. Thicken the gravy with the cornstarch mixture and pour over the chicken wings.

Yield: 4–10 servings.

SCALLION STUFFED CHICKEN

Good cooking ideas travel swiftly or perhaps they are simultaneously arrived at in many different cuisines. The gentle flavor imparted to a whole chicken stuffed with scallions, leeks, or garlic has been appreciated by many cultures. This is the Chinese version.

11 scallions	2 tablespoons dry sherry
1½ tablespoons kosher salt	1 chicken, about 3 pounds
1 tablespoon minced ginger-root	

Preparation

Chop 10 of the scallions into three parts. Mix the salt, gingerroot, and sherry. Rub this mixture thoroughly inside and outside the chicken. Stuff the chopped scallions into the chicken cavity and let it stand for 1 hour.

Cooking

Place the chicken on a heatproof plate. Put in steamer and steam over boiling water for 40 minutes. Chop the chicken into bite-size pieces. Finely chop the remaining scallion to garnish the chicken.

Yield: 3–8 servings.

CHICKEN WITH BROWN BEAN SAUCE

¼ cup diced Chinese black mushrooms	⅓ cup chicken stock
2 whole chicken breasts	2 tablespoons peanut oil
1½ tablespoons brown bean sauce	1 teaspoon minced garlic
	1 teaspoon minced gingerroot
¾ teaspoon light brown sugar	¼ cup diced bamboo shoots
⅓ cup dry sherry	2 teaspoons cornstarch mixed with 1 tablespoon water
1 teaspoon dark soy sauce	

Preparation

Soak the mushrooms in water until soft or about 30 minutes, and drain. Cut off and discard the tough stems. Dice the mushrooms into ¼-inch squares. Skin and bone the chicken breasts. Dice into ¼-inch cubes. Gently mash the brown bean sauce and combine with the sugar, sherry, soy sauce, and chicken stock

Cooking

Heat a wok or skillet over high heat until a drop of water immediately sizzles into steam. Add the oil, garlic, and gingerroot. Stir for 30 seconds or until garlic becomes pungent. Add the chicken. Stir-fry for 1 minute. Add the mushrooms and bamboo shoots. Stir-fry for two minutes. Add the brown bean sauce mixture. Lower heat to medium and stir for 1 minute. Thicken with the cornstarch mixture.

Yield: 3–8 servings.

TAI CHI CHICKEN

½ chicken, about 1½ pounds	½ teaspoon sugar
2 fresh pimentos	Dash of pepper
2 tablespoons peanut oil	1 teaspoon hot oil
1 slice gingerroot, the size of a quarter	½ cup chicken stock or water
1 tablespoon dark soy sauce	2 teaspoons cornstarch mixed with 1 tablespoon water

Preparation

Chop chicken into pieces of 1 by 1½ inches. Remove seeds from pimentos and cut in 1-inch squares.

Cooking

Heat a wok or skillet over high heat until a drop of water immediately sizzles into steam. Add the peanut oil and gingerroot. Just before the oil begins to smoke, add the chicken and pimentos. Stir-fry for 1 minute. Add all the remaining ingredients except the cornstarch mixture. Reduce heat to low. Cover and simmer for 20 minutes. Thicken the sauce by stirring in the cornstarch mixture.

Yield: 2–4 servings.

CHICKEN WITH HAM AND BROCCOLI

This dish is a visual delight of red ham, white chicken, bordered by the green broccoli. The sauce of slightly thickened chicken stock enriched with a dab of rendered chicken fat is characteristic of the region.

4 thin slices cooked Smithfield ham
1½ pounds Chinese broccoli
3 scallions
2 quarts chicken stock
1 chicken, about 4 pounds, preferably freshly killed
6 slices gingerroot, the size of a half-dollar

¼ teaspoon salt or to taste
⅛ teaspoon white pepper
2 tablespoons rendered chicken fat
½ teaspoon light soy sauce
½ teaspoon sugar
1 tablespoon cornstarch mixed with 2 tablespoons water

Cooking

In a large pot or wok bring the chicken stock to a boil. Add the chicken, scallions, and gingerroot. When the chicken stock again comes to a boil, reduce heat and simmer the chicken for 35 minutes or until done. Turn the chicken from time to time to insure even cooking.

Remove the chicken from the pot. Remove the wings and the legs. Chop the wings into 3 sections and the legs into 1-inch pieces. Debone the remaining meat from the chicken and cut into 1½-inch squares. Pair each piece of chicken with a piece of ham and arrange in the center of a large, warm serving dish.

Remove the scallions and gingerroot from the chicken stock. Bring the chicken stock to a boil over high heat. Add the broccoli. When the chicken stock comes to a boil again, reduce heat and simmer for 3 minutes or until the broccoli has come to the peak of its color, a bright emerald green. Remove the broccoli from the chicken stock and place it around the edge of the chicken and the ham.

Remove all but 1 cup of the chicken stock used to cook the broccoli. Bring the remaining chicken stock to a boil. Add the salt, pepper, chicken fat, soy sauce and sugar. Add the cornstarch mixture and stir until thickened, about 30 seconds. Pour this sauce over the chicken, ham, and broccoli. Serve immediately.

Yield: 4–10 servings.

BRAISED CHICKEN IN RED WINE PASTE

The rich flavor of the red wine paste comes as a pleasant surprise in the course of a subtly flavored Fukienese dinner.

½ chicken, about 2 pounds
2 tablespoons red wine sediment paste
½ tablespoon sugar
1 tablespoon light soy sauce
2 tablespoons dry sherry
2 tablespoons peanut oil
½ teaspoon salt

1 scallion, cut into 1-inch lengths
1 teaspoon shredded gingerroot
½ cup bamboo shoots, thinly sliced in 1-inch squares
½ cup chicken stock
1 teaspoon sesame oil

Preparation
Chop the chicken into pieces 1 by 1½ inches. In a small bowl combine the wine sediment paste, sugar, soy sauce, and sherry.

Cooking
Heat a wok or skillet over high heat until a drop of water immediately sizzles into steam. Add the peanut oil, salt, scallion, and gingerroot. Just before the oil begins to smoke, add the chicken and bamboo shoots. Stir-fry for 1 minute.

Add the wine sediment paste combination. Stir well for 1 minute and then add the chicken stock. Reduce heat to low. Cover and simmer for 20 minutes.

Remove the chicken and bamboo shoots to a serving plate. Bring remaining sauce to a boil and add the sesame oil. Stir once or twice and pour over the chicken.

Yield: 2–4 servings.

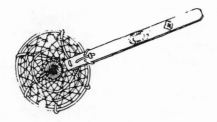

SHREDDED CHICKEN AND SPINACH

Again the red wine paste, but this time its richness is neatly contrasted with the slightly tart flavor of the spinach.

¾ pound boned and skinned
   chicken breast
1 egg white
2 tablespoons red wine sediment paste
1 tablespoon cornstarch
½ teaspoon sugar

½ teaspoon salt or to taste
1 tablespoon chicken stock
10 ounces spinach
3 tablespoons peanut oil
   Dash of pepper
1 tablespoon dry sherry

Preparation
   Shred the chicken breast. Place the chicken in a mixing bowl with the egg white, wine sediment paste, cornstarch, sugar, ¼ teaspoon of the salt and the chicken stock. Mix well and let stand for ½ hour. Rinse the spinach and trim off any tough stems.

Cooking
   Heat a wok or skillet over high heat until a drop of water immediately sizzles into steam. Add 1 tablespoon of the oil and the remaining salt. Just before the oil begins to smoke, add the spinach and pepper. Cover for 2 minutes or until the spinach has turned a deep glossy green. Remove excess moisture and arrange the cooked spinach around the border of a serving plate.
   Clean the wok or skillet and bring heat up again to very hot. Add the remaining oil. Just before the oil begins to smoke, add the chicken. Sprinkle the sherry over the chicken. Sir-fry for 2 minutes. Place the cooked chicken in the center of the serving platter.

Yield: 2–4 servings.

DUCK WITH BUDDHIST VEGETABLES

20 golden needles
1½ tablespoons cloud ears
2 ounces dried bean curd
1 ounce dried lotus root
20 dried lotus nuts
1 duck, about 5 pounds
½ cup and 4 teaspoons dark soy sauce
1 tablespoon and 1 teaspoon salt
1 cup flour

Oil for deep-frying
3 tablespoons five-flavor powder
3 tablespoons sugar
1 quart boiling water and 1 cup water
2 tablespoons peanut oil
½ cup sliced bamboo shoots
1 teaspoon light soy sauce
1 tablespoon sesame oil

Preparation

In a small pot cover the golden needles, cloud ears, bean curd, lotus root, and lotus nuts with boiling water. Put the lid on and let these dried ingredients soak for 30 minutes. Drain off the water and rinse under running water. Discard any hard ends of the golden needles.

Cut through the back of the duck. Rinse the duck under running water. Pat dry with paper towels. Rub the 4 teaspoons dark soy sauce and 1 tablespoon salt into the duck. Sprinkle flour all over the duck.

Cooking

Deep-fry the duck in very hot oil for ten minutes. Add the five-flavor powder, sugar, and ½ cup dark soy sauce to 1 quart boiling water. Simmer the duck in this mixture for ½ hour. Remove the duck from the pot, allow it to cool, and then carefully remove all the bones except for the wings and legs.

Heat a wok or skillet over high heat until a drop of water immediately sizzles into steam. Add the peanut oil and 1 teaspoon salt. Just before the oil begins to smoke, add the vegetables and bamboo shoots and stir-fry for 2 minutes. Add 1 cup of water and the light soy sauce. Let the sauce come to a boil, then cover and reduce the heat. Simmer for 10 minutes. Remove the pan from the heat, stir in the sesame oil. Place the vegetables on a serving platter. Chop the boned duck into bite-size pieces and reassemble it on top of the vegetables with the skin side up.

Yield: 6–10 servings.

BRAISED DUCK IN RED WINE PASTE

The addition of five-flavor powder gives a different quality to the red wine paste.

½ duck, about 3 pounds
½ teaspoon five-flavor powder
3 tablespoons red wine sediment paste
½ teaspoon sugar
1 tablespoon light soy sauce
2 tablespoons dry sherry

2 tablespoons peanut oil
½ teaspoon salt
3 scallions, cut into 1-inch lengths
2 slices gingerroot, the size of a quarter
½ cup chicken stock

Preparation
Rub the duck with five-flavor powder. Chop into pieces of 1 by 1½ inches. In a small bowl combine the wine sediment paste, sugar, soy sauce, and sherry.

Cooking
Heat a wok or skillet over high heat until a drop of water immediately sizzles into steam. Add the oil, salt, scallions, and gingerroot. Just before the oil begins to smoke, add the duck and stir-fry for 1 minute. Add the wine sediment paste mixture and stir well for 1 minute. Pour in the chicken stock. Reduce heat to low, cover, and simmer for 40 minutes. Add more chicken stock if the pan becomes dry.

Yield: 3–8 servings.

NANKING SALT DUCK

This is a simple but tasty dish. The salt serves both to flavor and partially cure the perishable duck.

3 tablespoons Szechwan peppercorns
½ cup kosher salt
1 duck, about 5 pounds

2 tablespoons dry sherry
1 cup chopped coriander to garnish

Preparation
Mix the peppercorns with the salt. Toast the mixture in a dry pan over low heat, shaking the pan from time to time until the peppercorns are fra-

grant. Let cool. Crush the peppercorns with the handle of a Chinese knife or with a rolling pin.

Wipe the duck with paper towels and rub inside and out with the salt mixture. Cover and refrigerate overnight. The next day rinse off all of the salt with cold water.

Cooking

Put the duck in a heatproof bowl. Rub outside of the duck with the sherry. Cover the heatproof bowl. Place a trivet on the bottom of a very large pot. Place the heatproof bowl on top of the trivet. Put enough water into the pot so that the water reaches halfway up the heatproof bowl. Bring the water to a boil, then lower to simmer. Cook in this manner for 1½ hours. Check regularly to see if there is enough water.

Let the duck cool to room temperature. Remove from the heatproof bowl and drain excess liquids from inside of the duck into the heatproof bowl. Chop the duck into bite-size pieces and arrange on a serving platter. Pour the remaining liquid over the duck and refrigerate for 2 hours before serving. Garnish with coriander.

Yield: 6–10 servings.

SHANGHAI DUCK

8 scallions, cut into 2-inch lengths	1 duck, about 5 pounds
2 star anise (16 sections)	1 cup dark soy sauce
2 slices gingerroot, the size of a half-dollar	1 cup light soy sauce
	1 cup water
	¾ cup sugar

Preparation and cooking

Put the scallions, star anise and gingerroot in a heavy pot. Place the duck breast side up in the pot. Mix the remaining ingredients and pour over the duck. Cover and bring to a boil. Simmer for about two hours or until tender, turning every half-hour. Chop into bite-size pieces.

Yield: 6–10 servings.

LION'S HEAD

This dish has become popular at many Chinese restaurants and is typical of the robust casseroles of the eastern region. The name comes from the fanciful notion that the meatballs resemble a lion's head and the shredded vegetables its mane.

6 water chestnuts
2 scallions
1 pound ground pork
1 egg, beaten
1 teaspoon finely chopped
   gingerroot
½ teaspoon sesame oil
1 tablespoon dry sherry
3 tablespoons dark soy sauce

1½ pounds Chinese cabbage
   (*bok choy*) or celery cabbage
2 tablespoons peanut oil
3 tablespoons cornstarch
½ teaspoon sugar
   Dash of pepper
½ cup chicken stock
2 teaspoons cornstarch mixed
   with 1 tablespoon water

Preparation

Mince the water chestnuts and scallions and combine with the pork, beaten egg, gingerroot, sesame oil, sherry, and 2 tablespoons of the soy sauce. Mix thoroughly with a large spoon or your hands. Shape into 6 balls and set aside. Slice the cabbage diagonally at ¼-inch intervals.

Cooking

Heat a wok or skillet over high heat and, when hot, add the peanut oil. While the pan is heating, dip the meat balls in the cornstarch. Brown the meat balls until they are golden brown.

Remove the meatballs to a flameproof casserole. Add the remaining soy sauce, the sugar, pepper, and chicken stock to the casserole. Bring to a boil over high heat. Cover and simmer for 20 minutes. Add the cabbage and simmer for 10 minutes more.

To serve, place the cabbage on a serving dish. Arrange the meatballs on top. Bring the sauce to a boil, add the cornstarch mixture, and stir to thicken. Pour the sauce over the dish.

Yield: 4–6 servings.

SHANGHAI HAM

This delicious, meaty dish is perfect for a dinner party because it does not require close attention. A variation on the red-cooking method of the eastern region, the ham is steamed in soy sauce after it has been browned. The untrimmed fat provides a special treat.

6 large Chinese black mushrooms
  Scallions or coriander to garnish
½ cup light soy sauce
½ cup dark soy sauce
1½ cups water
1½ star anise (12 sections)
½ teaspoon five-flavor powder

4 tablespoons light brown sugar or rock sugar
½ fresh ham with the fat left untrimmed, 4-6 pounds
¼ cup peanut oil
1 cup thinly sliced bamboo shoots
2 cups chopped celery cabbage (1-inch pieces)

Preparation

Soak the mushrooms in water for 30 minutes or until soft and then trim off and discard the stems. Chop the scallions or coriander into 1-inch pieces.

In a small pot combine the soy sauces, water, star anise, five-flavor powder, and sugar. Over low heat, stir the mixture gently until the sugar has dissolved. Rub the ham well into this sauce and reserve the remainder.

Cooking

Set a large skillet over high heat for ½ minute. Add the oil and swirl it around the skillet over high heat for another ½ minute. Add the ham and thoroughly brown until it has turned a deep chestnut color. It may be necessary to lower heat to medium if the oil begins to smoke.

Put the ham, its drippings, and the remaining sauce into a large heat-proof bowl and steam it over rapidly boiling water for approximately 3 hours. When properly done the meat should be so tender that it can be pulled away with chopsticks.

During the last ½ hour of cooking, add the mushrooms, bamboo shoots, and cabbage. Serve the ham (sliced or whole) and the vegetables on a platter. Garnish with either the scallions or coriander. The sauce may be served in a separate bowl for those who wish it.

Yield: 12–18 servings.

RED-COOKED PIG'S FEET

Pig's feet have a rather lowly reputation because of the large proportion of bone to meat, but the gelatinous meat is delicious—the problem is solved by the unorthodox technique of stuffing them. This dish makes an excellent hors d'oeuvre or first course.

2 pig's feet	4 tablespoons sugar
½ pound ground pork	1 star anise (8 sections)
1 clove garlic	½ teaspoon five-flavor powder
1 cup dark soy sauce	1 slice gingerroot, the size of a
1 cup light soy sauce	half-dollar
3 cups water	

Preparation

Carefully make a slit lengthwise along the pig's feet. Remove the bone and the hoof. Fill the cavity with chopped pork. Roll the meat back to its original shape and secure with string at two-inch intervals.

Peel the garlic and bruise it with the side of a knife or cleaver.

Cooking

In a large pot bring all the remaining ingredients including the garlic to a boil. Add the stuffed pig's feet and simmer for 2 hours.

To serve, remove the pig's feet and cool to room temperature. Cut the meat into ¼-inch slices and arrange on a platter. Do not refrigerate, for this toughens the pig's feet.

Yield: 3–8 servings.

PORK WITH CHINESE BROCCOLI

1 pound Chinese broccoli	¼ cup peanut oil
½ pound boned pork	1 tablespoon shredded
2 tablespoons light soy sauce	gingerroot
¼ cup dark brown sugar	½ teaspoon minced garlic
1 tablespoon dry sherry	½ teaspoon salt or to taste
Dash of pepper	

Preparation

Cut the broccoli diagonally to make thin slices about ⅛ inch thick. Cut the pork against the grain into thin slices ⅛ inch thick, 2 inches long, and

¾ inch wide. Mix together the soy sauce, sugar, sherry, and pepper in a small bowl.

Cooking

Heat a wok or skillet over high heat until a drop of water immediately sizzles into steam. Maintain high heat throughout the cooking process. Add 2 tablespoons of the oil, the gingerroot, and garlic. Stir for 30 seconds or until the odor of the garlic is pungent. Add the pork and stir-fry for 2 minutes or until it is done. Remove the pork to a warm platter.

Reheat the pan. Add the remaining oil and the salt. Just before the oil begins to smoke, add the broccoli. Stir-fry for 1 minute or until the broccoli has almost reached its peak of color, a bright deep green.

Add the sauce, and then the pork. Stir briefly to dissolve the sugar and serve immediately.

Yield: 2–6 servings.

PORK WITH SESAME SEEDS

A delicious hors d'oeuvre or first course and quite simple to make. The only precaution is to keep the oil from becoming too hot, for then the sesame seeds will sputter.

3 scallions	2 tablespoons light soy sauce
¼ cup shredded gingerroot	1 pound boned pork
2 tablespoons dry sherry	1 egg white
2 teaspoons sugar	2 tablespoons cornstarch
½ teaspoon salt or to taste	2 cups white sesame seeds
¼ teaspoon pepper	Oil for deep-frying

Preparation

Chop scallions into ½-inch lengths. In a large bowl, combine the scallions, gingerroot, sherry, sugar, salt, pepper, and soy sauce. Set aside.

Slice the pork into strips measuring ¼ by ¾ by 2½ inches. Add the pork strips to the sherry and soy sauce mixture. Marinate for an hour, turning them every now and then.

Combine the egg white and cornstarch. Dredge each pork strip in this mixture and then in the sesame seeds to coat both sides.

Cooking

Deep-fry the pork strips four or five at a time in moderately hot oil at about 300 degrees for 7 minutes or until done. Drain the strips on paper towels and keep them warm while the rest of the batch is being fried. Serve warm with a saucer of light soy sauce for a dip.

Yield: 3–8 servings.

SHANGHAI RED-COOKED PORK

The cinnamon and star anise give a special richness to the sauce.

1½ pounds pork butt	3 slices gingerroot, the size of a
3 tablespoons light soy sauce	quarter
2 tablespoons dark soy sauce	1 tablespoon gin
1 cup chicken stock	1 star anise (8 sections)
1 piece stick cinnamon, 1½	2 scallions
inches long	1½ teaspoons light brown sugar

Cooking
Put all the ingredients into a pot. Bring to a boil. Cover and simmer for 1½ hours. Turn the pork every 15 minutes. Cool and slice.

Yield: 4–10 servings.

BRAISED PORK AND BEAN CURD

3 bean curds	2 tablespoons peanut oil
1 pound boned pork	½ cup button mushrooms
2 teaspoons brown bean	½ cup peas
sauce	½ cup diced bamboo shoots
1 tablespoon light brown sugar	1 tablespoon gin
1½ tablespoons hoisin sauce	⅓ cup chicken stock

Preparation
Cut each bean curd into 9 pieces. Cut the pork into ½-inch cubes. Mash the brown bean sauce and combine with the sugar and hoisin sauce.

Cooking
Heat a wok or skillet over high heat until a drop of water immediately sizzles into steam. Add the oil. Just before the oil begins to smoke, add the diced pork and stir-fry for 2 minutes.

Add the mushrooms, peas, bamboo shoots, and gin. Stir-fry for 2 minutes. Add the brown bean sauce mixture. Mix well. Add the chicken stock. Bring to a boil. Lower heat to simmer. Add the bean curds. Cover and cook for 10 minutes.

Yield: 3–8 servings.

BRAISED SHANGHAI SPARERIBS

1 pound spareribs
1 tablespoon dark soy sauce
1 tablespoon light soy sauce
1 tablespoon dry sherry
1 teaspoon light brown sugar
¾ cup chicken stock

2 tablespoons vegetable oil
3 slices gingerroot, the size of a quarter
2 scallions, cut into 1-inch lengths

Preparation
Chop the spareribs into 1-inch pieces. Mix the soy sauces, sherry, sugar, and chicken stock in a bowl.

Cooking
Heat a wok or skillet over high heat until a drop of water immediately sizzles into steam. Add the oil, gingerroot, and scallions. Stir for 30 seconds. Add the spareribs. Stir-fry for 2 minutes. Add the soy sauce mixture. Bring to a boil. Lower heat, cover, and simmer for 30 minutes.

Yield: 2–8 servings.

The following two recipes are for sweet-and-sour spareribs. Every region—and indeed every province—has devised its own recipe based on one that originated according to legend in the province of Honan in north China. The Shanghai version is rather predictable, but still good. The Fukienese added several distinctive and original twists of their own. It is a delicious and—as explained in the recipe note—an amusing conceit.

SHANGHAI SWEET-AND-SOUR SPARERIBS

1½ pounds spareribs
2 tablespoons cornstarch
⅓ cup red wine vinegar
⅓ cup dark brown sugar
1 teaspoon dark soy sauce
Oil for deep-frying

½ teaspoon salt or to taste
¼ cup chopped scallions (1½-inch lengths)
½ cup thinly sliced carrots
1 teaspoon cornstarch mixed with 1 tablespoon water

Preparation

Chop the spareribs into 1½-inch lengths. Roll the spareribs in the cornstarch. Combine the vinegar, sugar, and soy sauce in a small bowl.

Cooking

Heat the oil to 375 degrees and deep-fry the spareribs for 2 to 3 minutes. Remove and drain on paper towels. Place the ribs on a serving dish.

In a hot skillet add 2 tablespoons of the oil and the salt. Stir for 30 seconds. Add the sweet-and-sour soy sauce mixture, the scallions, and carrots. Bring the liquid to a boil and cook for 30 seconds. Stir in the cornstarch paste to thicken. Pour over the spareribs.

Yield: 3–8 servings.

FUKIENESE SCALLION BEADED "SPARERIBS"

This recipe is an amusing conversation piece. The trick in this dish is to fool the eater into thinking that you have taken the trouble to remove the bones from the "spareribs" and replaced them with pieces of scallion. The pork should be sweet, but the sauce should be sour.

1 pound lean pork	½ cup chicken stock
20 scallions	⅓ cup red wine vinegar
Oil for deep-frying	

Marinade

¼ teaspoon salt	1 tablespoon orange-flavored
1½ teaspoons finely chopped gingerroot	liqueur
	1 teaspoon rice flour
4 teaspoons light brown sugar	½ teaspoon dark soy sauce
¼ teaspoon minced garlic	¼ teaspoon five-flavor powder
¼ cup dry sherry	(optional)
¼ cup dry red wine	1 teaspoon grated tangerine or
1 tablespoon tomato paste	orange peel

Preparation

Slice the pork, approximating the shape of bite-size spareribs—1½ inches long, 1 inch wide, and ½ inch thick. In a small pan over medium heat blend together the ingredients for the marinade for 10 minutes. Marinate the pork for 6 hours or overnight. Poke a hole lengthwise through the pork pieces with a chopstick, and allow the scallion to stick out for ½ inch on each side. Slice off the excess green part.

Cooking

Heat the oil to 375 degrees. Deep-fry the pork pieces for 5 minutes, or until done. Remove to a serving platter and keep warm. To make the sauce, stir the chicken stock with the vinegar over medium heat until hot. Pour the sauce over the "spareribs."

Yield: 3–8 servings.

FUKIENESE PORK WITH SCALLION SAUCE

A lovely, subtle dish with not quite identifiable flavors.

2½ tablespoons red rice wine vinegar
½ teaspoon five-flavor powder
¼ teaspoon sugar
¼ teaspoon light soy sauce
4 scallions, chopped into ¼-inch lengths

⅓ cup chicken stock or water
½ teaspoon salt
2 tablespoons peanut oil
1 slice gingerroot, the size of a quarter
¾ pound shredded pork

Preparation

In a bowl combine the vinegar, five-flavor powder, sugar, soy sauce, scallions, chicken stock, and salt.

Cooking

Heat a wok or skillet over high heat until a drop of water immediately sizzles into steam. Add 1 tablespoon of the oil and the gingerroot. Just before the oil begins to smoke, add the pork. Stir-fry for 2 minutes or until all the pieces have turned white. Remove the pork from the pan and drain on paper towels. Add the remaining oil to the pan.

Allow the pan to cool to medium heat. Add the sauce and stir for 2 minutes until the five-flavor powder and the sugar have dissolved. Add the pork and cook over medium heat for 2 minutes.

Yield: 2–6 servings

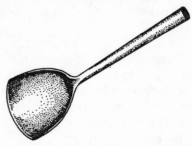

SWEET AND PUNGENT FUKIENESE LYCHEE PORK

1 pound boned pork
¼ cup red wine sediment paste
1 tablespoon cornstarch
   Oil for deep-frying
1 cup canned lychee
¼ cup shredded cucumbers

1 carrot, sliced into paper-thin slices
½ cup chicken stock
⅓ cup red wine vinegear
2 tablespoons light brown sugar

Preparation
Cut the pork into 1-inch cubes. Marinate it in wine sediment paste for 6 hours or overnight.

Cooking
Dust the pork cubes lightly with cornstarch. Deep-fry in very hot oil about 375 degrees for 5 minutes or until done. Remove and set aside.

Put all the remaining ingredients in a wok or large skillet over medium heat until the mixture starts to boil. Add the pork cubes. Lower heat to a simmer. Cover and cook for 2 minutes.

Yield: 3–6 servings.

FUKIENESE PORK LIVER

Even people who generally do not like liver will like this gentle sauce which tames the robust flavor of the liver.

1 pound pork liver
1 egg white
½ cup red wine vinegar
2 tablespoons light brown sugar

2 tablespoons minced garlic
1 tablespoon minced ginger root
1 tablespoon dark soy sauce
¼ cup shredded cucumber

Preparation
Clean and then cut the pork liver into slices ¼ inch thick. Cut each slice into 2-inch squares. Carefully make diagonal slashes across each piece of liver until it resembles a checkerboard. This will make the liver less tough. Brush with egg white.

Cooking
Mix together the vinegar, sugar, garlic, gingerroot, and soy sauce. Bring the mixture to a boil in a pan. Lower to medium heat, maintaining a

low boil. Add the pork liver and cucumbers. Cover and cook for 10 minutes or until done.

Yield: 4–8 servings.

RED-COOKED BEEF

This is a very useful recipe, for the dish can be served hot or cold for a buffet or large dinner party.

1 clove garlic	2 star anise (16 sections)
2 tablespoons peanut oil	2½ cups light soy sauce
½ teaspoon salt	2 cups dark soy sauce
2 slices gingerroot, the size of a	7 cups chicken stock
quarter	½ cup rock sugar or light sugar
5 pounds boned beef	3 tablespoons dry sherry

Preparation and cooking

Peel and bruise the garlic. Bring the heat under a deep, heavy pot to high. Add the oil, salt, gingerroot, and garlic. Just before the oil begins to smoke, place the beef in the pot and sear in order to seal in the juices. Add all the remaining ingredients. Bring to a boil. Cover and simmer for 1½ hours. The meat should be tender enough so that a chopstick can pierce it. Slice the meat and serve either cold or hot with the sauce in which it was cooked.

Yield: 10–20 servings.

SHANGHAI RED-COOKED FISH

1 fish, about 2 pounds	1 tablespoon dry sherry
½ teaspoon salt	2 tablespoons dark brown
5 scallions, chopped into 1½-	sugar
inch lengths	¾ cup chicken stock
2 slices gingerroot, the size of a	¼ cup sliced bamboo shoots
quarter	½ cup peanut oil
4 tablespoons dark soy sauce	

Preparation

Clean and scale the fish. Dry it inside and outside with paper towels. Make three diagonal slashes on each side of the fish for more even cooking. Rub the salt on the inside and outside of the fish. In a bowl combine the scallions, gingerroot, soy sauce, sherry, sugar, chicken stock, and bamboo shoots.

Cooking
Heat a wok or skillet until it is very hot. Add the oil. When the oil is very hot, fry the fish for 3 to 5 minutes on each side to brown and partially cook it. Remove all but 3 tablespoons of the oil. Add the soy sauce mixture. Bring to a boil, cover, and simmer for 10 minutes. Remove the cover and cook over high heat, basting the fish until only ½ cup of the sauce remains.

Yield: 2–4 servings.

POACHED SWEET-AND-SOUR WEST LAKE CARP

The serenely beautiful West Lake of Hangchow has been a source of pleasure for generations. The carp that live in its waters have been similarly prized.

1 fresh carp, about 3 pounds
2 slices gingerroot, the size of a half-dollar
4 scallions, chopped into 3-inch lengths
1½ cups water
½ cup red wine vinegar
2 tablespoons dark soy sauce
½ cup dark brown sugar
1 tablespoon chopped garlic
3 tablespoons finely shredded fresh gingerroot
3 tablespoons peanut oil
1 tablespoon cornstarch mixed with ¼ cup water
½ teaspoon pepper

Preparation
Clean and scale the carp and be sure to remove the gills from inside the head. Carefully split the fish from head to tail so that the fish becomes one flat piece.

Cooking
Place the fish in a large covered pot skin side up and add enough water to cover the fish. Add the 2 slices of gingerroot and half the chopped scallions. Bring the water to a simmer. Cover and simmer for 4 minutes. Remove the pot from the heat, but leave the fish in the water, covered, for 6 to 8 minutes longer until done. Remove the fish carefully to a large platter.
In a saucepan combine the 1½ cups water, the vinegar, soy sauce, sugar, the remaining chopped scallions, the garlic, shredded gingerroot, and

oil. Bring to a boil while stirring. Stir in the cornstarch mixture to thicken. Pour the sauce over the fish and sprinkle with the pepper.

Yield: 3–6 servings.

DEEP-FRIED SWEET-AND-SOUR FISH

A marvelous combination of flavors: sweet, sour, salty, and hot. This is a deluxe dish that requires special efforts, but they are well worth the result. The double frying process gives the fish an unusual crispness.

1 fish, about 2 pounds	½ cup red wine vinegar
½ teaspoon salt	½ cup dark brown sugar
2 tablespoons dry sherry	1 tablespoon dark soy sauce
1 tablespoon minced ginger-root	3 tablespoons cornstarch
	Oil for deep-frying
6 Chinese black mushrooms	2 tablespoons diced Smithfield
½ green bell pepper	ham
2 fresh hot red peppers	1 teaspoon cornstarch mixed
¼ cup diced bamboo shoots	with 1 tablespoon water
½ cup chicken stock	

Preparation

Clean, scale, and then dry the fish with paper towels. Rub the inside and outside of the fish with the salt. Sprinkle the fish with the sherry and gingerroot. Let stand for 30 minutes.

Meanwhile, soak the mushrooms in warm water for 30 minutes or until they are soft. Dice the mushrooms, green pepper, and hot peppers. Combine with the bamboo shoots.

In a bowl combine the chicken stock, vinegar, sugar, and soy sauce. Sprinkle the fish with the cornstarch to coat.

Cooking

Heat the oil to 375 degrees. Lower the fish carefully with wire basket. Allow it to fry for 3 minutes. Remove the fish and drain it on paper towels. Allow the fish to cool for 15 minutes. Repeat the frying process, this time for 5 minutes. Remove the fish and place it on a serving platter.

Heat a wok or skillet over high heat until a drop of water immediately sizzles into steam. Add 2 tablespoons of the oil and stir for 30 seconds.

Add the ham and the vegetables and stir-fry for 1 minute. Add the sauce and bring to a boil. Stir in the cornstarch mixture to thicken. Pour over the fish and serve.

Yield: 2–4 servings.

NINGPO FRIED FISH ROLL WITH BEAN CURD SHEETS

A very simple dish but unbelievably good! Bean curd sheets can be purchased at Chinese grocery stores. They are dried, thin, and fragile. When deep-fried, as in this recipe, they become very flaky and crisp.

2 scallions	¾ pound fish fillets, sliced very
2 tablespoons light soy sauce	thin
2 sheets dried bean curd	Oil for deep-frying

Preparation

Chop the scallions into ½-inch pieces. Pour the soy sauce over the scallions in a little dish. Sprinkle the bean curd sheets lightly with water to soften them. Trim off the hard rolled edges that refuse to soften. Divide into pieces approximately 6 inches square.

Brush one of the fillets with the soy sauce and scallion mixture. Place a second fillet on top of the first one. Wrap the fillets with a piece of bean curd sheet as one would wrap an egg roll with the ends tucked in. Repeat the process until all the fillets are used.

Cooking

In a wok or deep-fryer heat the oil to 375 degrees or almost to the point of smoking. Place the prepared fillets in the oil and cook about 2 minutes or until the bean curd sheet has turned a golden brown and is flaky. Repeat with the remaining prepared fillets. The fillets can be served either whole or cut up into 2-inch segments.

Yield: 3–6 servings.

SCALLION STUFFED FISH

The stuffing is made of ground pork and scallions. The robust and aromatic sauce and stuffing complements the delicate flesh of the fish.

1 fish, about 2 pounds	¾ cup chicken stock or water
1 teaspoon salt	2 tablespoons dark soy sauce
5 scallions, chopped into ¼-	2 tablespoons minced ginger-
inch lengths	root
½ pound ground pork	1 teaspoon sugar
1 cup peanut oil	Dash of pepper

Preparation

Clean and scale the fish. Dry with paper towels. Rub the inside and out-side of the fish with ¾ teaspoon of the salt. Mix half the scallions thoroughly with the ground pork, adding the remaining salt. Stuff this mixture into the cavity of the fish.

Cooking

Heat a wok or skillet until it is very hot. Add the oil. When the oil is very hot, fry the fish for 3 to 5 minutes on each side to brown. Loosen the skin from the pan carefully with a spatula when turning the fish over. Remove all but 2 tablespoons of the oil. Lower heat and add the chicken stock, soy sauce, gingerroot, sugar, the remaining scallions, and the pepper. Cover and simmer for 20 minutes.

Yield: 2–4 servings.

FISH WITH STRAW MUSHROOMS
AND MINIATURE CORN

½ pound fish fillets	Liberal dash of pepper
½ cup chicken stock	½ teaspoon salt
2 slices gingerroot, the size of a	¾ teaspoon sugar
half-dollar	1 tablespoon dry sherry
4 ounces straw mushrooms	½ teaspoon light soy sauce
4 ounces miniature corn	1 teaspoon sesame oil
1 tablespoon rendered chicken	
fat	

Preparation and cooking
Slice the fish into strips ¼ inch thick. In a hot skillet add the chicken stock and gingerroot. Add fish fillet strips and bring to a light boil. Simmer for 1 minute. Add the remaining ingredients except for the sesame oil. Lower heat to medium and cover for 2 minutes. Stir in the sesame oil and serve.

Yield: 2–4 servings.

FISH HEAD CASSEROLE

For Fukienese fishermen this inexpensive dish was common. The soup and ingredients were poured over individual bowls of rice for a one-dish meal.

1½ to 2 pounds fish heads	½ cup dry sherry
3 scallions	1 tablespoon light soy sauce
3 slices gingerroot, the size of a half-dollar	½ teaspoon sugar
	½ teaspoon red wine vinegar
3 cups rich chicken stock	2 bean curds
½ teaspoon salt	

Preparation and cooking
Remove the gills from the fish heads and rinse thoroughly. Quarter the bean curds. Bring the chicken stock to a boil. Add all the ingredients except the bean curds. Cook at a light boil for 30 minutes. Add the bean curds and simmer for 5 minutes longer.

Yield: 2–4 servings.

FUKIENESE FRIED FISH ROLLS

Typically Fukienese, the seasoning is light and the fish is allowed to "speak" for itself.

¾ pound lace fat	1 teaspoon sugar
6 Chinese black mushrooms	3 scallions, cut into 1½-inch lengths
1 pound fish fillet	
1 teaspoon light soy sauce	Cornstarch
¼ teaspoon pepper	1 egg white
1 teaspoon dry sherry	Oil for deep-frying

Preparation

Cut the lace fat into 6-inch squares. Set aside. Soak the mushrooms for half an hour or until soft. Dice the mushrooms. Slice the fish into pieces measuring 1 by 3 inches. In a large bowl combine the mushrooms, fish, and all the remaining ingredients except the lace fat, cornstarch, oil, and egg white. Spread out a piece of lace fat and sprinkle whth about 1 teaspoon of cornstarch. Place about ½ cup of the fish mixture formed into a rectangular shape in the center of a square of lace fat. Fold narrower sides of the lace fat over the mixture and then fold the longer sides over the filling. Brush the roll with the egg white and dust with cornstarch. Proceed in the same way with the remaining lace fat and filling.

Cooking

Deep-fry each roll in moderately hot oil (300 degrees) for 10 minutes or until golden brown.

Yield: 3–6 servings.

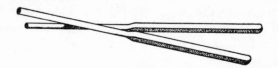

FUKIENESE DEEP-FRIED FISH WITH RED WINE PASTE

The fruity and musty flavor of the red wine sediment paste complemented by the aromatic five-flavor powder provides a new dimension of taste.

1 pound fish fillet	¼ cup red wine sediment paste
½ teaspoon salt	Oil for deep-frying
¼ teaspoon five-flavor powder	2 scallions, diced, to garnish

Preparation

Rub the fish with the salt and five-flavor powder. Marinate the fish in the wine sediment paste for four hours.

Cooking

Deep-fry in very hot oil for three to four minutes or until done. Remove from the oil and cut the fish into thick pieces of 2 by 1½ inches and arrange on a serving platter. Garnish with scallions.

Yield: 3–6 servings.

FUKIENESE DEEP-FRIED FLOUNDER

A flounder, when deep-fried in very hot oil, produces fins and tails that are more delectable than peanuts. If available, use a wire basket to lower the flounder into the oil so that the skin of the fish does not stick to the pan. Otherwise, try to keep the fish from the bottom of the pan until the skin has hardened.

1 fresh flounder, about 2 pounds
Oil for deep-frying
½ cup red wine vinegar
2 tablespoons light brown sugar
1 tablespoon Worcestershire sauce

1 tablespoon ketchup
1 tablespoon minced garlic
1 tablespoon shredded ginger-root
1 teaspoon salt
2 scallions, sliced into 1-inch pieces

Preparation
Clean and scale the fish. Pat dry with paper towels.

Cooking
Bring the oil to as high a heat as possible. Deep-fry the flounder for 10 minutes on each side. Place the fish on a serving platter.

Mix together all the remaining ingredients in a pan. Bring the mixture to a boil. Lower to medium heat, maintaining a low boil. Stir until all the ingredients have blended. Pour over the fish.

Yield: 2–6 servings.

FUKIENESE STEAMED FISH WITH PORK

8 Chinese black mushrooms
¼ pound thinly shredded pork
1 fresh bass or carp, 2–3 pounds
2 teaspoons sesame oil
1½ teaspoons salt
4 scallions
1 teaspoon light soy sauce
2 teaspoons shredded ginger-root

2 tablespoons peanut oil
1 teaspoon dark soy sauce
1 teaspoon sugar
2 tablespoons dry sherry
3 tablespoons chicken stock
1 teaspoon cornstarch mixed with 1 tablespoon water

Preparation

Soak the mushrooms in water for 30 minutes or until soft. Cut off and discard the tough stems. Slice the mushrooms thinly and set them aside by the shredded pork. Clean and scale the fish. Dry with paper towels. Rub the fish inside and out with the sesame oil and 1 teaspoon of the salt. Place in a heatproof dish. Chop the scallions into 1-inch lengths. Put the white parts in with the pork; place the green parts on top of the fish. Sprinkle the light soy sauce and gingerroot over the fish.

Cooking

Place the fish in a steamer over rapidly boiling water for 20 to 30 minutes or until the fish is done. Remove the fish to a heated serving platter.

Heat a wok or skillet over high heat until a drop of water immediately sizzles into steam. Add the peanut oil and the remaining salt. Just before the oil begins to smoke, add the pork with the white parts of the scallions, and the Chinese mushrooms. Stir-fry for 1 minute. Add the dark soy sauce, sugar, sherry, and chicken stock. Stir for ½ minute. Add the cornstarch mixture to thicken slightly. Pour over the fish and serve immediately.

Yield: 3–6 servings.

SHRIMP TOAST

A deservedly famous dish which makes an excellent hors d'oeuvre for any meal. Some recipes say that the chopping may be done in a blender. It can be, but the chopping by hand gives the shrimp an exquisite texture that a blender can never match.

1½ pounds shrimp	1 egg
½ cup finely minced onion	1½ teaspoons salt or to taste
6 water chestnuts	1 tablespoon cornstarch
3 tablespoons unsalted pork fat	1 tablespoon dry sherry
1 tablespoon minced ginger-root	2 tablespoons water
½ teaspoon sugar	⅛ teaspoon pepper
	18 slices very thin stale bread
	Oil for deep-frying

Preparation

Shell and devein the shrimp. Chop the shrimp very finely and combine with the onion. Mince the water chestnuts and pork fat. Combine all the prepared ingredients with the remaining ingredients, except for the bread and the oil, and mix thoroughly. Spread this mixture on the slices of stale bread. Cut each slice diagonally twice to make four bite-size triangles.

Cooking
Heat the oil to 375 degrees or until it is very hot. Deep-fry the pieces a few at a time, first on the shrimp side and then on the bread side, for 2 to 3 minutes or until the pieces have turned a golden brown. Remove from the pan with a slotted spoon and drain on several thicknesses of paper towels. The pieces of shrimp toast may be kept warm in a 200-degree oven, but the sooner they are served the better.

Yield: 6 dozen pieces.

SHANGHAI DEEP-FRIED SHRIMP BALLS

These fluffy and light shrimp balls are always a hit. They can also be served as appetizers.

1 pound shrimp	½ teaspoon sugar
½ cup minced water chestnuts	1 tablespoon cornstarch
½ teaspoon light soy sauce	1 egg white
½ teaspoon sesame oil	Oil for deep-frying
½ teaspoon salt	2 wedges lemon

Preparation
Shell and devein the shrimp. Chop the shrimp very finely so that they almost become a paste. Mix the shrimp and all the remaining ingredients together except for the egg white, oil, and lemon. Place 1 tablespoon of the mixture on the palm of one hand and roll between both palms to form a ball. Repeat until all of the mixture has been used.

Cooking
Heat the oil to 375 degrees. Dip each shrimp ball into the egg white just before putting it into the oil. They will float when done. Sprinkle with lemon at the table.

Yield: 6–8 servings.

YANGCHOW GOLD COIN SHRIMP

1 pound shrimp	3 tablespoons peanut oil
3 ounces fatback	½ pound spinach
2 tablespoons finely minced scallions	3 tablespoons water
	½ cup chicken stock
1 egg white	⅓ teaspoon sugar
1 teaspoon salt or to taste	Dash of pepper
1 tablespoon dry sherry	2 teaspoons cornstarch mixed
2 teaspoons cornstarch	with 1 tablespoon water

Preparation
Shell and devein the shrimp. Dry between paper towels. Mince the shrimp and fatback with a Chinese knife or in a meat grinder. Mix throughly with the scallions, egg white, ¾ teaspoon of the salt, the sherry, and the 2 teaspoons cornstarch. Form into 20 or so patties, about the size of a silver dollar.

Cooking
Heat a wok or skillet to medium heat with 2 tablespoons of the oil. Fry the patties for 2 minutes on each side. Place in the center of a serving platter.

Heat a wok or skillet to very hot. Add the remaining oil and the remaining salt. Just before the oil begins to smoke, add the spinach and stir-fry for 1 minute. Add the water. Cover for 1 minute. Remove the cover and stir-fry for ½ minute. Place the spinach around the shrimp patties on the platter.

To make a gravy for the shrimp patties, place the chicken stock, sugar, and pepper in a saucepan. Bring to a boil. Thicken with the cornstarch mixture. Pour over the shrimp patties.

Yield: 4–8 servings.

HANGCHOW GLAZED SHRIMP

1 pound small shrimp	1 tablespoon light soy sauce
1 teaspoon salt	2 tablespoons peanut oil
1 egg white	3 slices gingerroot, the size of a quarter
½ teaspoon baking soda	
1 tablespoon cornstarch	2 tablespoons minced scallions to garnish
1 tablespoon dry sherry	

Preparation

Shell and devein the shrimp. In a mixing bowl add the salt to the shrimp. Mix well and let stand for 30 minutes. Let the shrimp dry on paper towels. Return the shrimp to the mixing bowl, adding the egg white, baking soda, cornstarch, sherry, and soy sauce. Mix well and marinate for 15 minutes.

Cooking

Heat a wok or skillet over high heat until a drop of water immediately sizzles into steam. Add the oil and gingerroot. Just before the oil begins to smoke, add the shrimp and stir-fry for 3 minutes or until they are done. The shrimp should be almost crunchy but not tough. Garnish with scallions.

Yield: 3–6 servings.

SIZZLING SHRIMP WITH RICE

1 pound small shrimp	1 tablespoon white rice wine
1 tablespoon cornstarch	vinegar
1 tablespoon dry sherry	1 cup chicken stock
4 water chestnuts	1 tablespoon light soy sauce
4 scallions	Dash of pepper
1 tablespoon shredded ginger-	1 cup rice crusts (see recipe on
root	page 271)
1 teaspoon minced garlic	2 or more tablespoons peanut
⅓ cup ketchup	oil
1 tablespoon Worcestershire	½ teaspoon salt
sauce	½ cup peas
1½ tablespoons sugar	Oil for deep-frying

Preparation

Shell and devein the shrimp. Combine the shrimp with the cornstarch and sherry. Dice the chestnuts and scallions. Combine the gingerroot and garlic and set beside the stove. In a bowl, combine the ketchup, Worcestershire sauce, sugar, vinegar, chicken stock, soy sauce, and pepper. Break the rice crusts into 2-inch-square pieces.

Cooking

Heat a wok or skillet over high heat until a drop of water immediately sizzles into steam. Add the peanut oil and the salt, the garlic and gingerroot. Stir until the odor of the garlic is pungent. Add the shrimp and stir until they turn pinkish and are almost done. Add more peanut oil if necessary to keep the shrimp from sticking. Add the peas, water chestnuts, and scallions. Stir briefly to coat the vegetables with oil. Add the ketchup mixture immediately and, stirring, allow the sauce to come to a boil. Reduce heat to very low to keep the sauce warm.

Deep-fry the rice crusts in very hot almost smoking oil until they have turned a light golden brown. Remove the crusts to a serving bowl and rush them to the table. Immediately pour the shrimp and sauce over the still very hot rice crusts which will crackle and hiss vigorously on contact with the sauce.

Yield: 4–8 servings.

CRAB WITH EGGS

This simple dish, in which the smooth and subtle sweetness of crab meat is complemented by scrambled eggs, is excellent for brunch.

1 cup crab meat, preferably backfin	2 tablespoons peanut oil
3 eggs	1 tablespoon finely minced gingerroot
1 tablespoon light soy sauce	½ teaspoon salt or to taste
1 tablespoon dry sherry	¼ cup minced scallions
1 teaspoon sugar	

Preparation
Pick over the crab meat to remove any pieces of cartilage or shell. Beat the eggs in a mixing bowl. Add the crab meat, soy sauce, sherry, and sugar. Mix.

Cooking
Heat a skillet or wok to medium. Add the oil, gingerroot, and salt. Add the egg and crab mixture. Stir slowly to cook. After 3 minutes, when the eggs have pretty much set, add the scallions. Continue to stir for 1 minute. Eggs should still be moist and slightly runny.

Yield: 2–4 servings.

FUKIENESE CRAB ROLLS

Lace fat is not always easy to find, but it makes an ideal wrapper, for in the frying it half melts away but leaves a very special hint of its presence.

1½ pounds lace fat	½ teaspoon salt or to taste
12 ounces crab meat, preferably backfin	1 teaspoon sugar
	Dash of pepper
12 ounces ground pork	1 tablespoon light soy sauce
3 tablespoons minced Smithfield ham	½ teaspoon sesame oil
2 minced scallions	1 egg white
¼ cup minced water chestnuts	1 tablespoon cornstarch
¼ cup minced bamboo shoots	Oil for deep-frying

Preparation

Cut the lace fat into 8-inch squares. In a large bowl, combine all the remaining ingredients except for the egg white, cornstarch, and oil for deep frying. Spread out a piece of lace fat and sprinkle with about 1 teaspoon of cornstarch.

Place about ½ cup of the crab mixture (shaped like a rectangle) in the center of a square of lace fat. Fold two opposite sides of the square over the mixture and then roll the remaining lace fat around the mixture as one would in preparing an egg roll. Brush the roll with the egg white and dust with cornstarch. Repeat the procedure for the remaining pieces of lace fat.

Cooking

Deep-fry each roll in moderately hot oil (300 degrees) for 15 minutes or until golden brown.

Yield: 6–12 servings.

FUKIENESE HARD-SHELL CRABS

6 large, live hard-shell crabs	½ teaspoon salt
2 tablespoons salt	½ teaspoon light soy sauce
2 eggs, beaten	1 cup peanut oil
3 tablespoons all-purpose flour	2 slices gingerroot, the size of a half-dollar
¾ teaspoon sugar	

Preparation

Place the live crabs in a pot of cold water with the 2 tablespoons salt for an hour so that the crabs will clean themselves. With a heavy butcher knife split each crab in half. Discard the small claws. Chop off the large claws and set aside. Remove the spongy lungs and rinse the inside under a running faucet. Mix the eggs with the flour, sugar, the ½ teaspoon salt, and the soy sauce. Dredge the crabs and the large claws in the egg mixture.

Cooking

Heat a wok or skillet over high heat. Add the oil and gingerroot. Just before the oil begins to smoke, add the crabs and claws. Spoon the oil over the crab pieces and cook for about 3 minutes.

Yield: 3–6 servings.

SHARK'S FIN WITH SEAFOOD TREASURE SAUCE

This is a dish that will be appreciated by the true gourmet. The subtleties of flavor and texture are extraordinary. The ingredients are expensive and the preparation time considerable, but the result is well worth the effort.

4 ounces shark's fin (in one piece)
6 slices gingerroot, the size of a half-dollar
3 scallions
¼ cup frozen peas
1½ cups crab meat
1 egg, beaten
1 teaspoon sesame oil
2 tablespoons peanut oil
¼ teaspoon salt or to taste
3 cups very rich chicken stock
½ teaspoon sugar
½ teaspoon light soy sauce
¼ cup thinly sliced canned abalone
1 tablespoon cornstarch mixed with ¼ cup water

Preparation

Rinse the shark's fin in cold water. Soak in warm water for 1 hour. Drain. Place the shark's fin in a pot with water to cover to a depth of 3 inches above the fin. Bring to a boil. Cover and simmer for 2 hours. Allow to soak for 24 hours. Rinse the shark's fin and discard any foreign particles. Wrap the shark's fin with cheesecloth. Place it in a pot with water to cover to a depth of 3 inches above the fin. Add 2 slices of the gingerroot and 1 of the scallions. Bring to a boil, then simmer for 2 hours. Allow the fin to cool in the water, then drain. Discard the liquid. It may be necessary to repeat this process another two times until the shark's fin is soft. Use a fresh slice of gingerroot and another scallion each time. When the shark's fin is as soft as cooked noodles, discard the cheesecloth and set the shark's fin aside in a bowl.

Allow the frozen peas to defrost. Pick over the crab meat to remove any pieces of cartilage or shell. Mix the crab meat with the sesame oil and egg.

Cooking

Heat a skillet or wok with the peanut oil and salt. Just before the oil begins to smoke, add the crab meat and egg mixture. Stir-fry for 1 minute or so until the egg has cooked. Break into pieces of ½ to ¾ inches with a spatula. Add the chicken stock. When it comes to a boil, lower heat to simmer. Add the shark's fin, sugar, and soy sauce. Cover and simmer for 30 minutes. Add the abalone and peas and cook for 5 minutes. Carefully stir in the cornstarch mixture to thicken.

Yield: 4–8 servings.

STIR-FRIED SCALLOPS AND PORK KIDNEYS

¾ pound pork kidneys	2 tablespoons dry sherry
½ pound scallops	¼ cup diced scallions
2 tablespoons vegetable oil	2 teaspoons light soy sauce
½ teaspoon salt or to taste	1 teaspoon sugar
1 slice gingerroot, the size of a quarter	1 teaspoon cornstarch mixed with 1 tablespoon water

Preparation

With a sharp knife remove the tough outer membrane covering the kidneys. Split the kidneys in half lengthwise. Place on a chopping block, flat side down, and score the surface by cutting halfway through diagonally to create a crisscross pattern. Space the cuts about ¼ inch apart. Then slice the kidneys into 1-inch-wide pieces.

Wash the scallops under cold water and pat dry with paper towels.

Cooking

Heat a wok or skillet over high heat until a drop of water immediately sizzles into steam. Add the oil, salt, and gingerroot. Just before the oil begins to smoke, add the kidney pieces. Stir-fry for 2 minutes. Add the scallops and all the remaining ingredients except for the cornstarch mixture.

Stir-fry for 1 minute or until the scallops are white but not too firm. Thicken with the cornstarch mixture.

Yield: 4–8 servings.

ABALONE WITH MINIATURE CORN
AND STRAW MUSHROOMS

This is a very simple dish taking full advantage of the natural subtle sweetness of abalone, miniature corn, and straw mushrooms. Vegetable oil can be substituted for rendered chicken fat, but a degree of richness and body will be lost in the sauce.

1 pound canned abalone
4 ounces straw mushrooms
4 ounces miniature corn
½ cup chicken stock
2 teaspoons light soy sauce
2 teaspoons dry sherry
½ teaspoon salt or to taste

2 tablespoons rendered chicken fat
1 teaspoon sugar
2 teaspoons cornstarch mixed with 1 tablespoon water
½ teaspoon sesame oil

Preparation
Slice the abalone into pieces ⅛ inch thick and about 1 inch square. Drain the mushrooms and the corn. Combine the chicken stock, soy sauce, sherry, salt, chicken fat, and sugar in a skillet or saucepan.

Cooking
Bring the chicken stock mixture to a boil. Add the abalone, corn, and mushrooms. Lower heat to medium. Cover and cook for 2 minutes. Thicken with the cornstarch mixture. Stir in the sesame oil and serve.

Yield: 4–8 servings.

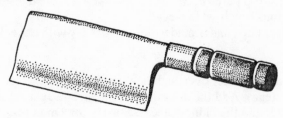

BUDDHIST VEGETABLE DISH

Pilgrimages used to be made to Buddhist monasteries as much for gastronomic as for spiritual reasons. Strict vegetarians, the monks had devised ingenious ways to vary their special diet.

25 golden needles	½ pound winter melon
1½ tablespoons cloud ears	¼ pound snow peas
2 ounces dried bean curd	4 bean curds
20 dried lotus nuts	½ cup sliced bamboo shoots
1 ounce dried lotus root	3 tablespoons peanut oil
6 Chinese black mushrooms	1 tablespoon light soy sauce
2 ounces cellophane noodles	1 teaspoon salt
¼ pound Chinese cabbage (*bok choy*)	1 cup water
	1 tablespoon sesame oil

Preparation

In a bowl cover the golden needles, cloud ears, dried bean curd, lotus nuts, and lotus root with warm water. Let them soak for 30 minutes or until completely soft. Drain off the water and rinse well under running water. Discard the hard ends of the golden needles, if present.

In a separate bowl soak the mushrooms in water for 30 minutes or until soft. Squeeze them gently to get rid of any excess water and then discard their hard stems. Quarter the mushrooms.

In a third bowl cover the cellophane noodles with warm water. Soak them for 30 minutes or until completely soft. Cut the noodles into 6-inch lengths.

Slice the cabbage diagonally into strips ½ by ½ inches. Cut the winter melon into pieces ½ inch thick by 1 inch square, and combine with the cabbage.

String the snow peas. Cut the bean curds into 6 sections. Cut the bamboo shoots into squares.

Cooking

Heat a wok or skillet over high heat until a drop of water immediately sizzles into steam. Maintain high heat throughout the cooking process. Add the peanut oil. Just before the oil begins to smoke, add the cabbage and winter melon and stir-fry for 1 minute.

Add the remaining vegetables and stir-fry for 2 minutes. Add the soy sauce, salt, and water. Let the sauce come to a boil, then cover and reduce the heat. Simmer for 10 minutes.

Remove the pan from the heat, stir in the sesame oil, and serve immediately.

Yield: 6–10 servings.

STIR-FRIED BROCCOLI

1 pound broccoli	2 tablespoons water
2 teaspoons light soy sauce	½ teaspoon salt or to taste
2 tablespoons dark brown	2 tablespoons peanut oil
sugar	1 teaspoon shredded ginger-
1 tablespoon dry sherry	root
Dash of pepper	

Preparation
Cut the broccoli flowerets from their stems and set aside. Cut the broccoli stems diagonally to make thin slices about ⅛ inch thick. Mix together the soy sauce, sugar, sherry, pepper, and water.

Cooking
Heat a wok or skillet over high heat until a drop of water immediately sizzles into steam. Add the salt, oil, and gingerroot. Stir for 30 seconds or until the gingerroot begins to brown. Add the broccoli stems and stir-fry for 1 minute or until they have almost reached their peak of color, a bright deep green. Add the flowerets and the soy sauce mixture. Stir for 30 seconds to dissolve the sugar.

Yield: 4–8 servings.

FUKIEN FISHBALL SOUP

Fukien is known for its soups and its fish dishes. This is a simple every-day soup that captures the flavor of that coastal region. A cup of shredded lettuce or Chinese cabbage can be added if vegetables are desired.

½ pound fish fillet	1 tablespoon dry sherry
1 tablespoon minced ginger-	½ teaspoon salt or to taste
root	½ teaspoon sugar
1 tablespoon light soy sauce	Liberal dash of pepper
2 tablespoons minced scal-	½ teaspoon sesame oil
lions	6 cups fish or chicken stock

Preparation

Mince the fish very finely and put into a mixing bowl. Add all the other ingredients except the fish or chicken stock and mix thoroughly. Shape fishballs between the palms of the hands into the size of a walnut.

Cooking

Bring the stock to a boil. Add the fishballs. Simmer for four minutes.

Yield: 6 servings.

FUKIEN FISH AND VEGETABLE SOUP

½ pound fish fillet
1½ teaspoons light soy sauce
⅛ teaspoon pepper
1 teaspoon cornstarch
½ teaspoon salt
1 tablespoon sesame oil

½ teaspoon sugar
1 quart chicken stock
2 slices gingerroot, the size of a half-dollar
2 cups thinly sliced Chinese cabbage (*bok choy*)

Preparation

Slice the fish into ¼-inch slices. Blend the fish with the soy sauce, pepper, cornstarch, salt, oil, and sugar. Let stand for 15 minutes.

Cooking

Bring the chicken stock to a boil. Add the gingerroot and cabbage. Lower heat to simmer for five minutes. Gently add the fish mixture and stir carefully. Cover and simmer for five minutes.

Yield: 6 servings.

FUKIENESE SEA TREASURES SOUP

The unusual ingredient in this soup is fish maw, which has no flavor of its own but offers an interesting spongy texture.

⅛ pound fish maw	½ teaspoon salt or to taste
1 teaspoon white wine vinegar	½ teaspoon sugar
1 tablespoon sherry	½ teaspoon light soy sauce
¼ pound crab meat	¼ cup thinly sliced bamboo
12 snow peas	shoots
¼ pound shrimp	Dash of pepper
1 quart chicken stock	½ teaspoon sesame oil
4 Chinese black mushrooms, soaked and shredded	

Preparation

Soak the fish maw for 3 hours in cold water. It will expand 3 to 4 times in size. Place the fish maw in boiling water with the vinegar and sherry. Simmer for 10 minutes. Drain. Rinse thoroughly in cold water and squeeze dry. Cut into 1-inch cubes. Flake and pick over the crab meat to remove any pieces of cartilage or shell. String the snow peas. Shell and devein the shrimp, then dice them.

Cooking

Bring the chicken stock to a boil. Add the fish maw, mushrooms, salt, sugar, and soy sauce. Cover and simmer for 30 minutes. Add the shrimp, crab meat, bamboo shoots, snow peas, pepper, and oil. Stir. Cover and simmer for 5 minutes.

Yield: 6 servings.

CRAB-MEAT SOUP

A very simple but elegant soup, this is the Fukienese variation of egg drop soup.

1 cup crab meat	½ teaspoon salt or to taste
2 egg whites	½ teaspoon light soy sauce
1 quart chicken stock	1 tablespoon cornstarch mixed
Dash of pepper	with ¼ cup water

Preparation and cooking

Flake and pick over the crab meat to remove any pieces of cartilage or shell. Beat the egg whites very lightly. Bring the chicken stock to a boil. Add the pepper, salt, soy sauce, and crab meat. Cover and simmer for 5 minutes. Stir in the cornstarch mixture until the soup thickens and is smooth. Slowly pour the egg whites into the broth while stirring the broth. Serve.

Yield: 6 servings.

CRAB-MEAT, WATERCRESS, AND BEAN-CURD SOUP

1 bunch watercress	Dash of pepper
2 bean curds	½ teaspoon sugar
1 cup crab meat	½ teaspoon salt or to taste
1 quart chicken stock	½ teaspoon light soy sauce

Preparation

Wash, drain, and trim the watercress. Slice the bean curds into 1-inch squares. Flake and pick over the crab meat to remove any pieces of cartilage or shell.

Cooking

Bring the chicken stock to a boil. Add the pepper, sugar, salt, soy sauce, watercress, and crab meat. Cover and simmer for 5 minutes.

Yield: 6 servings.

SIZZLING RICE SOUP

1 quart chicken stock	½ cup peas
½ teaspoon salt or to taste	½ cup button mushrooms
½ teaspoon light soy sauce	Oil for deep-frying
½ teaspoon sugar	1 cup rice crusts (see recipe on page 271)
Dash of pepper	
1 tablespoon cornstarch mixed with ¼ cup water	3 tablespoons minced scallions
½ cup diced cooked shrimp	
½ cup cooked, boned, and diced chicken breast	

Cooking

Bring the chicken stock to a boil and add the salt, soy sauce, sugar, and pepper. Stir in the cornstarch mixture until the soup thickens and is smooth. Add the shrimp, chicken, peas, and mushrooms. Simmer for 5 minutes.

In the meantime, deep-fry the rice crusts in the oil heated to 375 degrees until they have turned golden brown. Pour the soup into a tureen. Sprinkle with the scallions and serve immediately. Serve the rice crusts in a separate dish at the same time. Drop the rice crusts into the soup at the table. They will sizzle or "sing" delightfully to entertain your dinner companions.

Yield: 6–8 servings.

FUKIENESE "WONTON" SOUP

The Fukienese housewives make a dumpling skin (like a wonton *skin) out of meat. It is difficult to believe such a skin is possible until you try it.*

1 pound boned pork	½ pound ground pork
2 cups cornstarch	Dash of pepper
¾ cup chopped, shelled, and deveined raw shrimp	½ teaspoon sugar
	3 scallions, chopped
½ cup chopped bamboo shoots	6 cups chicken stock

Preparation

Mince or grind the 1 pound of boneless pork very finely. Add the cornstarch a little at a time and knead it into the pork thoroughly before adding a bit more. When the "dough" is no longer sticky but still elastic, roll it into a long sausage about 1¼ inches thick. Pull off a large enough piece from the sausage so that when it has been rolled out into a thin circle it will be 3 inches in diameter.

In a bowl combine the remaining ingredients with the exception of the chicken stock. The bits of shrimp, bamboo shoots, and scallions (when chopped) should be less than ¼ inch in size to correspond to the size of the grains of ground pork.

Fill each of the meat circles with a tablespoon of the filling. Fold the skin in half and seal by pressing the edges firmly together.

Cooking

Bring the chicken stock to a boil in a large pot. Add the "wontons."

When the chicken stock again comes to a boil, reduce the heat and simmer for 15 minutes. Serve as a soup.

Yield: 8–10 servings.

YANGCHOW FRIED RICE

Fried rice is usually little more than a dish containing leftovers, although a very good one when properly done. Yangchow fried rice, however, rises far above its humble origins and becomes worthy of inclusion in the finest banquets owing to its variety of flavors and restrained seasoning.

1 tablespoon peanut oil	¼ cup chicken stock or water
½ teaspoon salt	2 teaspoons dry sherry
1 egg, lightly beaten	2 tablespoons diced scallions
¼ cup diced cooked shrimp	1 cup shredded lettuce
¼ cup diced Chinese roast pork	Dash of pepper
2 tablespoons diced Smithfield ham	¼ teaspoon sugar
	1 teaspoon light soy sauce
3 cups cooked rice, preferably 1 day old	

Cooking

Heat a wok or skillet over high heat until a drop of water immediately sizzles into steam. Add the oil and salt. Stir until the oil is hot and then scramble the egg. Break up with a spatula into 1-inch pieces.

Add the shrimp, pork, ham, rice, chicken stock, and sherry. Break up the clumps of rice and stir-fry for 2 minutes.

Add the scallion, lettuce, pepper, sugar, and soy sauce. Stir-fry for 1 minute more.

Yield: 4–8 servings.

CHICKEN FRIED RICE

1 tablespoon peanut oil	¼ cup diced cooked chicken
¼ teaspoon salt	3 cups cooked rice, preferably 1 day old
1 egg, beaten	Dash of pepper
¼ cup bean sprouts	1 teaspoon dark soy sauce
¼ cup diced onions	¼ teaspoon sugar
¼ cup chicken stock or water	

Cooking

Heat a wok or skillet over high heat until a drop of water immediately sizzles into steam. Add the oil and salt. Stir briefly. Add the egg and scramble it until done. Break up the egg with a spatula into 1-inch pieces. Add the bean sprouts and onions and, after a stir or two, the chicken stock. Stir-fry for 1 minute.

Add the chicken, rice, pepper, soy sauce, and sugar. Break up the lumps of rice and stir-fry for 2 minutes more.

Note: For Roast Pork Fried Rice, substitute ¼ cup Chinese roast pork for the chicken. For Shrimp Fried Rice, substitute ½ cup diced cooked shrimp for the chicken.

Yield: 4–8 servings.

YANGCHOW WOH MEIN

3 chicken livers	½ cup thinly sliced Chinese
3 chicken gizzards	roast pork
12 snow peas or ½ cup peas	¼ cup thinly sliced chicken
1 pound Chinese egg noodles	breast
1½ quarts chicken stock, seasoned to taste	¼ cup soaked and shredded Chinese black mushrooms
¼ cup thinly sliced canned abalone	½ cup thinly sliced bamboo shoots
½ cup shelled and deveined shrimp	½ teaspoon sesame oil
	3 scallions, diced

Preparation

Wash the livers and gizzards and cut them into quarters. String the snow peas.

Cooking

Place the noodles in boiling water for 3 to 5 minutes until tender. Do not overcook. Drain. Rinse with cold water in a colander. Place the noodles in a tureen. Bring the chicken stock to a boil. Add all the remaining ingredients except the scallions. Cook for 2 minutes. Ladle over the noodles in the tureen. Sprinkle with the scallions.

Yield: 4–6 servings.

SHANGHAI SPRING ROLLS

Spring rolls are less well known than their southern cousins, the Can-
tonese egg rolls. The Shanghai rolls are more restrained in flavor and have
more delicate skins. Although the skins can be made at home with consid-
erable practice and diligence, it is infinitely easier to buy them at a Chinese
food shop.

The Filling

8 Chinese black mushrooms	Dash of pepper
2 pressed bean curds	1 cup bean sprouts
1 cup cubed, shelled, and de-veined raw shrimp	1 teaspoon sugar
	½ cup shredded bamboo shoots
2 teaspoons dry sherry	½ cup shredded water chest-nuts
2 teaspoons cornstarch	
2 tablespoons peanut oil	½ cup shredded snow peas
½ teaspoon salt or to taste	1 cup chopped Chinese chives or scallions
½ pound ground pork	
1 tablespoon light soy sauce	2 teaspoons sesame oil

The Spring Rolls

20 square Shanghai spring roll skins	Beaten egg for sealing
	1 cup peanut oil for pan-frying

Preparation

Soak the mushrooms for 30 minutes in water or until soft. Remove the stems and dice the mushrooms. Cut the bean curds into matchstick slivers. Combine the shrimp with 1 teaspoon of the sherry and 1 teaspoon of the cornstarch.

Cooking the filling

Heat a wok or skillet over high heat until a drop of water immediately sizzles into steam. Maintain high heat throughout the cooking process. Add the peanut oil and salt. Stir for 30 seconds. Add the pork and shrimp. Stir for 1½ to 2 minutes until the pork turns white.

Add the remaining sherry, the soy sauce, and pepper. Stir in the bean sprouts, mushrooms, sugar, bamboo shoots, water chestnuts, and snow peas. Stir-fry for 1 minute. Turn off heat and stir in the bean curds, chives or scallions, and sesame oil. Allow the filling to cool completely.

Preparing the spring rolls

The spring roll skins should be covered with a damp cloth as you work to prevent them from drying out. To fill the spring roll skins, place a square of skin in front of you with one corner pointing toward you. Spoon 3 to 5 tablespoons of the filling horizontally an inch or so below the center of the skin. Cover the filling with the corner of the skin facing you. Roll the skin for one turn to enclose the filling. Moisten the far corner from you with beaten egg. Roll the skin into a cylinder. Press gently and seal. Repeat the process until all of the filling has been used.

Pan-frying the spring rolls
Heat the 1 cup peanut oil for frying in a skillet until it is almost smoking. Add several spring rolls, allowing enough room to turn them over. Cook until the skins are crisp and golden brown. Place the fried rolls on paper toweling to drain the excess oil. Do not stack on top of one another because this will cause steam to collect and the rolls will become soggy.
Serve with small dishes of mustard, hot oil, vinegar, or plum sauce.

Yield: 20 large rolls.

SPRING ROLL SKINS

2 cups all-purpose flour, sifted   1 cup water

Preparation
Gradually add the flour to the water, stirring constantly to keep lumps from forming. A French wire whisk is an ideal tool but, admittedly, not very Chinese. When the thick batter is completely smooth, cover the bowl with a damp cloth and let it stand 1 hour to rest.

Cooking
Heat a heavy, very lightly greased skillet over low heat. Take a handful of the batter and press it onto the skillet. Then pull back the excess so that only a thin layer of batter adheres to the skillet. After about 30 seconds the skin is cooked and may be pulled gently from the skillet. Place the skin on a plate covered with a damp cloth. Repeat this process until all the batter is used up.

Yield: About 20 skins.

RED WINE SEDIMENT PASTE

1½ tablespoons red bean curd
1 teaspoon finely chopped
  gingerroot
4 teaspoons light brown sugar
1 teaspoon minced garlic
¼ cup dry sherry
¼ cup dry red wine

1 tablespoon tomato paste
1 tablespoon orange-flavored
  liqueur
1 teaspoon rice flour
½ teaspoon dark soy sauce
1 teaspoon finely grated tangerine peel

Cooking

Blend all the ingredients together in a small pot over low-medium heat for 10 minutes. Stored in the refrigerator, this paste will keep for about a month.

Yield: About ¾ cup.

2

NORTH CHINA

Kansu, Shensi, Shansi,
Honan, Hopeh, Shantung

The north is China's ancient heartland. It was here, along the Yellow and Wei rivers, that the Chinese people first emerged thousands of years ago. It was in the north that Confucius, Mencius, and the great classic philosophers lived and taught centuries before the birth of Christ. For all but a few of its thousands of years of history, the Chinese have chosen the north for their capital which drew people from all of China. It was from the north, during the great Han Dynasty (197 B.C.–A.D. 220) that the first camel caravans departed through the Kansu corridor along the famed Silk Road with goods that would ultimately find their way to India and even to Roman Europe. On their return journeys, these caravans brought new products and goods, new ideas, and tales of the strange lands at the other end of the earth.

Yet the north is very different from the rest of China. The difference is so dramatic that Marco Polo gave the north the name of Cathay in contrast to the south which he called Manji. One of the reasons for this difference is that the Tsinling Mountains which form most of the southern border of this region cut off the warm moist winds that moderate the climate of the rest of China. The north is a land of extremes. The winters are cold, dry, and windy, marked by frequent dust storms that almost hide the sun. The summers, on the other hand, are oppressively hot with the temperature frequently rising to above 100 degrees. Here the summer rains are cruelly variable. Peking has recorded July rainfalls of more than thirty inches in some years and less than a third of an inch in others. As a result, every year holds the possibility of famine, whether from flood or drought.

Since the Ch'in dynasty of the third century B.C., the Great Wall has marked the northern border of China. It stretches for 2,500 miles from the province of Kansu in the west to the sea in the east. It was built to protect the Chinese farmlands from incursions by the nomads of the north. Unfortunately, although physical boundaries such as walls stay put, climatic ones do not. Over the centuries the land on either side of the Great Wall has cyclically changed from desert to pastureland to agriculturally viable land and back again. During humid periods the Chinese farmers moved outside the Wall, but during dry periods when the pastureland outside the Wall turned to desert, the nomads invaded China.

The vast majority of the northern Chinese live on the great alluvial plain formed in the east by the Yellow River. The land is flat, except for dikes and ancestral burial mounds that dot the carefully tended fields. An occasional grove of trees surrounds a temple or monastery, but otherwise the plain is treeless, the result of early Chinese agricultural exuberance. Houses are made of pounded earth or sun-dried bricks, and during the dusty winter they become almost invisible against the yellow earth and yellow sky. Until recently the houses have been unheated except for the practice of circulating the warm smoke from the kitchen stove through a baffle beneath a brick sleeping platform in an adjoining room—a scant but welcome relief on frigid winter nights.

The peculiarities of the Hwang Ho or Yellow River dominate the plain. As it descends from its source in Tibet to the Yellow River plain, the Hwang picks up immense amounts of yellowish silt as it winds through the western loess and this silt begins to drop to the riverbed when the Hwang enters the plain so that, over a period of time, the river actually rises above the surrounding plain. Contained only by its bed, the river sometimes breaks through its banks and flows to lower ground, completely inundating the land for as much as hundreds of square miles in any direction. Small wonder the Hwang Ho is known as China's sorrow.

From earliest times, the Chinese have energetically built dikes to contain the flood waters. This practice has only encouraged a greater accumulation of silt and a higher riverbed. Despite inevitable disaster, land-hungry Chinese persisted in setting up farms along the river, even within the dikes themselves.

If left to its own devices, the Hwang, when it breaks its banks, would seek a new and lower course and throughout history this has happened repeatedly. At least fifteen times the mouth of the river has changed locations over a 350-mile stretch of coast. An amusing story is told of a British fleet which blockaded the mouth of the river to improve the British negotiating position with the Chinese. After waiting for some weeks and finding no traffic on the river, the British discovered to their chagrin that they were opposite the most recent but not the current mouth.

The chief city of the plain is Peking, also the capital of China. Although many cities have occupied its site, the present city with its broad avenues, regular plan, and impressive gates was laid out by Kublai Khan in the thirteenth century. The choice of Peking as capital was a logical one for the Mongols as well as the later Manchus because of its proximity to their northern homelands. But the Chinese found it a useful spot as well for keeping a watchful eye on their sometimes rambunctious neighbors to the north.

Peking is an interesting city, really four cities in one. The major portion, called the Tartar City, lies within a fifty-foot-high wall. Within this city is the walled Manchu City, and within it the Forbidden City, once the imperial compound. Since the Chinese were at one time forbidden to live within the Tartar City, they built another city to the south called, of course, the Chinese City.

Life in Peking was long dominated by the court and by the offices of government. To Peking have come people from all over China. Restaurants sprang up to cater to these visitors and semipermanent residents from distant regions of China. Exposure to many different styles of cooking has given the so-called Mandarin or northern cuisine an eclectic, cosmopolitan quality that explains the presence of Szechwan, Shanghai, and other regional dishes on the menus of nominally northern restaurants.

The imperial court dishes, of course, influenced the food of the upper classes, and it is these dishes that have given Peking its gastronomic reputation. Characteristic of court cooking was the heavy use of wine and *kaoliang*, a grain-based liquor. The food was usually gently cooked and the flavoring restrained. The overall effect was almost austere to some tastes although the main ingredient might have been quite exotic, such as fish lips, bear's paw, and the like.

In contrast, the food of the common people was simple and often pungent. Noodles and pancakes of wheat and millet flour were the basic starch and filler. Rice was a luxury reserved for the upper classes or for special occasions. Onions, scallions, garlic, and leeks were used with enthusiasm and often combined with brown bean sauce or a mixture of soy sauce and vinegar. It is snidely said by Chinese from other regions that the northerners tend to be so tall and heavily built because the vast amounts of onions and garlic they eat keep the "germs" away.

Some have suggested that a true regional cuisine is lacking, that the northerners have simply adopted the best of the rest of China as their own. Others claim that everything good and delicious in Chinese cooking was created in the north, citing the fact, for example, that the many sweet-and-sour dishes first originated in Honan province. Still others focus on Shantung province as the source of the best of the Peking or northern cuisine.

Shantung province is little more than a hilly promontory extending into the Yellow Sea. Because of its proximity to the sea, its climate is moist and quite moderate. It has been particularly famous for its fruits. Apples and hard sweet pears are grown along with the indigenous peach and imported grapes. Pongee silk is produced by silkworms fed on oak leaves. The sacred mountain, T'ai Shan, is located there. It was believed to hold the springs of life and to control man's activities after death. Emperors worshiped here. Confucius lived near its base and thousands of tourists still climb the six thousand stone steps which lead to the temples at the summit. Once most of Shantung was forested, but the trees were cut down and serious erosion followed, ruining much of the land for agriculture and leading to major immigration to Manchuria.

The broad loessland in the west is the least populated region of northern China. (Loess refers to the windborn silt which covers and levels most of the rolling terrain to depths of as much as three hundred feet.)

The loess itself is very fertile, but the scantiness of rainfall makes agriculture difficult except in river valleys where irrigation is possible. There fruit and even rice is grown. Where there is some rainfall, wheat, millet, *kaoliang,* sweet potatoes, and corn are grown. Where there is less rain, the loess is used as pastureland for livestock.

The loess is very fine in texture and has the curious property of standing vertically. Here ordinary roads have become canyons of up to forty feet in depth as every passing cart cuts deeper into the loess. Another curious phenomenon was the cave dwellings carved out of the loess, where the farmer could literally live beneath his farm. These would be cool in summer and well insulated in the winter. Small shafts for smoke led from stoves in the cave dwellings to the field above. Thus one might see smoke curling up from cultivated fields without house or person in sight.

The people of the loessland are diverse. After the Revolution of 1911, China adopted a flag with five stripes to signify each of the major peoples of China. Yellow was for the Chinese, white for the Moslems, red for the Manchus, blue for the Mongols, and black for the Tibetans. The northwest is the only section where all five groups live together. The Moslems, a particularly interesting group, originally came from Middle Asia during the Mongol regime. While face veils for women were abolished, in fairly recent times a very short veil or hat can still be seen and the men wear a white skull cap. Over the centuries they have remained largely unassimilated. The Chinese attribute this to their aversion to pork which plays such a central role in Chinese cooking. This theory may not be completely simplistic for there was at one time common intermarriage between the small but ancient Jewish community in Kaifang and the Moslems, who shared their dietary taboos, but not with the Chinese.

In the loessland one finds agricultural and pastoral peoples living together in relative peace, for this has traditionally been a frontier area with land enough for all to live according to their own styles. Here the sophistication of elegant cutting and stir-frying of the Yellow River plain gives way to the simpler techniques of roasting and simmering. Beef and lamb are available and more widely used than elsewhere in China. Perhaps the main contribution of this region to Chinese cooking is the notion of the hot pot where each person cooks his own combination of meat and vegetables in a simmering caldron of soup.

DRUNKEN CHICKEN

This simple but elegant dish takes its name from the quantity of wine used to marinate the chicken. The quality of the ingredients is essential to the success of this recipe—a freshly killed and tasty pullet and a good dry sherry that was intended for drinking and not just cooking. If one is feeling extravagant, substitute additional sherry for the reserved chicken stock. Sherry is the preferred substitute for good rice wine which is still almost impossible to find.

2 slices gingerroot, the size of a half-dollar
1 scallion
1 chicken, preferably freshly killed, about 4 pounds

3 tablespoons kosher salt, or more if needed
2 cups dry sherry
    Chopped coriander or scallions to garnish

Preparation
Place the gingerroot and the scallion in the cavity of the chicken.

Cooking
Steam the chicken in a heatproof bowl over rapidly boiling water for 40 minutes or until done, that is, when the juices run clear. Remove the bowl from the steamer and let both the chicken and the chicken stock cool to room temperature. Reserve the chicken stock.

Chop the chicken into eight pieces, i.e., two wings, two drumsticks, two thighs, and two breasts. Sprinkle both sides of the chicken parts well with salt. This will serve to partially cure them. Let the chicken parts stand at room temperature in a covered dish overnight.

The next day combine 2 cups of the reserved chicken stock with the sherry. Pour this mixture over the chicken parts and refrigerate in a covered dish at least overnight or for as long as a week. If the chicken is not completely covered by this marinade, either add more sherry and chicken stock at a one-to-one ratio or turn the pieces over from time to time.

When ready to serve, chop the chicken parts into 1- to 2-inch pieces. Garnish with coriander or scallions. Serve cool.

Yield: 4–10 servings.

CHICKEN VELVET

One might call Chicken Velvet the Chinese answer to the French soufflé. Both are somewhat tricky to make, but when well made incredibly delightful. Like the preceding recipe for Drunken Chicken, this is a court dish probably first served to an emperor. The snow peas are not authentic, but give some visual color to an otherwise monochromatic dish. The variations on Chicken Velvet are many, including poaching the dumplings in soup.

12 snow peas (optional)	2 cups chicken stock
1 teaspoon dry sherry	Oil for deep-frying
¾ teaspoon salt	2 tablespoons rendered chick-
2 tablespoons cornstarch	en fat
4 egg whites	2 tablespoons minced cooked
1 whole chicken breast	Smithfield ham to garnish

Preparation
Wash and string the snow peas. In a medium bowl, combine the sherry, ½ teaspoon of the salt, 1 tablespoon of the cornstarch, and 1 egg white. In a separate bowl, beat the remaining egg whites until they are frothy.

Bone the chicken breast and remove the skin and gristle. Dice the meat finely. Chop the meat very thoroughly and, while chopping, slowly add teaspoon by teaspoon ¼ cup of the chicken stock. Do not add another teaspoon of the chicken stock until the previous one has been absorbed into the meat. The result will be a very thick, smooth paste.

Place the chicken in the bowl with the cornstarch and egg-white mixture. Stir well to combine. Blend in ¾ cup of the chicken stock a little at a time to this mixture, stirring constantly.

Fold the frothy egg whites into the chicken paste mixture.

Cooking
Heat the oil over moderate heat to 300 degrees. Gently put a tablespoon of the chicken mixture into the oil. Repeat until the pan is full of these little dumplings. Remove the dumplings with a slotted spoon when they have become white and firm. They should not be allowed to brown. Place the cooked dumplings in a colander over a bowl to drain. Repeat this process until all the chicken mixture has been used. Place the drained dumplings on a hot serving platter and keep them warm.

Mix the remaining cornstarch with ¼ cup of the chicken stock. Reserve the remaining ¾ cup of chicken stock. Pour off all but 2 tablespoons of the oil from the pan.

Heat the oil over high heat and add the remaining salt. Just before the oil begins to smoke, add the snow peas and stir to coat well with the oil. Add the remaining chicken stock and bring to a boil. Add the cornstarch mixture and stir until thickened. Sprinkle with the chicken fat. Pour the snow peas and sauce over the chicken. Garnish with the ham and serve immediately.

Yield: 2–4 servings.

PAPER-WRAPPED CHICKEN

An amusing dish that is fun although not particularly filling to eat. The ingredients may be altered to suit one's mood or the state of one's larder. The waxed paper protects the meat from the very hot oil while allowing the heat to penetrate and cook the meat.

1 pound boned and skinned chicken breast	Waxed paper
1 teaspoon sugar	20 very thin slices bamboo shoots
2 tablespoons gin	20 very thin slices cooked Smithfield ham
⅛ teaspoon white pepper	20 very thin slices leek, white part only
2 tablespoons sesame oil	Oil for deep-frying
1 tablespoon dark soy sauce	
2 tablespoons light soy sauce	

Preparation

Slice the chicken meat as thinly as possible into slices approximately ¾ by 1½ inches. In a small bowl combine the sugar, gin, pepper, sesame oil, and soy sauces. Cut the waxed paper into about 20 4- or 5-inch squares.

To assemble the packages, take a square of waxed paper and grease the side facing you. Take a slice of chicken, dredge it in the soy sauce mixture, and place it diagonally in the middle of the square. On top of the chicken put a slice of bamboo shoot, a slice of ham, a slice of leek, and finally another slice of chicken also dredged in the soy sauce mixture. Take the corner of the waxed paper below the chicken and pull it up over the chicken until it almost meets the corner above the chicken. Fold the other two corners over the chicken to form an envelope. Take the flap of this "envelope" and pull it over the chicken. Tuck the flap under to secure the package.

Cooking

Heat the oil to 375 degrees or until it is almost smoking. Deep-fry the packages a few at a time for about ½ minute on each side or until they reach a light brown color. Drain the packages and serve immediately. The packages can be easily opened with chopsticks or fork to reach the succulent morsels inside.

Yield: 20 packages.

STEAMED CHICKEN LEGS AND WINGS WITH WINE

2 pounds chicken legs and wings
1 tablespoon salt
2 tablespoons shredded gingerroot

4 scallions, chopped in 2-inch lengths
½ cup dry white wine

Preparation
Clean the chicken and dry with paper towels. Rub the salt into the chicken. Place in a heatproof dish. Sprinkle the gingerroot and scallions over the chicken. Pour the wine over the chicken.

Cooking
Steam in a steamer over boiling water for 25 minutes or until done.

Yield: 3–6 servings.

PEKING SALT-CURED CHICKEN

1 chicken, preferably freshly killed, about 4 pounds
2 tablespoons kosher salt

1 tablespoon shredded gingerroot
2 scallions

Preparation
Clean the chicken and dry with paper towels. Mix the salt and the gingerroot together and rub inside and outside of the chicken. Stuff the scallions into the cavity. Place the chicken in a bowl and cover with aluminum foil. Refrigerate for two days.

Cooking
Steam over rapidly boiling water for 40 minutes or until done. Chop into bite-size pieces.

Yield: 3–6 servings.

BROWN-SUGAR SMOKED CHICKEN

The Chinese have been smoking meats from time immemorial but in the following recipes burning sugar provides the flavoring rather than fragrant wood. The flavor is unique. Fish steaks are also delicious cooked in this manner—salmon is particularly good. Unless your pot has a very tight lid do not try smoking in this manner if windows cannot be opened or an efficient exhaust fan cannot be turned on.

1 chicken, about 4 pounds	1½ tablespoon kosher salt
1 tablespoon finely minced gingerroot	4 scallions
	¾ cup dark brown sugar

Preparation
Clean the chicken and dry with paper towels. Mix the gingerroot with the salt. Rub the mixture thoroughly both inside and outside of the chicken. Let stand overnight in the refrigerator. Place the scallions in the cavity of the chicken.

Cooking
Place the chicken in a heatproof dish and steam for 40 minutes or until done. Allow it to cool and pat it dry.
For the next step you will need a Dutch oven with a tight lid. Line the inside with aluminum foil. Also line the inside of the cover. Spread the sugar evenly on the bottom. Place a rack on top of the sugar. Set the steamed chicken on top of the rack. Cover and smoke over medium heat for 20 minutes. Remove from heat and let stand for 30 more minutes. Chop into bite-size pieces and serve.

Yield: 3–6 servings.

TEA SMOKED CHICKEN

A variation on the preceding recipe is achieved by throwing in some tea leaves along with the brown sugar. Try experimenting with flavored teas such as jasmine and lychee.

2 tablespoons kosher salt	⅓ cup dark brown sugar
1 tablespoon Szechwan peppercorns	⅓ cup fresh tea leaves
1 chicken, about 3 pounds	1 tablespoon sesame oil

Preparation

In an ungreased pan over moderate heat toast the salt and peppercorns for 4 minutes, stirring steadily. At the end of this time the peppercorns should be fragrant and the salt slightly browned. Crush the mixture with the handle of a cleaver or between two layers of waxed paper using a rolling pin.

Remove any excess fat from the cavity of the chicken. Rinse the chicken under running water and pat dry with paper towels. Rub the chicken inside and out with the peppercorn mixture. Wrap the chicken in plastic wrap and let it sit in the refrigerator for at least 6 hours or overnight.

Cooking

Steam the chicken over rapidly boiling water for 40 minutes or until done, that is, when its juices run clear. Remove the chicken from the steamer and pat dry with paper towels.

Thoroughly line a heavy pot with aluminum foil. Also line its lid. Sprinkle the bottom of the pot with the sugar and tea leaves. Place a rack in the pot to keep the chicken above the tea and sugar. Put the chicken in the pot.

Place the pot over high heat. When the sugar begins to smoke, cover the pot, lower the heat slightly, and smoke the chicken for 15 minutes. At the end of that time, turn off the heat and let the covered pot stand for 30 minutes more.

Brush the chicken with the oil. Either carve the chicken in the American manner or chop it into bite-size pieces with the bone in according to the Chinese manner. Serve either hot or at room temperature.

Yield: 3–6 servings.

JULING CHICKEN

The rendered chicken fat in the following sauce both binds the flavors and gives body to the sauce. The combination of dark soy sauce and wine vinegar is typically northern.

3 tablespoons dark soy sauce	2 tablespoons white rice wine
½ chicken, about 1½ pounds	vinegar
¼ cup rendered chicken fat	Oil for deep-frying

Preparation

Rub 1 tablespoon of the soy sauce into the chicken and let it stand for 10 minutes. Put the remaining soy sauce, the chicken fat, and vinegar in a small pot.

Cooking

Deep-fry the chicken in the oil heated to 375 degrees for 5 minutes on each side. Chop the chicken into 1½- by 1-inch pieces and place them in a serving dish.

Heat the soy sauce mixture over medium to low heat, stirring constantly until the mixture almost comes to a boil. Pour over the chicken.

Yield: 2–4 servings.

SHANTUNG CHICKEN WITH HOT HOISIN SAUCE

Hoisin sauce is a widely used condiment in the north. Its rich fruity quality goes admirably with chicken.

2 whole chicken breasts	1 teaspoon minced gingerroot
2 tablespoons hoisin sauce	1 cup diced bamboo shoots
1½ tablespoons dry sherry	2 tablespoons scallions (¼-
1 tablespoon dark soy sauce	inch lengths)
¼ teaspoon crushed red pepper	¼ cup chicken stock
or to taste	2 tablespoons peanut oil

Preparation

Bone the chicken breasts and remove the skin. Dice into ¼-inch cubes. Mix well with the hoisin sauce, sherry, and soy sauce. Combine the remaining ingredients with the exception of the oil.

Cooking

Heat a wok or skillet over high heat until a drop of water immediately sizzles into steam. Add the oil. Stir for 30 seconds. Add the chicken with the marinade and stir-fry for 2 minutes. Add the remaining ingredients and stir-fry for 2 minutes.

Yield: 4–8 servings.

CHILLED CHICKEN SALAD

½ spring chicken, about 1	1 tablespoon minced gingerroot
pound	2 tablespoons light soy sauce
3 cucumbers	2 tablespoons red wine vinegar
1 leek or 3 scallions, white	1 tablespoon sesame oil
parts only	2 tablespoons sugar
1 tablespoon sesame seeds	1 teaspoon crushed red pepper

Preparation

Boil the chicken for about 30 minutes. Let it cool. Remove the meat from the bones and shred the meat and skin. Wash the cucumbers and shred into matchstick pieces. Shred the white part of the leek or scallions. Toast the sesame seeds in a dry, hot frying pan for 5 minutes, shaking from time to time to keep the seeds from burning.

Mix the shredded chicken with the cucumbers and place in a serving dish. Sprinkle with the leek or scallions and gingerroot. Place in the refrigerator. Mix the remaining ingredients and add the sesame seeds. Pour over the chicken and cucumbers just before serving. Toss well.

Yield: 2–6 servings.

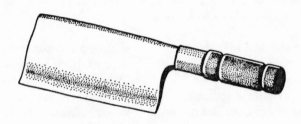

FRIED TIENTSIN DUCK

1 duck, 4 to 5 pounds	2 eggs, beaten
2 tablespoons kosher salt	2 teaspoons light soy sauce
1 teaspoon five-flavor powder	¼ cup cornstarch
2 tablespoons dry sherry	Oil for deep-frying

Preparation

Rinse the duck under cold water and dry well with paper towels. Mix the salt and five-flavor powder. Rub this mixture inside and outside of the duck. Put a rack on the bottom of a heatproof dish and place the duck on the rack. Mix the sherry with the eggs and soy sauce.

Cooking

Cook the duck in a steamer over rapidly boiling water for 1 to 1½ hours. Remove and let it cool. Bone the duck and cut it into bite-size pieces. Coat the pieces with the egg, soysauce, and sherry mixture and dredge in the cornstarch. Heat the oil to 375 degrees and deep-fry for 2 minutes until brown and crisp.

Yield: 6–10 servings.

DUCK WITH POTATOES

The humble potato, both sweet and white varieties, has been widely grown in China ever since its introduction from the Americas several centuries ago. It is prized for its ability to thrive where other crops will not. However, the Chinese consider it inferior food fit only for livestock and the very poor. Nevertheless, a few potato dishes have been created that are definitely not humble, and this is one of them.

1 duck, about 5 pounds	3 tablespoons dry sherry
6 tablespoons light soy sauce	1 tablespoon salt
2 pounds white boiling potatoes	1 tablespoon sugar
	⅛ teaspoon black pepper
2 tablespoons brown bean sauce	1 quart water
	¼ cup peanut oil
¼ cup red bean curd	2 teaspoons cornstarch mixed with ¼ cup water
2 star anise (16 sections)	

Preparation

Wash the duck and dry thoroughly with paper towels. Rub 2 tablespoons of the soy sauce into its skin. Peel the potatoes and cut them into 1½-inch cubes. Thoroughly mix the remaining soy sauce with the brown bean sauce, red bean curd, star anise, sherry, salt, sugar, pepper, and water to form a sauce.

Cooking

Set a wok or large skillet over high heat for ½ minute. Add the oil and swirl it around the pan over high heat for another ½ minute. Add the duck and brown it on all sides until it has turned an amber color. Remove the duck.

Pour 1 cup of the sauce into the cavity of the duck and truss the duck well. Bring the remaining sauce to a boil. Add the duck and the potatoes. Cover the pan and simmer for 20 minutes on each side, basting occasionally.

Remove the duck, and when cool, chop it into 1½-inch pieces. Put the chopped duck in the center of a large serving platter and surround the duck with potatoes.

Bring the sauce to a light boil and, stirring constantly, add the cornstarch mixture. Stir until thickened. Remove the sauce from the heat and pour over the duck and the potatoes.

Yield: 6–10 servings.

PEKING DUCK

Peking duck, one of the best-known dishes in the Chinese repertoire, must be served sizzling hot from the oven. This requisite is one of the reasons why restaurant versions are almost always disappointing. The original recipe is more than fifteen thousand words long and almost every direction is dedicated to making the skin as crisp as possible. The pumping up operation separates the skin from the moist flesh. The bath in boiling water tightens the skin. The honey dries to make a hard, slightly sweet glaze when the duck is hung for at least a day in a cool, breezy place. The searing in a hot oven finishes the job. All these steps, while not difficult, do take time, but the final combination of textures and flavors makes them worth the effort.

1 duck, about 5 pounds	6 to 12 scallions
¼ cup honey	1 dozen Mandarin Pancakes
2 to 4 tablespoons water	(see recipe on page 123)

Preparation

Remove excess fat from the cavity of the duck. Rinse the duck well inside and out under cold running water. Skewer or sew the duck closed leaving only one small hole. Insert the tube of a bicycle pump into the cavity of the duck and pump until the duck is visibly enlarged. (A bamboo tube and human windpower were used in China before the advent of the bicycle pump.)

Remove the pump tube from the duck and place the duck in a sink. Pour boiling water over the skin of the duck, top and bottom. Pat the skin dry with paper towels.

Combine the honey with 2 to 4 tablespoons water to make a syrup. Pour or brush this mixture over the skin of the duck. Hang the duck up by its tail to dry for at least six hours but preferably overnight in a cool, dry, breezy place. (An unheated room with a fan directed on the duck would serve well.) At the end of this time, the skin should be dry to the touch.

Cut the white parts of the scallions into 2-inch pieces. Shred one or both ends with a sharp knife and place in ice water. In about one hour, the shredded part of the scallions will have opened up to make a bushy tip.

Cooking

Preheat the oven to 450 degrees. Place the duck breast side up on a rack in a roasting pan. Put the duck in the oven, reduce the heat to 350 degrees, and cook for 1¼ hours or until done. The duck should be turned over every 15 minutes (with a towel to protect the hand) to insure even browning. The goal is a rich, even chestnut brown skin. If some of the skin appears to be browning too rapidly, cover that section with aluminum foil. After an hour or so, the skin of the duck should be dry and hard to the touch. If it is not, briefly turn the temperature back up to 450 degrees for a finishing blast of dry heat.

Remove the duck from the oven. If you wish to be completely authentic, simply remove the skin from the duck, serving the skin and saving the meat for another meal. Or, if you prefer, carve the skin and the meat together into 1½-inch-square pieces. The duck carcass is traditionally used to make a soup (see recipe on page 117).

To eat the duck, take a pancake and place a piece of the skin in its center. Take one of the scallion brushes and brush on one of the sauces given below on the duck. Wrap the pancake around the duck skin and the scallion and eat the package with your fingers.

Yield: 6–10 servings.

SAUCE FOR PEKING DUCK I

¼ cup brown bean sauce   1 tablespoon light brown sugar
1 teaspoon dark soy sauce   1 teaspoon sesame oil

Mash the brown bean sauce well and combine with the remaining ingredients.

SAUCE FOR PEKING DUCK II

¼ cup hoisin sauce   1 teaspoon sesame oil
1 tablespoon dark soy sauce

Combine the ingredients and spoon into two or three saucers.

TEA EGGS

1 dozen eggs   5 sections star anise
4 teaspoons salt   2 sticks cinnamon
3 tablespoons dark soy sauce   4 tablespoons black tea

Cooking
Cover the eggs with cold water and bring them to a simmer. Simmer gently for 20 minutes. Remove the pan from the heat. Leave the eggs in

the water until they are cool enough to handle. Crack the shell of each egg all over as though you were preparing to peel it but do *not* peel.

Return the eggs to the pan and cover them again with cold water. Add all the remaining ingredients to the pan and simmer with the cover on for 2 to 3 hours. Add more water if necessary to keep the eggs covered.

Turn off the heat and leave the eggs in the liquid at room temperature for at least 8 hours. When peeled, the eggs will be covered with a network of fine lines where the tea has seeped in. Serve the eggs cold.

Yield: 1 dozen eggs.

PEKING EGG YOLKS

What does one do with egg yolks left over from Chicken Velvet, a soufflé, or an angel food cake? If your cholesterol count can take it, by all means try this dish.

½ cup egg yolks
1 cup chicken stock
½ cup minced water chestnuts
½ teaspoon sugar
½ teaspoon salt or to taste

2 tablespoons cornstarch
3 tablespoons peanut oil
4 tablespoons minced
    Smithfield ham to garnish

Preparation
Beat the egg yolks thoroughly and then add all but the last 2 ingredients. Blend well.

Cooking
In a wok or skillet, heat the oil until it is moderately hot. Add the egg mixture. Stir gently to cook the eggs through but beware of overcooking. The eggs should be smooth and creamy, not dry and tough.

Remove the eggs to a warm platter. Sprinkle with the ham and serve immediately.

Yield: 2 servings.

MOO SHU ROO

Typically northern, this dish has achieved a remarkable popularity in recent years. The golden needles and cloud ears impart textural interest to this dish. As with many Peking dishes the flavoring is restrained. Chicken is often substituted for the pork.

4 eggs	3 tablespoons peanut oil
¼ cup dried cloud ears	1 slice gingerroot, the size of a
½ cup dried golden needles	quarter
3 scallions, shredded	1 teaspoon salt
1 tablespoon dark soy sauce	½ cup shredded lean pork
2 teaspoons sugar	1 cup shredded bamboo shoots
¼ cup water	1 teaspoon sesame oil
Dash of pepper	1 dozen Mandarin pancakes
1 tablespoon dry sherry	(see recipe on page 123)

Preparation
Beat the eggs lightly. In a small pot cover the cloud ears and golden needles with boiling water. Cover the pot and allow to soak for 15 minutes. Discard the water. Cut off the hard ends of the golden needles. In a small bowl, combine the scallions, soy sauce, sugar, water, pepper, and sherry.

Cooking
Heat a wok or skillet over high heat. Add 1 tablespoon of the peanut oil and the gingerroot. Reduce heat to medium. Add the beaten eggs and scramble them until they are dry. Transfer the eggs to a small bowl and break them up into small pieces. Discard the gingerroot.

Clean the wok and heat it over high heat until a drop of water immediately sizzles into steam. Add the remaining peanut oil and the salt. Just before the oil begins to smoke, add the pork and bamboo shoots. Stir-fry for 2 minutes.

Add the golden needles, cloud ears, and the scallion sauce mixture. Stir-fry for 1 minute. Add the scrambled eggs and sesame oil. Stir briefly to mix and remove from heat. The sauce should be scant.

This dish is normally served with Mandarin Pancakes. Each person spreads a pancake flat on his plate and places 2 to 3 tablespoons of the cooked ingredients in the center. The pancake is rolled up and eaten with the fingers.

Yield: 4–8 servings.

THRICE-COOKED PORK

The Chinese are masters of the art of preparing dishes requiring multiple cooking processes, and this recipe is a famous example of the technique. The poaching cooks the meat. The frying gives the outside a distinct texture which stands up even under the extended steaming that gives the meat its lovely gelatinous final form. Like Peking duck, each step has its reason, and if one is left out the dish loses some of its special quality.

2 teaspoons minced garlic
½ teaspoon five-flavor powder
4 tablespoons light soy sauce
¼ cup red bean curd
1 tablespoon dry sherry
½ teaspoon salt or to taste
3 tablespoons light brown
   sugar
2 taro or 3 medium mature
   potatoes

2 pounds unsalted pork belly
2 slices gingerroot, the size of a
   quarter
2 tablespoons honey
   Oil for deep-frying
2 tablespoons white rice wine
   vinegar

Preparation
In a small bowl combine the garlic, five-flavor powder, soy sauce, red bean curd, sherry, salt, and sugar. Peel the taro or potatoes, slice them into pieces no more than ¼ inch thick and about 1½ inches across. Place the slices in cold water until ready to use.

Cooking
Bring enough water to boil in a large pot so that it will cover 1 inch over the pork belly and gingerroot when they are added. Add the pork belly and gingerroot and, when the water boils again, reduce the heat to medium and simmer for 1 hour or until the pork is tender when pierced with a fork.

Drain the pork, prick it all over with a fork, and brush it with honey. Let it stand until it has cooled and then slice it into pieces ¼ inch thick.

Heat the oil to 375 degrees. Add the pork and deep-fry it for 2 minutes or until it has turned golden brown. Remove the pork with a slotted spoon and marinate it in the vinegar.

Heat the oil again to 375 degrees and deep-fry the taro or potato slices for 5 minutes or until crisp. Remove the slices from the pan with a slotted spoon. Slice the pork into pieces the same size as the taro or potato. In a heatproof bowl, arrange alternate layers of pork and taro or potato. Pour the soy sauce mixture over the pork and starch layers.

Steam over rapidly boiling water for 1 hour or until the pork has become transparent and gelatinous. Replenish the water as needed in the bottom of the steamer.

Yield: 6–10 servings.

STIR-FRIED PORK AND SCALLIONS

¾ pound boneless pork	12 snow peas
1 tablespoon dark soy sauce	2 tablespoons peanut oil
1 tablespoon dry sherry	½ teaspoon salt or to taste
Dash of pepper	1 slice gingerroot, the size of a
1 egg white	quarter
12 scallions	½ cup shredded bamboo shoots

Preparation
Slice the pork across the grain very thinly into pieces 1 by 2 inches. Marinate in a bowl with the soy sauce, sherry, pepper, and egg white.

Wash the scallions. Discard the green part and slice the white part lengthwise into 1½-inch slices. String the snow peas and shred them into 1½-inch lengths.

Cooking
Heat a wok or skillet over high heat until a drop of water immediately sizzles into steam. Add the oil, salt, and gingerroot. Stir for 30 seconds. Just before the oil begins to smoke, add the pork and marinade. Stir-fry for 2 minutes. Add the scallions, snow peas, and bamboo shoots. Stir-fry for 1 minute.

Yield: 2-4 servings.

COLD SPICED BEEF

4 pounds boned shin of beef	1 tablespoon salt
3 quarts water	3 tablespoons gin
6 star anise (48 sections)	Coriander leaves or scallions
6 tablespoons dark soy sauce	to garnish
6 tablespoons sugar	

Preparation
Trim the beef of fat and tough membrane. Make into a roll lengthwise and tie with string at three or four places.

Cooking

Bring the water to a boil and add the star anise and the beef. Cover the pot and boil briskly for 2 hours. Add the soy sauce, sugar, and salt. Simmer for 2 hours with the cover on, turning the meat occasionally. Remove the cover, add the gin and raise heat to medium for about 30 minutes until only 1½ cups of sauce remain. Remove the beef, allow to cool, and refrigerate. The sauce will turn into a jelly. Cut the meat into ¼-inch slices. Cover the meat with the jelly which has been cut into little cubes. Garnish with coriander or scallions. Serve cold.

Yield: 8-12 servings.

STIR-FRIED LAMB AND LEEKS

Lamb is a popular meat only in the north. Perhaps this is because sheep are grazing animals and only the north has the large expanses of grasslands on which to raise them. Or perhaps the appreciation of lamb is a legacy from the nomads who regularly breached the Great Wall. In any event, the northern Chinese early on discovered how delicious lamb was with garlic or onions.

1 pound boned shoulder or leg of lamb	¼ teaspoon five-flavor powder
1 tablespoon dark soy sauce	3 leeks
3 tablespoons chicken stock	2 tablespoons peanut oil
1 teaspoon light brown sugar	1 teaspoon chopped garlic
1 tablespoon gin	½ teaspoon salt or to taste

Preparation

Slice the lamb across the grain very thinly into pieces measuring 1 by 2 inches. Marinate in a bowl with the soy sauce, chicken stock, sugar, gin, and five-flavor powder for 15 minutes. Wash the leeks. Discard the green part and slice the white part lengthwise into 1½-inch slices.

Cooking

Heat a wok or skillet over high heat until a drop of water immediately sizzles into steam. Maintain high heat throughout the cooking process. Add the oil, garlic, and salt. Stir for 30 seconds or until the odor of the garlic has become pungent. Add the lamb and marinade. Stir-fry for 2 minutes. Add the leeks and stir-fry for 1 minute.

Yield: 2–4 servings.

LAMB WITH BROWN BEAN SAUCE

Brown bean sauce is widely used in the north, and here it is combined with lamb, another typically northern ingredient. The recurring use of gin in these recipes is a substitute for the hard-to-find liquor called kaoliang.

¾ pound boneless lamb
1½ tablespoons brown bean sauce
½ tablespoon red wine vinegar
1 tablespoon dark soy sauce
1 tablespoon gin

½ teaspoon minced gingerroot
1 scallion
4 tablespoons sesame oil
1 tablespoon light brown sugar
2 teaspoons cornstarch mixed with 1 tablespoon water

Preparation
    Cut the lamb across the grain into thin slices measuring 1 by 2 inches. Mash the brown bean sauce. Combine the brown bean sauce, vinegar, soy sauce, gin, and gingerroot. Chop the scallion into ¼-inch pieces.

Cooking
    In a moderately hot wok or skillet add 2 tablespoons of the oil. Just before the oil begins to smoke, add the lamb and stir-fry for 2 minutes. Remove the lamb. Add the remaining oil and the sugar. Continuing on moderate heat, stir for 30 seconds.
    Add the brown bean sauce mixture. Stir for 1 minute. Return the lamb to the pan and mix well. Thicken with the cornstarch mixture. Garnish with the scallion.

Yield: 2–4 servings.

SHREDDED LAMB WITH VEGETABLES

¾ pound boneless lamb
12 snow peas
2 tablespoons peanut oil
½ teaspoon salt or to taste
¼ cup shredded leeks, white part only
¼ cup shredded bamboo shoots
¼ cup sliced water chestnuts

⅛ cup soaked and shredded Chinese mushrooms
2 teaspoons dark soy sauce
1 tablespoon gin
1 teaspoon sesame oil
3 tablespoons chicken stock
1 teaspoon cornstarch mixed with 1 tablespoon water

Preparation
    Slice the lamb across the grain into thin pieces measuring 1 by 2 inches. Shred these slices into matchstick pieces. String the snow peas.

Cooking
  Heat a wok or skillet over high heat until a drop of water immediately sizzles into steam. Maintain high heat throughout the cooking process. Add the peanut oil and salt. Stir for 30 seconds. Add the leeks and the lamb. Stir for 1½ to 2 minutes until the lamb turns white. Add the remaining ingredients except the cornstarch mixture. Stir for 1 minute. Add the cornstarch mixture to thicken.

Yield: 2–4 servings.

BRAISED LAMB

Northerners are fond of mildly spicy food. The braising process blends the flavors nicely and the pepper flakes cut through any greasiness in the lamb.

1 pound boned lamb
2 tablespoons dark soy sauce
1 tablespoon light brown sugar
1 tablespoon rice wine vinegar
   or cider vinegar
1 cup chicken stock
½ teaspoon salt or to taste
2 tablespoons peanut oil

1 tablespoon shredded gingerroot
1 tablespoon dry sherry
2 scallions, cut into 1-inch
   pieces
1 teaspoon red pepper flakes
1 teaspoon cornstarch mixed
   with 2 tablespoons water

Preparation
  Dice the lamb into 1-inch squares. Blend the soy sauce, sugar, vinegar, and chicken stock. Set aside.

Cooking
  Heat a wok or skillet over high heat until a drop of water immediately sizzles into steam. Add the salt and oil. Just before the oil begins to smoke, add the gingerroot and lamb. Stir-fry the lamb for 2 minutes.
  Add the sherry and stir for 30 seconds. Add the scallions and red pepper flakes. Stir to blend the ingredients. Add the chicken stock mixture. When the sauce comes to a boil, stir to blend the ingredients. Cover the pan and lower heat to simmer for ¾ hour. Thicken with the cornstarch mixture.

Yield: 3–6 servings.

CLEAR SIMMERED LAMB

A very simple dish that shows the Mongol influence in the northwest.

2 quarts water
4 pounds lamb shoulder
3 slices gingerroot, the size of a half-dollar
1 leek, white part only

1 tablespoon light soy sauce
1 teaspoon salt or to taste
¾ cup diced scallions to garnish

Cooking
Bring the water to medium boil in a large pot. Add the lamb and let the water come back to a boil. Skim off the scum. Add the gingerroot and leek. Reduce heat and cover the pot. Simmer for 2½ hours. Add the soy sauce and salt during the last 15 minutes. The lamb should be tender enough to pierce through easily with a chopstick. Remove the lamb and allow to cool slightly before slicing into thin pieces. Serve with the scallions as a garnish and dishes of light soy sauce as a dip.

Yield: 8 servings.

JELLIED LAMB LOAF

An elegant dish that serves nicely as an hors d'oeuvre or first course.

1 pound boned lamb
2 tablespoons crushed garlic
1 star anise (8 sections)
2 tablespoons dark soy sauce
½ teaspoon salt

1 tablespoon sugar
¼ cup dry sherry
3 cups water
2 tablespoons unflavored gelatin

Preparation
Trim the lamb of any fat and cut into 1-inch cubes.

Cooking
Combine the lamb, garlic, star anise, soy sauce, salt, sugar, sherry, and water in a 2-quart saucepan. Bring to a boil over high heat. Skim off the scum from the surface. Reduce heat and simmer for 1½ hours or until the meat is very, very tender. Remove from heat. With a splotted spatula, discard the garlic and star anise. Remove the lamb to a mixing bowl. Shred the meat into small pieces. Soften the gelatin for 5 minutes in ¼ cup cold water, then stir into the cooking liquid. Bring to a boil, then lower

heat to simmer. Stir until the gelatin has completely dissolved and has been well mixed into the liquid. Turn off heat and stir in the pieces of meat. Pour the mixture into a medium loaf pan. Put into the refrigerator to set firm (about 3 to 4 hours).

To serve, loosen the jellied lamb around the inside of the loaf pan with a sharp knife. Dip the bottom of the pan in hot water for a few seconds. Turn upside down over a chilled serving plate.

Yield: 3–8 servings.

SQUIRREL FISH

This well-known dish is called Squirrel Fish because the finished product is said to look like a squirrel. If the resemblance escapes you, as it does us, enjoy the dish anyway.

2 pounds sea bass or another firm white fish (cleaned and scaled, but with both head and tail left on)	Oil for deep-frying
	2 tablespoons thinly shredded gingerroot
½ tablespoons dry sherry	¼ cup soaked and sliced Chinese black mushrooms
1½ teaspoons salt or to taste	
Flour for dredging	¼ cup diced bamboo shoots
⅓ cup red wine vinegar	¼ cup peas (optional)
⅓ cup light brown sugar	1 tablespoon cornstarch mixed with 2 tablespoons water
2 teaspoons dark soy sauce	
½ cup chicken stock	¼ cup chopped scallions to garnish

Preparation

Wash the fish and dry inside and out with a paper towel. With a Chinese cleaver remove the head. Turn the head upside down and break the head bone in the middle, but do not cut completely through. Push down on top of the head until the head has flattened out. (This is the part, after it has been dredged in flour and deep-fried, which resembles the body of the squirrel with the filleted flesh serving as its tail.)

Bone the fish by cutting along the backbone on both sides, but do not remove the tail. Sever the backbone at the base of the tail. You should have two fillets joined at the tail.

Combine the sherry and 1 teaspoon of the salt. Rub over the fish fillet and head. Let stand for ½ hour, then coat generously with flour.

Combine the vinegar, sugar, soy sauce, and the chicken stock in a small bowl. Set aside.

Cooking

Heat the oil for deep-frying in a large fryer, wok, or skillet until it reaches 375 degrees or just before it begins to smoke. Lower the fish fillet and head into the oil. Deep-fry for 5 to 8 minutes until the fish is golden brown. Remove the fish and drain on paper towels. Place the flattened fish head at the end of an oblong serving dish. Place the fish fillet and tail, with the skin side up, on the serving dish as if the fish is reassembled but flattened.

Heat a wok or skillet over high heat until a drop of water immediately sizzles into steam.

Add 2 tablespoons of the oil used for frying, the remaining salt, and the gingerroot. Just before the oil begins to smoke, add the mushrooms, bamboo shoots, and peas. Stir-fry for 2 minutes. Add the vinegar mixture and bring to a boil. Stir and thicken with the cornstarch mixture. Pour over the fish. Garnish with the scallions.

Yield: 2–4 servings.

SHRIMP WITH HOISIN SAUCE

5 scallions	3 tablespoons peanut oil
¼ cup hoisin sauce	¼ teaspoon salt
1 tablespoon dark soy sauce	1 tablespoon shredded ginger-
1 tablespoon gin	root
1½ pounds raw shrimp	1 teaspoon minced garlic

Preparation

Chop the scallions into ½-inch lengths. Combine the hoisin sauce, soy sauce, and gin. Shell and devein the shrimp.

Cooking

Heat a wok or skillet over high heat until a drop of water immediately sizzles into steam. Maintain high heat throughout the cooking process. Add the oil, salt, gingerroot, and garlic. Stir for 30 seconds or until the odor of the garlic has become pungent. Add the shrimp and stir-fry for 3 minutes or until the shrimp have turned pinkish and have curled together.

Add the scallions and stir to coat them well with the oil. Add the hoisin mixture. Mix well to coat the shrimp with the sauce. Cook for 1 minute longer. Remove to a serving platter.

Yield: 4–6 servings.

STEWED CRAB MEAT

A true court dish that demonstrates the sublime simplicity of northern cooking. The natural sweetness of the crab is highlighted by the gentle stir-frying in rendered chicken fat and the judicious addition of leeks and sherry.

2 cups crab meat
3 tablespoons rendered chicken fat
3 slices gingerroot, the size of a quarter
1 cup chicken stock

3 tablespoons dry sherry
1 teaspoon sugar
2 teaspoons light soy sauce
1 teaspoon sesame oil
1 tablespoon cornstarch mixed with ¼ cup water

Preparation and cooking
Pick over the crab meat to remove any pieces of cartilage or shell. Heat the chicken fat in a skillet over moderate heat. Add the crab meat, leeks, and gingerroot. Stir-fry for 2 minutes.

Add all the remaining ingredients except the cornstarch mixture. Simmer for 5 to 10 minutes. Add the cornstarch mixture and stir until the liquid thickens.

Yield: 3–6 servings.

CHILLED HOT-AND-SOUR CUCUMBERS

Perhaps because of the difficulty of keeping dishes warm during chilly Peking winters, one finds a great number of cold vegetable dishes in this region. The use of a spicy dressing is also common. Cucumbers have been substituted for the more difficult to find fuzzy melon.

4 large Chinese black mushrooms
8 medium cucumbers
1 teaspoon salt
2 tablespoons sesame oil
4 fresh red hot peppers or 2 teaspoons crushed red pepper

1 tablespoon shredded gingerroot
2 tablespoons red wine vinegar
2 tablespoons light brown sugar
1 tablespoon cornstarch mixed with 2 tablespoons water

Preparation
Soak the mushrooms in water for 30 minutes or until soft. Cut off and discard the tough stems. Slice the mushrooms thinly.

Split each cucumber in half lengthwise. Remove the seeds. Place in boiling water for 1 minute. Drain in a colander and rinse thoroughly with cold water. Slice the cucumbers into semicircles ¼ inch thick. Season with 1 teaspoon salt.

Cooking

Add the oil to a moderately hot skillet or wok. When the oil just begins to smoke (sesame oil has a lower smoking point than vegetable oil), add the mushrooms, red peppers, and gingerroot. Stir-fry for ½ minute. Stir in the vinegar, sugar, and cornstarch mixture. Turn off heat and mix well. Toss the cucumbers with the sauce and chill in the refrigerator before serving.

Yield: 10 servings.

SPINACH SALAD

Generally speaking, the Chinese eat very few raw vegetables. Even the vegetables in their salads are frequently blanched both to remove the raw flavor and as a health precaution in a land where animal and human wastes have been universally used as fertilizer.

1 pound spinach	½ teaspoon red wine vinegar
2 tablespoons water	½ teaspoon salt
1 teaspoon dry mustard	1 quart water
¾ teaspoon sesame oil	

Preparation

Wash the spinach. Remove the tough parts of the stem. Gradually add the 2 tablespoons water to the mustard, stirring into a thin paste. Add the oil, vinegar, and salt to the mixture. Mix thoroughly.

Cooking

Bring the 1 quart water to a boil. Put the spinach in the boiling water for 1 minute. Drain the spinach through a colander and run cold water over the spinach until completely cool. Drain and squeeze out the excess water. Place in a serving dish and mix with the mustard dressing. Serve cold.

Yield: 4-8 servings.

SPICED CHINESE CABBAGE

1 pound Chinese cabbage (*bok choy*)
3 tablespoons red wine vinegar
3 tablespoons light brown sugar
1 tablespoon light soy sauce

1 teaspoon hot oil
2 tablespoons peanut oil
½ teaspoon salt or to taste
1 slice gingerroot, the size of a quarter

Preparation
Wash the cabbage. Slice the leaves and stalks diagonally into pieces 1 by 1½ inches. Mix the vinegar, sugar, soy sauce, and hot oil in a small bowl.

Cooking
Heat a wok or skillet over high heat until a drop of water immediately sizzles into steam. Add the peanut oil, salt, and gingerroot. Stir-fry 30 seconds or until the gingerroot begins to brown. Add the cabbage and stir-fry for 2 minutes. Remove the pan from heat and stir in the sauce mixture. Serve lukewarm.

Yield: 3–6 servings.

ASPARAGUS SALAD

1 pound young asparagus
1 tablespoon dark soy sauce
2 teaspoons sesame oil

½ teaspoon red wine vinegar
1 teaspoon sugar

Preparation
Snap off the tough root ends of the asparagus and discard. Slice the asparagus diagonally into 1½-inch lengths. Combine the soy sauce, oil, vinegar, and sugar. Stir to dissolve the sugar.

Cooking
Bring a pot of water to a boil. Drop the asparagus into water for 1 minute. Drain and rinse with cold water. Toss the asparagus with the dressing. Serve chilled.

Yield: 3–6 servings.

CREAMED CELERY CABBAGE

Dairy products are rarely used in China, but this recipe for a northern court dish is an exception. Perhaps it was first created for a milk-drinking Mongol or Manchu emperor, but in any event it has become a standard dish in the Chinese cuisine. In the north bok choy is often replaced by Tientsin cabbage, which is a first cousin to the celery cabbage in the supermarket.

1 pound celery cabbage
1 cup milk
Dash of pepper
2 tablespoons cornstarch
2 tablespoons rendered chicken fat or peanut oil

¼ teaspoon salt or to taste
1 cup chicken stock or water
2 tablespoons minced Smithfield ham to garnish

Preparation
Cut the cabbage stems into 1-inch segments and discard the leaves. Combine the milk, pepper, and cornstarch.

Cooking
Heat a wok or skillet over medium heat. Add the chicken fat and salt. Just before the fat begins to smoke, add the cabbage and stir briefly to coat well with the fat. Add the chicken stock. Cover the pan and cook until the cabbage is tender, about 4 minutes. Stir in the well-mixed milk and cornstarch solution. Continue stirring for 15 seconds or until the sauce has thickened. Garnish with the Smithfield ham.

Yield: 4–6 servings.

PEKING FRIED BEAN CURD

2 bean curds
1 cup peanut oil
¼ cup dark soy sauce
2 tablespoons red wine vinegar
1 tablespoon distilled white vinegar

1 teaspoon hot oil
3 tablespoons chopped fresh coriander or scallions

Preparation
Cut each bean curd diagonally in half. Cut the squares diagonally again

in the opposite direction to make a total of 8 triangles. Pat dry with paper towels.

Cooking
Heat the peanut oil until moderately hot (350 degrees). Carefully cook the bean curds until they are golden brown. Mix the remaining ingredients together in a sauce dish and serve with the bean curds.

Yield: 2–4 servings.

HOT-AND-SOUR SOUP

Like fried rice, Hot-and-Sour Soup originated as a way to use up leftovers and, like fried rice, it has emerged as a glorious dish in its own right, if well prepared. The term "to taste" occurs with unusual regularity in this recipe since the balance of hot-and-sour can be changed according to one's mood. We prefer a more sour flavor in the summer and a hotter one in the winter.

¼ cup cloud ears
¼ cup golden needles
¼ pound pork
3 tablespoons cornstarch
1 teaspoon dry sherry
½ cup water
2 bean curds
4 tablespoons white rice wine vinegar or to taste

½ teaspoon white pepper or to taste
½ teaspoon hot oil or to taste
2 teaspoons sesame oil
2 scallions to garnish
1 quart chicken stock
½ teaspoon salt or to taste
1 tablespoon light soy sauce
1 egg, beaten

Preparation
Soak the cloud ears and golden needles in hot water for 20 minutes or until they have increased in size several times. Drain. Shred the cloud ears and cut the golden needles in half.
Shred the pork into narrow strips 1½ inches long. Combine the pork with 1 tablespoon of the cornstarch and the sherry.
Mix the remaining cornstarch with the water and set aside. Cut each bean curd into 9 pieces.
Combine the vinegar, pepper, hot oil, and sesame oil in a bowl and set aside. Chop the scallions into ½-inch segments.

Cooking
Bring the chicken stock, salt, and soy sauce to a boil in a large pot. Add

the pork and boil for 1 minute. Add the cloud ears, golden needles, and bean curd. Boil for 1 minute more.

Add the cornstarch mixture and stir to thicken. Lower heat and add the vinegar mixture. Adjust the seasoning. Slowly stir in the beaten egg. Garnish with the scallions.

Yield: 6 servings.

MANDARIN CUCUMBER SOUP

1 medium cucumber	1 teaspoon cornstarch
⅓ cup shredded chicken breast	1 quart chicken stock
1 teaspoon light soy sauce	1 teaspoon sesame oil

Preparation
Peel the cucumber. Split in half lengthwise and discard the seeds. Cut into ¼-inch slices. In a bowl mix the chicken with soy sauce and cornstarch and set aside.

Cooking
Bring the chicken stock to a boil. Add the chicken and stir until the chicken stock comes back to a boil. Add the cucumbers. Remove from heat and stir for 1 minute. Mix in the oil and serve immediately.

Yield: 6 servings.

DUCK SOUP

1 pound celery cabbage	2 scallions
1 cooked duck carcass (left over, for example, from Peking Duck)	1 teaspoon light soy sauce
	¾ teaspoon sugar
	½ teaspoon salt
1 quart water	
1 slice gingerroot, the size of a quarter	

Preparation
Wash the cabbage and cut into 1-inch pieces. Crush the ribs and spine of the duck carcass. Break the thigh and wing bones in half.

Cooking

Bring the water to a rolling boil. Add the duck bones, gingerroot, and scallions. Cover and lower heat to medium for 30 minutes.

Skim off the scum, if any. Cover and simmer for 30 minutes more.

Remove the bones, scallions, and gingerroot with a slotted spatula. Add the cabbage, soy sauce, sugar, and salt. Cover and cook over medium heat for 30 minutes or until the cabbage is very tender.

Yield: 6 servings.

FUZZY MELON SOUP

1 fuzzy melon
4 cups chicken stock
¼ teaspoon light soy sauce

¼ cup shredded Smithfield ham
1 teaspoon sesame oil

Preparation

Peel and halve the melon. Do not seed. Slice across at ¼-inch intervals.

Cooking

Bring the chicken stock and soy sauce to a boil. Add the ham. When the chicken stock comes to a boil again, add the melon. Remove from heat, stir in the oil, and serve immediately.

Yield: 6 servings.

LAMB SOUP WITH DRIED BEAN CURD

2 quarts water
2 pounds lamb bones
2 ounces dried bean curd (sliced type)
2 slices gingerroot, the size of a quarter
1 tablespoon light soy sauce

¾ teaspoon salt
1 teaspoon sugar
3 scallions
½ pound celery cabbage
2 ounces dried lotus root
1 ounce dried lotus nuts

Cooking

Put all the ingredients into a soup pot. Bring to a boil. Remove the scum. Cover and simmer for 2 hours.

Yield: 10 servings.

HOT POT COOKING

Hot pot dinners are an exercise in participatory cookery. A pot of boiling stock is placed at the center of the dining table and raw ingredients are attractively arranged around the table. Each guest chooses the ingredients he or she wants and dips them in the stock for a minute or two to cook. The cooked ingredients are then returned to the plate where they are seasoned and garnished to taste. After all the meats have been eaten, any remaining vegetables such as spinach or celery cabbage are added to the stock. This is served as a soup to end the meal.

To hold and heat the stock the Chinese use an Oriental chafing dish which is heated by coal. These can be bought in many Oriental specialty stores, although one must make certain that it is designed for cooking, not just show. On the other hand, a large chafing dish or even an electric frying pan will serve as well.

It is important that all the ingredients are fresh and that they are carefully sliced or shredded. As to utensils, each guest will need a plate and a bowl for the soup at the end of the meal. Wooden chopsticks for the nimble or an orange juice strainer for the less expert are needed to hold the food while it is cooking. Garnishes should include scallions, coriander, and shredded gingerroot. The assortment of sauces should include soy sauce, red wine vinegar, oyster sauce, hot oil, and hoisin sauce.

Rice or fried rice can be served with the meal as a filler.

MONGOLIAN HOT POT

Mongolian Hot Pot is a simple dish served with steamed rolls and a strong condiment sauce for dipping.

3 pounds boned leg of lamb	3 slices gingerroot, the size of a quarter
2 pounds lamb liver	
2 pounds lamb kidney	3 leeks, shredded
1 pound spinach	2 tablespoons minced garlic
Bone from the leg of lamb	20 steamed rolls (see recipe on page 262)
2 quarts chicken stock	
3 tablespoons dry sherry	

Preparation

Trim the fat and gristle from the leg of lamb. Cut away the tough tissue from the liver and the kidneys. Cut the lamb, liver, and kidneys into pieces measuring ½ by 1½ inches. Arrange the pieces for each guest on separate plates. Wash the spinach and remove the tough parts of the stems.

Cooking

Add the bone to the chicken stock. Add the sherry and gingerroot and bring to a boil. Simmer for 1½ hours.

Add the leeks and garlic to the stock, pour into a Chinese hot pot or chafing dish, and continue to simmer the stock at the table. Each guest helps himself by cooking individual pieces of meat in the stock. When the meat is done, it is dipped into the sauce and then eaten with a steamed roll. When all or nearly all of the meat has been consumed, add the spinach to the hot pot. Serve the soup in individual bowls to complete the meal.

To prepare dipping sauce for Mongolian Hot Pot

Combine ¼ cup red wine vinegar, 1 tablespoon dark soy sauce, 2 teaspoons diced scallion, and 1 teaspoon shredded gingerroot.

Yield: 10–12 servings

PEKING PRECIOUS POT

This Peking Precious Pot is a "citified" version of the original Mongolian Hot Pot and it may be more to most people's taste.

1 pound chicken breasts, skinned and boned	2 ounces cellophane noodles
1 pound fillet of non-oily white fish	2 quarts chicken stock
½ pound lean beef	3 slices gingerroot, the size of a quarter
1 pound small shrimp, shelled, cleaned, and deveined	1 pound spinach
½ pound chicken livers	1 pound celery cabbage, cut into bite-size pieces
	½ cup diced scallions

Preparation

Cut the chicken breasts, fish, and beef into thin slices. Split the back of each shrimp. Cut the chicken livers into bite-size pieces. Arrange these raw ingredients attractively in plates around the table. Pour boiling water over the cellophane noodles and let stand for 20 minutes.

Cooking

Bring the chicken stock and gingerroot to a boil. Turn off heat and add spinach, cabbage, and cellophane noodles. Pour into a chafing dish or hot pot, sprinkle with the scallions, and bring to the table. Adjust the heat of the hot pot or chafing dish so that the stock continues to simmer. Each guest should have a saucer of one or more dipping sauces.

Yield: 8 servings.

DIPPING SAUCES FOR PEKING PRECIOUS POT

Chekiang vinegar: Combine ¼ cup red wine vinegar, 1 tablespoon dark soy sauce, 2 teaspoons diced scallions, and 1 teaspoon shredded ginger-root.

Soy-gingerroot-scallion: Combine ¼ cup light soy sauce, 1 tablespoon diced scallions (white parts only), 1 teaspoon shredded gingerroot, ¼ teaspoon sesame oil, and ⅛ teaspoon white pepper.

BROWN BEAN SAUCE NOODLES
(CHA CHIANG MEIN)

This robust noodle dish has no pretensions whatsoever; it is inexpensive to make, quite filling, and very tasty indeed. This makes a satisfying single dish meal or late night supper.

1 pound Chinese egg noodles	¼ teaspoon cayenne pepper
¼ cup brown bean sauce	(optional)
2 tablespoons hoisin sauce	1 tablespoon peanut oil
2 chopped scallions	½ teaspoon salt
½ cup chicken stock or water	1 tablespoon minced garlic
½ teaspoon sugar	1 pound ground pork

Garnishes

½ cucumber	4 scallions
10 radishes	2 tablespoons minced garlic

Preparation

Boil the noodles for 7 minutes, stirring occasionally. They should be drained in a colander under running water when they reach the *al dente* stage. Place in a serving bowl

Shred each of the garnishes and place each in its own bowl. Mash the brown bean sauce with the handle of a cleaver or the back of a spoon. To the brown bean sauce add the hoisin sauce, chopped scallions, chicken stock, sugar, and cayenne. Set aside.

Cooking

Heat a wok or skillet over high heat until a drop of water immediately sizzles into steam. Add the oil, salt, and garlic. When the odor of the garlic has become pungent, add the pork and stir-fry for 1 minute or until the pork has become gray.

Add the brown bean sauce and chicken stock mixture. Blend well with the pork. Cover and lower heat to medium. Cook for 5 minutes more. Remove to a separate serving dish.

To serve, let each guest help himself to some noodles and then to some sauce. If he or she prefers a salty dish, then a lot of sauce should be taken. The proportion of sauce to the bland noodles determines the degree of saltiness. Your guests may then garnish their noodles with as few or as many of the garnishes as you have provided.

Yield: 4–6 servings.

TWO SIDES BROWN NOODLES

1 pound Chinese egg noodles
1 cup shredded chicken breast
1 egg white
1 teaspoon dry sherry
½ teaspoon sugar
  Dash of pepper
½ cup chicken stock
2 teaspoons dark soy sauce
1 cup plus 2 tablespoons peanut oil
½ teaspoon salt
2 cups shredded Chinese cabbage (*bok choy*)
½ cup soaked and shredded Chinese black mushrooms
½ cup shredded bamboo shoots
1 tablespoon cornstarch mixed with ¼ cup water

Preparation

Place the noodles in boiling water for 3 to 5 minutes until tender. Do not overcook. Rinse with cold water in a colander. Drain the noodles and set aside.

Mix the chicken in a bowl with the egg white.

In a small bowl blend together the sherry, sugar, pepper, chicken stock, and soy sauce.

Cooking

Heat a 10-inch skillet and add 1 cup of oil. Just before the oil begins to smoke, add the noodles and flatten out into a round cake. Fry over medium heat until the bottom side is golden. Turn over to the other side. When the second side in golden, remove to a warm plate or to a slow oven.

Heat a skillet or wok over high heat with 2 tablespoons oil and the salt. Just before the oil begins to smoke, add the chicken, cabbage, mushrooms, and bamboo shoots. Stir-fry for 1½ minutes. Add the chicken stock mixture. Bring to a boil and stir. Add the cornstarch mixture slowly and stir until thickened. Pour over the fried noodles.

Yield: 4–6 servings.

COLD MANDARIN NOODLES

Cold noodles are splendid for summer buffets or light lunches. Serve it in place of macaroni or potato salad. Shredded Chinese roast pork or other cooked meats may be added if desired.

2 medium cucumbers	3 tablespoons light soy sauce
4 scallions	⅛ teaspoon pepper
½ pound Chinese egg noodles	1 cup bean sprouts
1 tablespoon peanut oil	½ teaspoon sugar
3 tablespoons sesame oil	½ teaspoon salt or to taste

Preparation and Cooking
Wash and skin the cucumbers. Shred them into pieces the size of a matchstick. Wash the scallions and chop into 1½-inch lengths. Cook the noodles. Rinse in cold water and drain. Mix all the ingredients together. Refrigerate.

Yield: 4-8 servings.

MANDARIN PANCAKES

2 cups all-purpose flour	2 tablespoons sesame oil
¾ cup boiling water	½ teaspoon peanut oil

Preparation
Place the flour in a bowl. Make a well in the flour and gradually add the boiling water, stirring briskly with a chopstick or a fork.

Turn the dough out onto a lightly floured board and knead 5 to 10 minutes or until it is smooth and fairly elastic. Roll the dough into a ball. Cover it with a damp tea towel and let the dough rest for at least 30 minutes.

Roll the dough into a long uniform cylinder. Carefully cut the roll into 16 or 24 uniform pieces depending on whether you want approximately 5-inch or 7-inch pancakes. Roll each of these sections into a ball and then flatten with the heel of your hand. Brush the tops of these flattened balls lightly with sesame oil. Place one oiled pancake on top of a second with oiled sides together. Repeat this process with the remaining pancakes making certain that each pair is carefully matched in size.

Using a thin rolling pin or an old broom handle, roll each pair of now bonded pancakes out as thinly and as evenly as possible. To insure that each pancake is rolled to the same thinness and remains the same size as its partner, turn the bonded pancake over and roll the other side from time to time. Keep the finished pancakes covered with a damp cloth.

Cooking

Heat a skillet over medium heat. Put a little bit of peanut oil on a paper towel and rub it lightly over the skillet. The oiling process is done only once. Put a pancake in the pan. After about 1 minute, turn the pancake over to cook on its other side for about another minute. Remove the pancake from the pan. Separate the two sides, and set them aside under a damp tea towel while you cook the remaining pancakes.

At no time should the pancakes be allowed to brown, although they may have lightly speckled brown spots on them. A sign that both pancakes are done is the appearance of air bubbles between the pancakes and a general willingness for the two sides to separate from each other.

The pancakes should be served immediately and hot. If they have cooled, put them into a steamer for a few minutes until they are soft and hot. They may also be wrapped tightly in foil and refrigerated. If they have been refrigerated, reheat them in a steamer for 10 minutes.

Yield: 16–24 pancakes.

JAO-TZE

Every region of China has its own form of stuffed dumpling which is served for lunch or for a snack at any time.

To make the wrappers
  2 cups all-purpose flour
  ¾ cup boiling water

Place the flour in a mixing bowl. Make a well in the flour and gradually add the boiling water while stirring with a chopstick or fork. Turn the dough out onto a lightly floured board and knead for 5 minutes or until smooth. Cover the dough with a damp cloth and let it rest for at least 30 minutes. Knead the dough for a second time about 3 minutes or until the dough becomes quite elastic.

Divide the dough in half. Put half the dough under a damp cloth to keep. it from drying out. Take the other half of the dough and shape it into a long cylinder. Pinch off enough dough from one end to make a ball 1 inch in diameter. Flatten the ball with the heel of your hand and then roll it out to make a 3-inch circle. The thinner your rolling pin, the easier this will be. A chopped-off broom handle is a good substitute. Flour the board, if necessary to keep the dough from sticking. Repeat until the dough is used up and you have about 36 wrappers. The finished wrappers should be covered by a damp cloth while you prepare one of the fillings that follow.

Yield: About 3 dozen wrappers.

PORK FILLING FOR JAO-TZE

Mix together the following ingredients and fill the skin as described below.

¾ pound ground pork	1 tablespoon dry sherry
½ cup minced bamboo shoots	¾ teaspoon salt or to taste
½ cup diced celery cabbage	1 tablespoon sesame oil
1½ tablespoons dark soy sauce	2 teaspoons cornstarch
½ teaspoon sugar	2 tablespoons chicken stock

Yield: About 3 dozen dumplings.

LAMB FILLING FOR JAO-TZE

Mix together the following ingredients and fill the skin as described below.

¾ pound ground lamb	½ teaspoon salt or to taste
1 cup chopped scallions	½ teaspoon sugar
½ cup diced celery cabbage	1½ tablespoons dark soy sauce
2 tablespoons finely minced gingerroot	1 tablespoon sesame oil
	2 teaspoons cornstarch
1 tablespoon dry sherry	¼ cup chicken stock

Yield: About 3 dozen dumplings.

TO FILL JAO-TZE WRAPPERS

Place a rounded teaspoon of the filling in the center of the wrapper and slightly moisten the edge of the wrapper with water. Fold the wrapper in half over the filling and pinch firmly in the center to seal. Make several small pleats in the dough on the side facing you to gather the dough over the filling. Pinch the two sides of the dumpling together. The dumpling will then sit solidly on its broad bottom. The crescent-shaped dumpling is ready to be either boiled or pan-fried.

TO PAN-FRY JAO-TZE

Heat a skillet to medium high. Add 2 tablespoons peanut oil. When the oil is moderately hot, arrange *jao-tze* in skillet bottom side down. Cook until golden brown on the bottom, about 2 to 3 minutes. Pour ¾ cup water around the edge of the skillet and cover. Cook over high heat for about 5 minutes until the water has almost boiled away. Turn heat to low for 7 minutes. Return heat to high briefly to remove all excess water. Transfer *jao-tze* to a serving plate, placing them on their sides, and serve with one or more sauces.

TO BOIL JAO-TZE

Carefully drop *jao-tze* into 1½ quarts boiling water for about 10 minutes. Remove with a slotted spatula to a colander to drain. Arrange on a serving platter and serve with one or more sauces.

SAUCE FOR JAO-TZE

Jao-tze can be served with small dishes of hot oil, light soy sauce, or red wine vinegar. A combination sauce which can be served is the following:

¼ cup light soy sauce	1 tablespoon minced garlic
¼ cup red wine vinegar	1 tablespoon hot oil
1 tablespoon minced ginger- root	1 tablespoon sesame oil

PEKING PORK ROLLS

Northerners are quite fond of spinach as a green vegetable, and one finds it used in many different ways. In this recipe it is used as part of a filling for a pastry. The unusual wrapper is little more than an omelet, but with the added binding strength provided by the cornstarch. The combination of egg, pork, and spinach simply seasoned is quite pleasant and satisfying.

To make the egg skin

6 teaspoons cornstarch mixed with 6 tablespoons water

½ teaspoon salt or to taste
6 eggs, lightly beaten

To make the filling

1 pound spinach
2 tablespoons (or more) peanut oil
1 teaspoon minced gingerroot
1 pound ground pork
3 tablespoons minced scallions

1 teaspoon light soy sauce
1 tablespoon dry sherry
½ teaspoon sesame oil
2 cups chicken stock

Preparation

Add the cornstarch mixture and salt to the eggs. Mix. Clean the spinach and discard the tough ends.

Cooking

Heat a 10-inch skillet over moderate heat and add the peanut oil. Add ¼ cup of the egg mixture and tip the skillet so that the egg mixture flows across it evenly. Cook for about 2 minutes and slide the egg skin off. Make 6 such egg skins, adding peanut oil if necessary. Allow the skins to cool.

Heat a wok or skillet over high heat until a drop of water immediately sizzles into steam. Add peanut oil and gingerroot. Just before the oil begins to smoke, add the pork, scallions, soy sauce, and sherry. Stir-fry for 2 minutes. Stir in the sesame oil. Remove from the skillet and allow to cool.

Place ⅙ of the pork mixture on each egg skin. Fold into an egg roll pancake.

In a skillet bring the chicken stock to a boil. Add the spinach. Carefully add the pork rolls. Cover and simmer for 2 minutes. Place on a serving platter. Carefully cut the pork rolls into thirds.

Yield: About 8 servings.

PEKING GLAZED APPLES

This is an exquisite dessert with a hard candy glaze encasing a still warm and crispy slice of apple. It is a bit of a bother to make but provides as impressive a finale to a dinner as one could wish. This dish most likely originated in Shantung Province with its many apple orchards.

2 medium apples	¼ cup water
1 egg white	Oil for deep-frying
¼ cup cornstarch	2 tablespoons toasted sesame
1½ cups sugar	seeds

Preparation

Peel and core the apples. Cut the apple into 8 wedges. Dredge the apple slices first in the egg white and then in the cornstarch.

Combine the sugar and water in a saucepan over high heat and stir until the sugar is dissolved. Continue boiling this syrup without stirring until it reaches the hard crack stage (325 degrees on a candy thermometer). At this point, a drop of the syrup will immediately harden when dropped in cold water and the syrup will spin a thick thread. Keep the syrup warm over low heat.

Cooking

Heat the oil to 375 degrees or to the point that a slight haze forms over the oil. Add half the apple slices and fry them unti they turn a light brown. Remove the slices from the oil with a slotted spoon or chopsticks and coat them well in the syrup. Place the slices on a serving platter that has been well greased to avoid sticking. Repeat this process with the other half of the apples. Sprinkle the apples with the sesame seeds.

Immediately bring the apples and a bowl of ice water to the table. There each guest will briefly dip a slice of apple in the ice water to harden the syrup to a crackly glaze around the still warm fruit.

Yield: 4 servings.

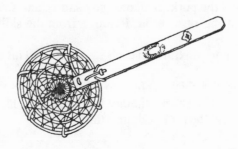

PEKING DUST

*A famous Chinese dessert, but somewhat strange to Western tastes.
The unauthentic addition of whipped cream helps bridge the gap.*

1 pound fresh chestnuts	1 cup heavy cream (optional)
½ cup sugar	Glazed fruit or preserved
¼ teaspoon salt	kumquats to garnish
1 teaspoon dry sherry	

Score the tops of the chestnuts by making a crisscross with a sharp
knife. Place the chestnuts in a pot. Cover with cold water. Bring to a boil.
Simmer for about 40 minutes or until the jackets have burst. Drain and
peel. Mince the chestnut meats and place in a mixing bowl. Add the sugar,
salt, and sherry. Mash thoroughly. Mound in the center of a serving plate.
Whip the cream and spread over the chestnut mixture. Garnish with
glazed fruit or preserved kumquats.

Yield: 6–8 servings.

3
WEST CHINA

Szechwan, Yunnan, Kweichow,
Hunan, Hupeh

THE western part of China is a world unto itself—tropical and mountainous, much of it too mountainous for cultivation or the support of a significant population. But the Red Basin of Szechwan is an exception. Ringed by rugged mountains, the Basin's only contact with the rest of China is through the spectacular Yangtze gorges with its turbulent rapids. There sheer cliffs rise over one thousand feet. In places the river narrows to less than two hundred yards. In a single day during summer floods the river may rise as much as fifty feet and crest more than two hundred feet above the low-water mark.

In the isolated Szechwan Basin, however, live 50 million people who have for centuries practiced perhaps the most intensive agriculture in China. Only about 5 percent of the area is flat, but the steep foothills have been laboriously terraced for as many as fifty levels. Despite generous rainfall, irrigation is widespread. The irrigation system of the Min River is particularly noteworthy for it dates back 2,200 years to the engineer Li Pong and his son Er Wang. Their motto—"Dig the channel deep, keep the spillway low"—has been carefully observed and every winter the waters are diverted channel by channel and the accumulated debris of the year removed. The result of this annual ritual has been an effective irrigation system in excellent working order for these many centuries, an unparalleled feat.

Szechwan efficiency is also exemplified in paddies which are used as storage ponds for the water the farmers will need for spring planting. Not content to let the water sit idly for these months, they stock these ponds with fish and freshwater shrimp.

In addition to the hard work of the Szechwan farmer, the climate helps enormously in allowing the land to support such a great number of people. The temperature is above freezing the year round with abundant rain and high humidity. There is almost constant cloud cover and fogs are frequent. Summers are oppressively hot and sticky, the winters are raw and chilly—an excellent environment for agriculture, but not always a pleasant one for man.

Szechwan is a major producer of rice, sugarcane, and citrus fruits. On the hills tea is cultivated which is later processed in brick form. Silk cultivation on the hills is also important with Chungking traditionally famous for its satin and Chengtu for its brocade. Wheat, corn, and potatoes are also widely grown on the steep hills and lower mountains. Fine edible fun-guses, notably cloud ears and the rare silver fungus, are gathered in this region. Practically anything that can be grown elsewhere in China can be grown here whether in the warm lowlands or cooler highlands.

The cooking of this region is famous for its liberal use of hot peppers, an incomprehensible practice to many Chinese not from this region and to anybody tasting such incredibly hot dishes for the first time.

An American friend of ours tells of being stationed in this part of China during World War II. At one point the Americans came under some criti-cism from their Chinese counterparts for never joining them over dinner, but the truth was that the Americans could not bear the unending series of spicy dishes. One officer, however, regularly went over to eat at the Chi-nese mess. He was finally cornered by his colleagues and asked how he could bear the food. "Actually, it's quite good," he replied, "but before I go, I eat a fresh hot pepper, wash it down with a shot of whiskey. After that, nothing bothers me."

Some say that the peppers are used to encourage cooling perspiration in a hot, damp climate. Others say that they are used to disguise putrefying unrefrigerated meat. Still others say that the hot peppers actually stimu-late the palate and sensitize it to the many flavors that emerge after the initial fires die down. The truth is that after the first few bites, which can bring tears to one's eyes, the sense of heat lessens and other flavors are discerned.

The best of Szechwan cooking is among the most interesting and so-phisticated in the world. Characteristic is the skillful contrasting of many different flavors in a single dish—hot, sour, and salty, for example. Gin-gerroot, often shredded, is an important and distinctive ingredient in the cooking of this region. Another unusual flavor is that of the Szechwan peppercorns—a mild, fragrant, almost flowery peppercorn that is first toasted in a dry pan and then crushed. Star anise, cinnamon, and other spices are used liberally as well. The citrus fruits grown in the region also find their way into numerous dishes such as Lemon Chicken and Spicy and Tangy Chicken. Little lamb is raised in this region, although some may be found on the steep upper slopes. Beef, on the other hand, is rela-tively available, for the cattle are used as beasts of labor in the many salt mines.

An unusual emphasis is placed on texture. Beef, for example, is often cooked to be deliberately chewy. On the other hand, there is the wonder-ful dish called Slippery Chicken with the texture of satin. The crunchy quality of the native fungi is similarly prized.

In this area a somewhat different stir-frying technique is used which in-volves cooking the meat first in a good deal of oil, and then finishing off the vegetables and the rest of the dish in only a tablespoon or so of oil.

Abundant gravy is rarely found. Instead, a scant sauce clings to rather than surrounds the meat or vegetables. Multiple cooking processes are also common—for example, first steaming then deep-frying a cut of meat.

How food was seasoned before the arrival of chili peppers in the sixteenth century from their native Central America is a matter of conjecture. Some authorities suggest that the pimento was widely used. The term "pimento" refers, however, either to the sweet red capsicum pepper or to the fruit of the pimento plant which is used to make allspice. Both plants are native to Central America. If one pursues the pimento-as-allspice clue, one may surmise that the reference may be to one or probably more of the many similar spices native to China such as cinnamon-like cassia and star anise which still are widely used even without chili peppers in Szechwan food.

To the south of Szechwan are the less populous provinces of Yunnan and Kweichow. Clear sunny days are common and temperatures are moderate. One writer has described the pleasant climate as spring running directly into fall. Yunnan, whose name means "south of the clouds" of Szechwan, is mostly high plateau deeply dissected by unnavigable rivers. As one travels eastward toward Kweichow the landscape becomes increasingly eroded and bizarre. In Kweichow one can find true examples of incredible landscapes that have been depicted so dramatically in Chinese paintings with their precipitous slopes, overhanging cliffs with caves, and strange rock formations. Vertical spires rise as much as six hundred feet and land is seldom level for more than a half mile. The picturesque wisps of clouds around these karst spires are also unfortunately accurate for it is foggy or cloudy on an average of seven or eight days out of ten.

Both provinces were among the last to be assimilated into China. While the Han dynasty gained brief suzerainty from Yunnan, it was not until the Mongol conquest under Kublai Khan in 1252 that it formally became a part of China as something of a colony. Full incorporation did not occur until the seventeenth century. Even today the Chinese remain a minority in Yunnan and Kweichow where they live mostly in the cities. In the hills are many non-Chinese tribes of Thais, Lolos, Miaos, and Liaos. Kweichow has eighty-two such groups, several of which are known for their fine embroidery. There is also a significant Moslem minority of half a million in Yunnan, the descendants of the Turkish Moslems brought in by Kublai's administration.

The cooking of this area reflects influence both from Szechwan to the north and from Burma, Thailand, and India to the south and west. Yunnan in particular enjoys the use of hot curried dishes and is also famous for its fine hams. Basically, though, this is a poor area that has not developed the culinary or cultural sophistication of Szechwan.

Hunan and Hupeh provinces border Szechwan on the east below the Yangtze gorges but share many of its traditions. Hunan is quite hilly and is known for its fine black teas, particularly the strong smoky Lapsang souchong. Its lowlands along the Yangtze are known for their excellent glutinous rice. Hupeh has more level land, much of it irrigated, and its agricultural products are traded with Honan and Hunan. Its people are reportedly quite warlike, whether by personality or by force of history, and perhaps for this reason they have not had the opportunity to develop their own distinctive cuisine beyond a few memorable home-cooked dishes.

KUNG PAO CHICKEN

Also known as Viceroy's Chicken, this dish honors a Peking bureaucrat who was either exiled or sent as an emissary to distant Szechwan. It has become deservedly popular along with the quite different Kung Pao Shrimp. Neither dish is overwhelmingly spicy, but each is so delectable that they have earned permanent standing in the Szechwan repertoire.

¾ pound boned chicken
1 egg white
2 teaspoons cornstarch
2 tablespoons brown bean
  sauce
1 tablespoon hoisin sauce
1 teaspoon sugar
2 teaspoons dry sherry

1 tablespoon white rice wine
  vinegar
2 tablespoons water
1 teaspoon minced garlic
1 cup peanut oil
1½ teaspoons crushed red
  pepper
½ cup roasted peanuts

Preparation

Cut the chicken into ½-inch squares. In a bowl combine the chicken with the egg white and cornstarch.

In another bowl mash the brown bean sauce, then add the hoisin sauce, sugar, sherry, vinegar, water, and garlic. Assemble the remaining ingredients by the stove.

Cooking

Heat a wok or skillet over high heat until a drop of water immediately sizzles into steam. Maintain high heat throughout the cooking process. Add the oil. Just before the oil begins to smoke, add the chicken and stir for 45 seconds or until the chicken turns light brown. Remove the chicken.

Drain off all but 2 tablespoons of the oil. Reheat the pan. Just before the oil begins to smoke, add the red pepper and stir 20 seconds or until the pepper darkens.

Return the chicken to the pan along with the brown bean sauce mixture and peanuts. Stir for 1 minute or until done.

Yield: 2–4 servings.

COLD LEMON CHICKEN

8 Chinese black mushrooms
¼ cup sugar
¾ cup chicken stock
½ cup lemon juice
½ teaspoon light soy sauce
2 whole chicken breasts
1 tablespoon peanut oil

½ tablespoon salt or to taste
¼ cup finely shredded gingerroot
¼ cup seeded and shredded
  fresh hot peppers
2 tablespoons grated lemon
  rind

Preparation
Soak the mushrooms in water for 30 minutes or until soft. Remove the tough stems and then shred the mushrooms very finely. In a bowl combine the sugar, chicken stock, lemon juice, and soy sauce.

Cooking
Over high heat bring a pot of water to a boil. Add the chicken to the pot. When the water again comes to a boil, reduce heat and simmer for 10 minutes or until the breasts are done. Remove the breasts and let them cool. Bone the breasts and cut them into 1-inch squares. Arrange the pieces on a serving platter.

Heat a wok or skillet over high heat until a drop of water immediately sizzles into steam. Add the oil and salt. Just before the oil begins to smoke, add the gingerroot and the mushrooms. Stir for 30 seconds.

Add the peppers and grated lemon rind. Stir for 15 seconds and then add the chicken stock mixture. Stir until the mixture has come to a boil. Remove from heat. Pour the sauce over the chicken and let it cool to room temperature.

Yield: 2–6 servings.

AROMATIC FRIED CHICKEN

1 chicken, about 3 pounds
2 star anise (16 sections)
1 teaspoon ground and toasted
  Szechwan peppercorns
1 3-inch stick cinnamon
1 teaspoon minced gingerroot
2 chopped scallions
1 tablespoon dry sherry
½ cup light soy sauce

½ teaspoon salt
7 teaspoons sugar
1 tablespoon minced garlic
3 tablespoons white rice wine
  vinegar
1 teaspoon sesame oil
½ teaspoon hot oil
3 tablespoons cornstarch
  Oil for deep-frying

Preparation

Chop the chicken into pieces approximately 1½ inches square. In a small pot, combine the star anise, ground peppercorns, the well-broken stick of cinnamon, gingerroot, scallions, sherry, ¼ cup of the soy sauce, ¼ teaspoon of the salt, and 1 teaspoon of the sugar. Stirring occasionally, heat but do not boil this mixture over low heat for 3 minutes to blend the flavors. Let the mixture cool to room temperature. Coat the chicken pieces well with this mixture and then let them marinate in the mixture for at least 3 hours, turning occasionally.

In a small pot, combine the remaining soy sauce, the remaining salt, the remaining sugar, the garlic, vinegar, sesame oil, and hot oil. Set this sauce aside.

Roll the chicken in the cornstarch.

Cooking

Heat the oil to 375 degrees or until it is very hot. Deep-fry the chicken several pieces at a time until they have turned golden brown. Drain the chicken pieces on paper towels and keep warm until ready to serve. Just before serving, heat but do not boil the sauce, stirring constantly to partially dissolve the sugar and warm the sauce. Pour the sauce over the chicken and serve immediately.

Yield: 3–8 servings.

CHUNKED CHICKEN IN GINGER SAUCE

A gentle dish, this recipe shows the way in which gingerroot comes into its own as a major ingredient in Szechwan cooking.

½ chicken, about 1½ pounds	5 tablespoons red rice wine
1 tablespoon dark soy sauce	vinegar
1 tablespoon minced ginger-	1½ tablespoons light brown
root	sugar
1 scallion, chopped into 1-inch	1 teaspoon minced garlic
pieces	Oil for deep-frying

Preparation

Rinse and dry the chicken with paper towels. Rub the soy sauce into the chicken and let it stand for 10 minutes. Put the remaining ingredients, except for the oil, into a small pot.

Cooking

Deep-fry the chicken in the oil heated to 350 degrees for 5 minutes on each side. Cut the chicken into 1½- by 1-inch pieces and place them in a serving dish.

Heat the remaining ingredients over medium heat, stirring constantly until the mixture almost comes to a boil. Pour over the chicken.

Yield: 2–3 servings.

PON PON CHICKEN OR HACKED CHICKEN

This is a famous Szechwan dish. To be authentic, sesame seed paste should be used instead of peanut butter, but the substitution works perfectly well and does not turn rancid as easily. The blending of flavors is wonderful. After the initial blast of heat from the cayenne pepper and crushed red pepper, three other flavors come through: the floweriness of the Szechwan peppercorns, the nutty flavor and fragrance of the sesame seeds and peanuts, and the saltiness of the soy sauce. This dish is served cold and can be prepared ahead of time as an appetizer or a main dish.

1½ pounds chicken breast
  3 tablespoons sesame seed paste thinned with 2 tablespoons chicken stock or
  3 tablespoons smooth peanut butter with 2 tablespoons sesame oil
  2 teaspoons light soy sauce
  1 tablespoon red wine vinegar
  2 tablespoons peanut oil

  2 teaspoons crushed red pepper
  2 teaspoons minced gingerroot
  1 tablespoon chopped scallion
  1 tablespoon chopped garlic
  1 tablespoon dry sherry
  ½ teaspoon cayenne pepper
  1 tablespoon toasted and ground Szechwan peppercorns

Preparation and cooking

Place the chicken breasts in simmering water for 10 minutes or until done. Remove, strain, and cool. Bone the chicken breasts and remove the skin. Cut into thin strips.

Place either the sesame seed paste mixture or peanut butter mixture in a small mixing bowl. Add the soy sauce and vinegar, stirring until blended. Then proceed to blend in the oil, red pepper, gingerroot, scallion, garlic, sherry, cayenne pepper, and ground peppercorns.

Mix the sauce with the chicken and serve at room temperature.

Yield: 4–8 servings.

SPICY AND TANGY CHICKEN

Hot, fruity, sour, and salty—a combination that provides an unusual taste experience.

1 chicken, about 3 pounds
1 tablespoon light soy sauce
1 tablespoon dark soy sauce
2 tablespoons dry sherry
1 teaspoon salt or to taste
2 scallions, cut into 1-inch lengths
3 tablespoons cornstarch
  Oil for deep-frying
2 tablespoons peanut oil
2 teaspoons crushed red pepper or to taste
½ teaspoon toasted and ground Szechwan peppercorns
3 teaspoons grated tangerine or orange rind
2 tablespoons white rice wine vinegar
¼ cup chicken stock

Preparation

Rinse and clean the chicken. Split the chicken in half, then cut into bite-size pieces. Marinate for 2 hours in a mixture of the soy sauces, sherry, ½ teaspoon of the salt, and the scallions. Remove the chicken, but reserve the marinade for later. Cover the pieces of chicken lightly with the cornstarch.

Cooking

Deep-fry the chicken in oil heated to 350 degrees for 2 minutes or until the pieces are golden brown. Remove and drain on paper towels.

Heat a wok or skillet over high heat until a drop of water immediately sizzles into steam. Add the 2 tablespoons oil. Just before the oil begins to smoke, add the remaining salt, the red pepper, ground peppercorns, and tangerine or orange rind. Stir for 30 seconds. Add the chicken and mix well. Add the vinegar and stir-fry for 2 minutes.

Add the chicken stock to the remaining marinade. Stir into the pan and mix well with the chicken. Lower heat to medium low and cook until all of the liquid has disappeared, about 5 minutes.

Yield: 3–8 servings.

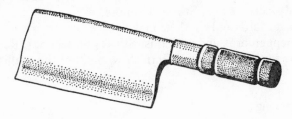

SLIPPERY CHICKEN

This spicy and aromatic dish plays up the smooth texture of bean curd with chicken meat. The effect is truly one of slippery chicken and quite novel.

1 tablespoon hot bean sauce	1½ tablespoons minced garlic
1 teaspoon dark soy sauce	½ teaspoon salt
4 bean curds	½ cup chicken stock or water
¾ pound boned chicken	1 teaspoon toasted and ground
1 tablespoon dry sherry	Szechwan peppercorns
1 egg white	¼ cup minced scallions
½ teaspoon sugar	1 teaspoon sesame oil
1 tablespoon cornstarch	Chopped scallions or
1 cup peanut oil	coriander to garnish
2 tablespoons minced ginger-root	

Preparation

In a bowl mash the hot bean sauce and combine with the soy sauce. Cut each bean curd into 9 pieces Shred the chicken and marinate in a mixing bowl with the sherry, egg white, sugar, and cornstarch.

Cooking

Heat a wok or skillet over high heat until a drop of water immediately sizzles into steam. Add the peanut oil. Just before the oil begins to smoke, add the gingerroot, garlic, and salt. Stir for 30 seconds or until the odor of the garlic has become pungent. Add the hot bean sauce mixture, the chicken, and chicken stock. Stir for 1 minute.

Add the bean curds and stir them in with care.

Add the peppercorns and scallions. Stir for 30 seconds. Remove from heat and stir in the sesame oil. Garnish with either the scallions or coriander.

Yield: 3–6 servings.

CHICKEN WITH SZECHWAN CHILI PASTE

An incredibly hot dish that gets most of its punch from the commercially prepared chili paste with garlic—a felicitous combination.

8 Chinese black mushrooms	1 cup peanut oil
¾ pound boned chicken	1 cup shredded bamboo shoots
1 tablespoon dry sherry	2 tablespoons shredded
1 egg white	gingerroot
1½ teaspoons sugar	½ cup shredded carrots
1 tablespoon cornstarch	1 teaspoon crushed red pepper
2 tablespoons chili paste	1 tablespoon cornstarch mixed
with garlic	with 3 tablespoons water
¼ cup water	1 teaspoon sesame oil
1 tablespoon light soy sauce	

Preparation

Soak the mushrooms in water for 30 minutes or until soft. Remove the tough stems and shred the mushrooms.

Shred the chicken and marinate in the sherry, egg white, ½ teaspoon of the sugar, and the cornstarch.

In a small bowl combine the chili paste, water, soy sauce, and the remaining sugar. Set aside.

Cooking

Heat a wok or skillet over high heat until a drop of water immediately sizzles into steam. Maintain high heat throughout the cooking process. Add the peanut oil. Just before the oil begins to smoke add the chicken and stir for 45 seconds or until the chicken turns light brown. Remove the chicken.

Drain off all but 2 tablespoons of the oil. Reheat the pan. Just before the oil begins to smoke add the bamboo shoots, mushrooms, gingerroot, carrots, and red pepper. Stir-fry for 1 minute. Add the chili paste mixture Stir and cook for 1 minute. Add the chicken and stir-fry for 1 minute. Lightly thicken the sauce with the cornstarch mixture as needed. Stir in the sesame oil and serve.

Yield: 2–4 servings.

CHUNGKING BRAISED CHICKEN

1 chicken, about 3 pounds
4 tablespoons dark soy sauce
4 fresh red or green hot peppers
1 cup chicken stock
1½ tablespoons light brown sugar
2 tablespoons white rice wine vinegar
1 cup peanut oil
½ teaspoon salt or to taste
4 slices gingerroot, the size of a quarter
1 teaspoon crushed red pepper
2 tablespoons dry sherry
1 tablespoon cornstarch mixed with 2 tablespoons water

Preparation

Clean the chicken. Split it in half and dry it with paper towels. Rub the chicken inside and out with 1 tablespoon of the soy sauce. Let it stand for 15 minutes and then chop it into bite-size pieces.

Split the fresh peppers and remove the seeds. Chop the peppers into ¼-inch lengths. In a small bowl combine the chicken stock, sugar, vinegar, and the remaining soy sauce.

Cooking

Heat a wok or skillet and add the oil. When the oil becomes hot, add the chicken and cook over high heat for 5 minutes or until nicely browned. Remove the chicken. Remove all but 3 tablespoons of the oil from the pan.

Reheat the wok or skillet and add the salt. Before the oil starts to smoke, add the gingerroot, fresh peppers, and red pepper. Stir-fry for ½ minute. Add the chicken and stir-fry for 1 minute. Add the sherry and stir-fry for ½ minute. Add the chicken stock mixture. Lower heat to simmer. Cover and simmer for 30 minutes. Thicken with the cornstarch mixture.

Yield: 3–6 servings.

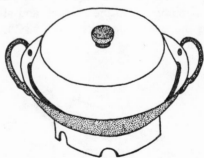

SZECHWAN DUCK

Szechwan duck is a favorite dish of ours. Its subtle fragrance satisfies everybody from lofty gourmets to a fussy child. The crisp skin is a special delicacy.

1 duck, about 5 pounds
1 tablespoon toasted and ground Szechwan peppercorns
2 tablespoons kosher salt
1 tablespoon minced gingerroot
2 star anise (16 sections)
2 whole scallions

1 tablespoon dark soy sauce
Oil for deep-frying
20 Steamed Rolls (see recipe on page 262)
Toasted salt and pepper
3 tablespoons finely minced scallions to garnish (optional)

Preparation
Remove the excess fat from the cavity of the duck. Rinse the duck under running water and pat dry with paper towels. Combine the ground peppercorns, salt, and gingerroot. Rub the duck inside and out with this mixture. Wrap the duck in plastic wrap and let it sit in the refrigerator overnight.

Cooking
Place the star anise and the whole scallions in the cavity of the duck. Steam in a heatproof dish over rapidly boiling water for 1 hour or until done, that is, when its juices run clear.

Remove the duck from the steamer. Dry it with paper towels and then rub its skin with the soy sauce. Let the duck dry uncovered in the refrigerator for 5 hours or until it is time for the final cooking process.

Heat the oil to 375 degrees (very hot). Carefully lower the duck into the oil and fry it until the skin is a deep golden color, turning the duck when necessary.

Carve the duck. Serve with steamed rolls and toasted salt and pepper. Each guest is then invited to make his own duck sandwich, optionally garnished with the minced scallions.

Yield: 4–8 servings.

TWICE-COOKED PORK

A classic dish in Chinese cuisine, Twice-Cooked Pork has a rare succulent crispness.

1 pound unsalted pork belly	1 tablespoon dry sherry
4 fresh green or red hot peppers	1 teaspoon sugar
½ green bell pepper	1 cup peanut oil
1 leek, white part only	2 teaspoons minced garlic
1 tablespoon brown bean sauce	2 slices fresh gingerroot, the size of a half-dollar
2 tablespoons chili paste with garlic	½ cup sliced bamboo shoots

Preparation

Place the pork belly in a pot and add water to 1 inch above the pork. Bring the water to a slow boil. Cover and simmer for 1 hour or until the meat is tender and can be easily pierced with a chopstick. Drain and cool completely. Cut against the grain into slices ⅛ inch thick. Remove the seeds from the hot peppers, then cut them into ¼-inch squares. Cut the bell pepper into 1-inch squares. Shred the leek into thin strips 1½ inches long.

Crush the brown bean sauce and combine with the chili paste, sherry, and sugar in a small bowl. Set aside.

Cooking

Heat a wok or skillet over high heat until a drop of water immediately sizzles into steam. Add the oil. Just before the oil begins to smoke, add the garlic and hot peppers. Stir until the odor of the garlic has become pungent. Add the pork and fry for 3 minutes or until the pork begins to turn golden brown. Remove the pork with a slotted spatula. Remove all but 2 tablespoons of the oil. Add the gingerroot. Stir for 15 seconds and add the bell pepper and bamboo shoots. Stir-fry for 1 minute. Return the pork to the pan. Add the leek and the brown bean sauce mixture. Stir-fry for 1 minute more.

Note: If the chili paste with garlic is not available, an interesting variation can be made by substituting 1 tablespoon hoisin sauce for the chili paste and increasing the hot peppers and minced garlic by one-half.

Yield: 3–6 servings.

SPICY GROUND PORK AND BEAN CURD

Neither ground pork nor bean curd is particularly outstanding, but the seasoning makes this a remarkable creation.

¾ pound ground pork
1 tablespoon chili paste with garlic
1 tablespoon dark soy sauce
1½ teaspoons sugar
4 bean curds
2 tablespoons peanut oil
2 tablespoons minced ginger-root
1½ tablespoons minced garlic
½ teaspoon salt
½ cup chicken stock or water
1 teaspoon toasted and ground Szechwan peppercorns
¼ cup minced scallions
2 teaspoons cornstarch mixed with 1 tablespoon water
1 tablespoon sesame oil
Chopped scallions or coriander to garnish

Preparation
In a bowl combine the pork, chili paste, soy sauce, and sugar. Cut each bean curd into 9 pieces.

Cooking
Heat a wok or skillet over high heat until a drop of water immediately sizzles into steam. Maintain high heat throughout the cooking process. Add the peanut oil, gingerroot, garlic, and salt. Stir for 30 seconds or until the odor of the garlic has become pungent. Add the pork mixture and stir-fry for 30 seconds or until the pork is white.

Add the chicken stock and cook for 1½ minutes. Add the bean curd and stir in with care. Cook for 2 minutes longer, stirring occasionally to avoid sticking.

Add the ground peppercorns, scallions, and cornstarch mixture. Stir for 30 seconds or until the mixture has thickened. Remove from heat and stir in the sesame oil. Garnish with either the scallions or coriander.

Yield: 4–8 servings.

MOCK SZECHWAN FISH

This and the recipe that follows are amusing variations on other recipes. Both take sauces originally intended for fish and use them for pork. However, the sauces' "fishy" origins are not forgotten, as is evident in the name of the dish—in this case, Mock Fish.

¾ pound boned pork
1 tablespoon cornstarch
1 tablespoon dry sherry
2 tablespoons brown bean sauce
1 tablespoon light soy sauce
1 tablespoon red rice wine vinegar
1 teaspoon sugar

1 teaspoon crushed red pepper
½ teaspoon sesame oil
1 tablespoon water
1 cup peanut oil
1 tablespoon minced ginger-root
1 teaspoon cornstarch mixed with ¼ cup water

Preparation

Cut the pork into strips measuring approximately 2 by ¼ by ⅛ inch. Combine the cornstarch and sherry. Marinate the pork strips in this mixture for 1 hour.

In a small bowl mash the brown bean sauce and stir in the remaining ingredients except for the gingerroot, cornstarch-water mixture, and peanut oil.

Cooking

Heat the peanut oil until it is very hot, almost smoking. Add the pork and fry the strips for 1 minute or until done. Drain the pork strips well. Remove all but 1 tablespoon of the oil from the pan.

Heat the remaining tablespoon of oil until very hot. Add the gingerroot and stir for 15 seconds. Return the pork to the pan. Add the brown bean sauce mixture and stir vigorously for 45 seconds to cook the beans.

Add the cornstarch mixture and stir until thickened. The sauce should be thick and fairly scant.

Yield: 2–4 servings.

YU SHIANG PORK

Yu shiang means aromatic fish, but the method of cooking and the sauce have been adapted to pork as in this recipe.

¾ pound boneless pork	2 tablespoons water
1 ball preserved turnip	Dash of pepper
1 teaspoon dark soy sauce	2 tablespoons peanut oil
2 teaspoons oyster sauce	½ teaspoon salt or to taste
½ teaspoon crushed red pepper	1 slice gingerroot, the size of a
1 teaspoon red wine vinegar	quarter
½ teaspoon sugar	1 teaspoon dry sherry

Preparation

Shred the pork into slivers the size of a matchstick. Unravel the ball of preserved turnip, rinse off the excess salt, and mince it finely. Mix the soy sauce, oyster sauce, red pepper, vinegar, sugar, water, and pepper in a bowl.

Cooking

Heat a wok or skillet over high heat until a drop of water immediately sizzles into steam. Add the oil, salt, and gingerroot. Stir for 30 seconds. Just before the oil begins to smoke, add the pork and sprinkle it with the sherry. Stir-fry for 2 minutes. Add the preserved turnip and the soy-and-oyster-sauce mixture. Stir for 1 minute.

Yield: 2–4 servings.

HUNAN CURRIED PORK ROLLS

1 medium onion	½ teaspoon light soy sauce
2 scallions	2 tablespoons water
1 pound lace fat	3 tablespoons chopped roasted
1 egg white	peanuts
1 tablespoon cornstarch	3 tablespoons curry powder
½ teaspoon sugar	½ pound ground pork
½ teaspoon salt or to taste	Oil for deep-frying

Preparation

Dice the onion into ¼-inch cubes. Dice the scallions. Cut the lace fat into 6-inch squares. Combine the egg white and cornstarch in a small bowl. In a second bowl combine the sugar, salt, soy sauce, water, scallions, and peanuts.

Cooking
In an ungreased wok or skillet toast the onions and the curry powder over medium-low heat for 1½ minutes or until pungent. Add the pork and stir well to mix. Raise heat to high. Add the seasonings and cook for 2 minutes. Let the mixture cool for a little while.

Place ½ cup of the pork mixture in the center of a square of lace fat. Fold opposite sides of the lace fat over the mixture and roll the remaining flaps of lace fat over the roll as one would with an egg roll. Brush the roll with the egg white and cornstarch mixture.

Deep-fry the rolls for 15 minutes in oil heated to 300 degrees. Drain on paper towels. Cut each roll into thirds for serving.

Yield: 4–6 servings.

HUNAN STEAMED SPARE RIBS

Although these ribs are steamed, they have a nice crunchy quality as a result of being rolled in rice flour.

1 sheet spare ribs, about 4 pounds	1 teaspoon five-flavor powder
2 tablespoons hot bean sauce	1 tablespoon dry sherry
¼ cup dark soy sauce	4 ounces rice flour

Preparation
Separate the ribs and, if you wish, chop them into 2-inch lengths. Mash the hot bean sauce with the handle of a Chinese cleaver and combine with the soy sauce, five-flavor powder, and sherry. Marinate the ribs in this mixture for 1 hour. Toast the rice flour in a small ungreased frying pan over low heat for 15 minutes. Remove the ribs from the marinade and roll them in the rice flour until they are well coated. Let the ribs dry for 4 hours.

Cooking
Steam over rapidly boiling water for 30 minutes.

Yield: 4–8 servings.

HONEY HAM

Many cultures have learned the delicious secret of a sweet glaze on cured meat. This particular sauce is sweet but not cloying.

1 slice smoked country ham, about 2 pounds
¼ cup lotus nuts
¼ cup rock sugar
¼ cup water
½ teaspoon light soy sauce
1 tablespoon honey
1 tablespoon cornstarch mixed with 2 tablespoons water

Preparation

Put the ham in a kettle with enough water to cover. Simmer for 2 hours. Drain the ham and cut into ½-inch-thick pieces. Remove the rind. Arrange the ham in a heatproof dish. Place the lotus nuts evenly over the ham. Sprinkle with rock sugar.

Cooking

Place the heatproof dish in a steamer. Cover and steam for 1 hour. Remove the ham to a serving platter. Drain the juices from the dish into a pan. Add the water, soy sauce, and honey. Bring to a boil. Thicken with the cornstarch mixture. Pour the sauce over the ham and lotus seeds before serving.

Yield: 4–8 servings.

PORK LIVER AND KIDNEY

This dish plays up the contrast in textures between liver and kidney.

½ pound pork liver
½ pound pork kidney
1 tablespoon chili paste with garlic
1 tablespoon dark soy sauce
1½ teaspoons sugar
2 tablespoons peanut oil
2 tablespoons minced ginger-root
1½ tablespoons minced garlic
½ teaspoon salt or to taste
¼ cup chicken stock
1 teaspoon toasted and ground Szechwan peppercorns
1 tablespoon sesame oil
¼ cup minced scallions to garnish

Preparation

Rinse the liver and kidney in cold water. Remove the tough membrane from the kidney. Cut both meats into thin slices. In a bowl combine the liver, kidney, chili paste, soy sauce, and sugar.

Cooking

Heat a wok or skillet over high heat until a drop of water immediately sizzles into steam. Maintain high heat throughout the cooking process. Add the peanut oil, gingerroot, garlic, and salt. Stir for 30 seconds or until the odor of the garlic has become pungent. Add the liver, kidney, and the sauce. Stir-fry for two minutes.

Add the chicken stock and ground peppercorns. Cover and cook for 1 minute. Remove from heat and stir in the sesame oil. Garnish with the scallions.

Yield: 4–8 servings.

SZECHWAN BEEF

In this recipe the beef is deliberately overcooked to achieve a tough, chewy consistency that contrasts nicely with the crisp texture of the carrots and celery. The beef must be very finely shredded which is most easily done if the meat is sliced when partially frozen.

1 pound flank steak	1 tablespoon crushed red pep-
2 tablespoons light soy sauce	per or to taste
1 tablespoon dry sherry	½ cup shredded carrot
1 cup peanut oil	¾ cup shredded celery
1 tablespoon shredded ginger-	½ teaspoon sugar
root	½ teaspoon salt or to taste

Preparation

Shred the beef into pieces the size of a matchstick. In a bowl combine the soy sauce and sherry. Marinate the beef in this mixture for 15 minutes to an hour.

Cooking

Place the oil in a wok or skillet over high heat. Just before the oil begins to smoke, add the beef but not the marinade. Fry for 3 minutes or until it has become dry and well browned. Remove and drain the beef.

Remove all but 2 tablespoons of oil from the pan. Reheat the pan and add the gingerroot and red pepper. Stir gently for 20 seconds or until the pepper flakes begin to brown.

Add the carrot and stir-fry for 15 seconds. Add the celery and stir-fry for 15 seconds. Add the beef, the reserved marinade, and sugar. Add the salt to taste, stirring to mix well. Remove to a warm serving dish and serve immediately.

Yield: 3–6 servings.

CHUNGKING BEEF WITH BLACK BEAN SAUCE

Like the Cantonese, the western Chinese appreciate the salty pungency of fermented black beans. The beans go well in beef dishes which have sufficient flavor to balance the powerful seasoning.

1 pound flank steak
1 egg white
1 tablespoon cornstarch
2 teaspoons light soy sauce
2 tablespoons black beans
1 tablespoon shredded ginger-root
1 tablespoon minced garlic
½ teaspoon salt or to taste
¼ cup chicken stock

1 tablespoon crushed red pepper
1 teaspoon light brown sugar
1 cup peanut oil
⅓ cup shredded cucumber
⅓ cup shredded bamboo shoots
⅓ cup shredded celery
1 leek, white part only, shredded
1 teaspoon sesame oil

Preparation
Cut the flank steak in half along the grain. Slice the beef across the grain to make thin strips ⅛ inch wide, ½ inch thick, and 1½ inches long. Then slice the beef into fine shreds. Combine the egg white, cornstarch, and 1 teaspoon of the soy sauce. Marinate the beef in this mixture.

Wash the black beans. Mash them with the handle of a Chinese knife and combine them with the gingerroot, garlic, and salt.

In a bowl combine the chicken stock, red pepper, sugar, and the remaining soy sauce.

Cooking
Heat a wok or skillet over high heat until a drop of water immediately sizzles into steam. Maintain high heat throughout the cooking process. Add the oil. Just before the oil begins to smoke, add the beef and stir for 30 seconds. Remove the beef.

Drain off all but two tablespoons of the oil. Reheat the pan. Just before the oil begins to smoke, add the black bean mixture. Stir for about 30 seconds or until the odor of the beans and the garlic has become pungent. Add the cucumber, bamboo shoots, celery, and leek. Stir-fry for 1 minute.

Add the chicken stock mixture. Stir for 30 seconds. Add the beef. Stir for 30 seconds more. Add the sesame oil. Stir briefly and serve.

Yield: 3–6 servings.

HUNAN BEEF WITH WATERCRESS

Meat and vegetable dishes are relatively uncommon in western China, while they are frequently served elsewhere. It is not unusual, however, for two separately cooked dishes to be served together for a similar effect.

¾ pound flank steak	2 tablespoons finely chopped
1 egg white	scallions
½ teaspoon salt	½ teaspoon cayenne pepper
1½ teaspoons cornstarch	1 teaspoon crushed red pepper
¼ cup dry sherry	¼ pound watercress
1 tablespoon sesame oil	4 dried red hot peppers
1 tablespoon dark soy sauce	2 tablespoons plus 1 cup pea-
1½ teaspoons white rice wine	nut oil
vinegar	1 teaspoon minced gingerroot
¼ teaspoon white pepper	1 tablespoon minced garlic

Preparation

Cut the flank steak into strips 2½ inches long, ¼ inch wide, and ½ inch thick. In a bowl combine the beef with the egg white, ¼ teaspoon of the salt, and the cornstarch.

In another bowl combine 3 tablespoons of the sherry, 1½ teaspoons of the sesame oil, the soy sauce, vinegar, white pepper, and scallions.

In a third bowl combine the remaining sesame oil with the cayenne and crushed red pepper.

Cut the watercress into 2½ inch-lengths, discarding the tough stems. Cut the dried red peppers into quarters.

Cooking

Heat a wok or skillet over high heat until a drop of water immediately sizzles into steam. Add 2 tablespoons of the peanut oil and the remaining salt. Just before the oil begins to smoke, add the watercress. Stir for a couple of seconds to coat the watercress with oil. Add the remaining sherry and continue to stir briskly for 15 seconds or until the stalks of the watercress have become slightly tender. Remove the watercress and place at one side of a warm serving plate.

Heat the remaining peanut oil until it is moderately hot, about 300 degrees. Add the beef strips and fry them gently for 15 seconds or until they are no longer pink on the outside. Remove the strips from the oil. Pour off all but 2 tablespoons of the oil.

Reheat the oil, add the dried red peppers, gingerroot, and garlic. Stir for 15 seconds. Return the beef to the pan and add the sherry and vinegar mixture. Stir for 15 seconds and add the sesame oil and crushed red pepper mixture. Stir well to blend and then remove from heat. The beef should still be pink inside. Arrange next to the watercress on the serving plate.

Yield: 2–4 servings.

CURRIED BEEF WITH POTATOES

3 pounds stew beef	1 teaspoon dark soy sauce
2 pounds white boiling potatoes	½ teaspoon sugar
	½ teaspoon salt or to taste
1 large onion	Dash of pepper
5 tablespoons curry powder	2 teaspoons cornstarch mixed
1 quart chicken stock	with ¼ cup water

Preparation
Cut the beef into 1½-inch cubes. Peel the potatoes and quarter them. Cut the onion into wedges.

Cooking
Place a heavy saucepan or wok over medium heat. Add the onion wedges and sprinkle them with the curry powder. Toast the curry powder in this manner for 2 minutes or until the odor of curry is pungent. Add the beef and stir for 3 minutes, but do not allow the curry powder to burn. Add the chicken stock, soy sauce, sugar, salt, and pepper. Simmer closely covered for about 2 to 3 hours or until meat can be easily pierced with a fork. During the last hour of cooking, add the potatoes. Thicken with the cornstarch mixture.

Yield: 6–12 servings.

LAMB WITH SZECHWAN PRESERVED VEGETABLE

Lamb is not as popular in the west as it is in the north, but some sheep are raised in the hills and a few interesting recipes have been developed.

½ pound Szechwan preserved
    vegetable
¾ pound boned lamb
1 tablespoon dry sherry
1 teaspoon sugar

1 tablespoon dark soy sauce
¼ cup water
2 tablespoons peanut oil
½ teaspoon salt or to taste

Preparation
Rinse the preserved vegetable well and pat dry. Cut it into fine shreds. Slice the lamb across the grain to make thin strips ⅛ inch wide, ½ inch thick, and 1½ inches long. Then shred the lamb. In a small bowl combine the sherry, sugar, soy sauce, and water.

Cooking
Heat a wok or skillet over high heat until a drop of water immediately sizzles into steam. Maintain high heat throughout the cooking process. Add the oil and salt. Just before the oil begins to smoke add the lamb. Stir-fry for 2 minutes. Add the preserved vegetable and the sherry and soy-sauce mixture. Stir over high heat for five minutes.

Yield: 2–4 servings.

YUNNAN LAMB WITH CURRY AND BLACK BEANS

Curry came to Yunnan from Burma. The genius who put together the unlikely combination of two rather dominant flavors from black beans and curry is unknown. But the result is a spectrum of tastes so fascinating it is surprising that this dish has not become better known.

½ pound boned lamb
1 tablespoon black beans
2 tablespoons peanut oil
½ teaspoon salt or to taste
1 tablespoon minced garlic

¾ cup sliced onions
1 tablespoon curry powder
½ cup chicken stock
1 teaspoon light soy sauce
½ teaspoon sugar

Preparation
Slice the lamb across the grain to make thin strips ⅛ inch wide, ½ inch

thick, and 1½ inches long. Rinse the black beans and mash with the handle of a Chinese knife.

Cooking
Heat a wok or skillet over high heat until a drop of water immediately sizzles into steam. Maintain high heat throughout the cooking process. Add the oil, salt, garlic, and black beans. Stir for about 30 seconds or until the odor of the beans and garlic has become pungent. Add the lamb and stir-fry for 2 minutes. Remove to a warm plate.

Heat a dry wok or skillet over medium-low heat. Spread the onions in the pan. Sprinkle the curry powder over the onions. Toast for 2 minutes or until the curry smells pungent, stirring occasionally to keep the curry powder from burning. Add the chicken stock, soy sauce, and sugar. Add the lamb and its black bean sauce and stir until the gravy thickens.

Yield: 2–4 servings.

HUNAN LAMB

1 pound boneless lamb	1 tablespoon white rice wine
2 tablespoons cornstarch	vinegar
1 egg white	4 fresh hot peppers
2 tablespoons water	1 leek, white part only
¼ cup dry sherry	1 cup peanut oil
2 tablespoons light soy sauce	1 tablespoon crushed red pepper
1 teaspoon sugar	per
⅛ teaspoon white pepper	1 tablespoon hot bean sauce

Preparation
Shred the lamb into strips 2 inches long by ¼ inch thick. Combine 1 tablespoon of the cornstarch with the egg white and dredge the lamb in this mixture. Combine the remaining cornstarch with the water, sherry, soy sauce, sugar, white pepper, and vinegar. Seed and shred the hot peppers. Also shred the leek.

Cooking
Heat the oil to 375 degrees or very hot. Add the lamb and fry for 30 seconds. Remove the lamb from the oil with a slotted spoon.

Remove all but 2 tablespoons of the oil from the pan. Reheat the oil and add the red pepper. Stir for 20 seconds or until the flakes darken.

Add the hot peppers and the leek. Stir for 20 seconds. Add the hot bean

sauce. Add the lamb to the pan along with the soy-sauce-and-vinegar mixture. Stir to blend for 15 seconds or until thickened. Serve immediately.

Yield: 3–6 servings.

HUNAN LAMB TRIPE

1 pound lamb tripe	3 tablespoons peanut oil
1 leek	½ teaspoon salt or to taste
1 tablespoon dry sherry	¼ cup shredded gingerroot
⅛ teaspoon white pepper	1 tablespoon crushed red
1 teaspoon dark soy sauce	pepper
½ teaspoon sugar	

Preparation

Wash and drain the tripe. Cut it into 2-inch-wide strips. Have a pot of water boiling. Lower heat to simmer. Add the tripe. Cover and simmer for 1 hour. Drain. When it is cool enough to handle cut the tripe into slices about ¼ inch wide and 2 inches long.

Discard green part and root of leek. Wash the white part of the leek thoroughly and slice diagonally into 2-inch strips.

Blend the sherry, white pepper, soy sauce, and sugar in a small bowl. Set aside.

Cooking

Heat a wok or skillet over high heat until a drop of water immediately sizzles into steam. Add the oil and salt. Just before the oil begins to smoke, add the leek, gingerroot, red pepper, and tripe. Stir-fry for 30 seconds. Add the sherry-and-soy-sauce mixture and sugar. Add more salt to taste if desired. Stir and cook until sauce is almost totally gone.

Yield: 4–8 servings.

FISH WITH SZECHWAN SAUCE AND VEGETABLES

1 tablespoon white rice wine vinegar
1 tablespoon crushed red pepper
8 fresh hot peppers
½ cup chicken stock
1 teaspoon sugar
1 tablespoon dry sherry
2 tablespoons minced scallions

1 fish, about 1½ pounds
½ teaspoon salt or to taste
1 cup peanut oil
¼ cup shredded gingerroot
1 cup shredded Chinese cabbage *(bok choy)*
Coriander to garnish

Preparation

In a small bowl mix the vinegar, red pepper, hot peppers, chicken stock, sugar, sherry, and scallions. Clean and scale the fish. Rinse under running water and pat dry.

Cooking

Heat a wok or skillet over high heat until a drop of water immediately sizzles into steam. Add the salt and oil. Just before the oil begins to smoke, add the fish. Lower heat to medium and fry for 5 minutes on each side. Remove the fish from the pan. Remove all but 2 tablespoons of the oil. Bring the pan to high heat. Add the gingerroot and then the cabbage. Stir-fry for 1 minute. Add the vinegar and chicken stock mixture and stir well.

Return the fish to the pan. Cover and cook for 2 minutes. Carefully turn the fish over and repeat for 2 minutes more.

Remove the fish and the sauce to a serving platter. Garnish with the coriander.

Yield: 2–4 servings.

SZECHWAN BRAISED FISH

Sweet, sour, and hot, this recipe provides a lovely blending of flavors.

8 Chinese black mushrooms
6 to 8 fresh hot peppers
2 tablespoons dark soy sauce
2 tablespoons red wine vinegar
1 cup chicken stock
1½ tablespoons light brown
    sugar
1 fish, about 2 pounds
1½ teaspoons salt or to taste

1 tablespoon cornstarch
3 cups peanut oil
4 dried red peppers
2 teaspoons shredded ginger-
    root
½ cup shredded bamboo shoots
2 teaspoons cornstarch mixed
    with 2 tablespoons water

Preparation

Soak the mushrooms in water for 30 minutes or until soft. Discard the tough stems and shred the mushrooms. Remove the seeds from the fresh hot peppers and cut the peppers into 1-inch pieces.

Blend the soy sauce, vinegar, chicken stock, and sugar in a bowl. Set aside.

Clean and scale the fish. Gently wash the fish and dry it with paper towels. Rub the fish on the inside and outside with 1 teaspoon of the salt. Dust the outside with the 1 tablespoon cornstarch.

Cooking

In a hot wok or skillet add the oil and red peppers. When the oil is 350 degrees or just before it smokes, add the fish carefully. As the fish is cooking on one side, spoon the hot oil over the other side with a spatula. Fry for 2 minutes on each side or until each side is brown.

Remove the fish. Remove the red peppers and discard. Remove all but 3 tablespoons of the oil. Heat the pan again. Just before the oil begins to smoke add the remaining salt and the gingerroot. Stir for 15 seconds and then add the bamboo shoots, mushrooms, and fresh hot peppers. Stir-fry for ½ minute. Add the chicken stock mixture and return the fish to the pan. Lower heat to a simmer. Cover and cook for 15 minutes, turning the fish over once.

To test for doneness the flesh should flake easily. Remove the fish to a serving dish. Add the cornstarch mixture to the pan and stir over high heat until the sauce has thickened. Pour the sauce over the fish and serve immediately.

Yield: 2–4 servings.

POACHED FISH WITH HOT PEPPER SAUCE

The Chinese are fond of poaching fish and then pouring a very hot oil-based sauce over the fish at the last minute. The heat of the oil cooking the scallions further flavors the sauce. Even with a spicy sauce, only the freshest of fish should be poached.

1 fish, about 2 pounds	6 tablespoons vegetable oil
1 slice gingerroot, the size of a half-dollar	3 tablespoons shredded gingerroot
2 tablespoons light soy sauce	⅛ teaspoon white pepper
4 scallions, cut into ¼-inch lengths	1 tablespoon crushed red pepper
2 teaspoons salt	

Preparation and cooking

Clean and scale the fish but leave the head intact. Place enough water in a pan so that the fish can float. Bring water to the boiling point, then lower to simmer. Add the slice of gingerroot and the fish. Poach for about 7 minutes. The fish is done when the eyes turn chalk-white or when the flesh will flake when tested with a chopstick. Place the fish in a serving dish. Sprinkle the soy sauce, scallions, and salt evenly over it.

In a hot skillet bring the oil almost to the point of smoking. Add the shredded gingerroot, white pepper, and red pepper. Stir for 15 seconds. Pour over the fish and serve immediately.

Yield: 2–4 servings.

YUNNAN FRIED FISH
WITH CURRY AND BROWN BEAN SAUCE

In this dish the saltiness and body of the brown bean sauce enhances the tang of the curry.

1 fish, about 2 pounds	1 cup chicken stock
1 egg, beaten	½ teaspoon salt or to taste
4 tablespoons cornstarch	¼ teaspoon sugar
3 cups peanut oil	2 tablespoons brown bean sauce
¼ cup coarsely chopped scallions	
2 tablespoons curry powder	2 teaspoons cornstarch mixed with 1 tablespoon water

Preparation

Clean and scale the fish. Dry with paper towels. Rub the egg over the outside of the fish. Dredge the fish in the 4 tablespoons cornstarch. Make three diagonal slashes on each side of the fish.

Cooking

In a skillet heat the oil to very hot, about 375 degrees. Fry the fish for 5 to 7 minutes on each side. To prevent the skin from sticking to the pan, try to keep the fish afloat with a slotted spatula until the skin has been somewhat cooked. Remove the fish to a serving plate.

Place the scallions and curry powder in a dry wok or skillet over medium-low heat. Toast the curry powder for 2 minutes or until pungent, stirring occasionally to keep the curry powder from burning. Add the chicken stock, salt, sugar, and brown bean sauce. Bring to a boil then simmer for 3 minutes. Add the cornstarch mixture to thicken. Pour the sauce over fish.

Yield: 2–4 servings.

YUNNAN STEAMED FISH WITH CURRY AND BLACK BEAN SAUCE

1 fish, 2 to 3 pounds	1 leek, white part only
1½ teaspoons salt	2 tablespoons curry powder
4 tablespoons peanut oil	1 tablespoon minced garlic
1 tablespoon shredded ginger-	1 cup chicken stock
root	1 teaspoon sugar
2 tablespoons black beans	

Preparation

Clean and scale the fish. Dry with paper towels. Rub the inside and outside of the fish with 1 teaspoon of the salt and 2 tablespoons of the oil. Make 3 diagonal slashes on both sides of the fish. Place the fish in a heatproof dish and sprinkle it with the gingerroot. Rinse the black beans. Mash with the handle of a Chinese knife. Shred the leek.

Cooking

Steam the fish for about 10 minutes. The fish is done when the flesh flakes and its eyes bulge. Remove from the stove to a warm platter.

While the fish is steaming, place the leek in a dry wok or skillet over medium heat and sprinkle the curry powder over it. Toast the curry powder for 2 minutes or until pungent, stirring occasionally to keep the curry powder from burning. Add the remaining oil and the remaining salt. Raise heat to high. Just before the oil begins to smoke, add the black beans and garlic. Stir. When the garlic becomes pungent, add the chicken stock and sugar. Bring the liquid to a boil and let it cook down by one-quarter. Pour the sauce over the fish and serve immediately.

Yield: 2–6 servings.

SZECHWAN SHRIMP

A delicious dish in which ketchup is used to give a tart tanginess and an attractive color. Although ketchup is a Western condiment, it has found its way to China. Interestingly, the word "ketchup" is derived from the Chinese words for "brine of pickled fish."

1 pound shrimp	8 scallions, chopped into ¼-inch lengths
1 tablespoon chili paste with garlic	¼ cup finely minced gingerroot
2 tablespoons ketchup	1 teaspoon crushed red pepper
1 tablespoon dark soy sauce	1 tablespoon minced garlic
2 tablespoons peanut oil	1 tablespoon dry sherry
½ teaspoon salt or to taste	1 teaspoon sugar

Preparation
Shell and devein the shrimp. Wash, drain, and pat dry with paper towels. In a bowl mix the chili paste, ketchup, and soy sauce.

Cooking
Heat a wok or skillet over high heat until a drop of water immediately sizzles into steam. Add the oil and salt. Just before the oil begins to smoke, add the scallions, gingerroot, red pepper, and garlic. Stir until the odor of the garlic has become pungent and the scallions have turned dark green. Add the shrimp and stir-fry for 1 to 2 minutes until the shrimp have become firm and pink. Add the sherry and sugar. Stir for 30 seconds. Add the chili paste mixture. Stir for about 1 minute until the sauce thickens somewhat.

Yield: 3–6 servings.

KUNG PAO SHRIMP

An exquisitely delicate balance of flavors. The sauce should cling lightly to the crisp but tender shrimp.

1 pound shrimp	1 tablespoon minced garlic
2 tablespoons cornstarch	2 tablespoons chopped
¼ cup white rice wine vinegar	scallions
¼ teaspoon salt	2 tablespoons minced ginger-
2 tablespoons light soy sauce	root
2 tablespoons sugar	1 cup peanut oil

Preparation
Shell and devein the shrimp. Lightly coat them in the cornstarch. In a small bowl combine the vinegar, salt, soy sauce, and sugar. In another bowl combine the garlic, scallions, and gingerroot.

Cooking
In a wok or skillet heat the oil to 375 degrees or very hot. Add the shrimp. Stir-fry for 1 minute or until they are pink. Drain the shrimp and remove all but 2 tablespoons of oil from the pan.

Reheat the 2 tablespoons of oil. Just before the oil begins to smoke, add the garlic, scallion, and gingerroot mixture. Stir until the odor of the garlic has become pungent. Add the vinegar mixture and bring it to a boil while stirring. Add the shrimp and stir briefly to warm them through and to reduce the sauce slightly.

Yield: 3–6 servings.

SHRIMP WITH TOMATO SAUCE

The tomato is a relative newcomer to China, having arrived from the New World. Although still not widely grown, the tomato has made its impact on Chinese cooking as is evident in this dish.

1 pound shrimp	2 tablespoons tomato paste
4 scallions, white part only	2 tablespoons chicken stock
1 tablespoon light brown sugar	½ teaspoon salt or to taste
1 tablespoon white rice wine	2 tablespoons peanut oil
vinegar	2 teaspoons minced garlic
1 tablespoon dark soy sauce	1 teaspoon minced gingerroot
1 teaspoon crushed red pepper	1 tablespoon dry sherry

Preparation

Shell and devein the shrimp. Pat dry with paper towels. Cut the white part of the scallions diagonally into pieces 1 inch long. In a small bowl combine the sugar, vinegar, soy sauce, red pepper, tomato paste, and chicken stock.

Cooking

Heat a wok or skillet over high heat until a drop of water immediately sizzles into steam. Add the salt and oil. Just before the oil begins to smoke, add the garlic, gingerroot, and scallions. Stir-fry for a few seconds. Add the shrimp and sprinkle them with the sherry. Stir and cover for 1 minute. Lower heat to medium and add the tomato paste mixture. Stir for 1 minute. The sauce should be relatively scant.

Yield: 3–6 servings.

SHRIMP PUFF IN GINGER SAUCE

½ pound shrimp	5 tablespoons red wine
4 water chestnuts	vinegar
1 egg, slightly beaten	1½ tablespoons light brown
1½ teaspoons cornstarch	sugar
1 scallion, minced	1 teaspoon minced garlic
½ teaspoon salt	1 tablespoon shredded
Oil for deep-frying	gingerroot
1 tablespoon dark soy sauce	

Preparation

Shell and devein the shrimp. Mince the shrimp and water chestnuts very finely. In a mixing bowl add the egg, cornstarch, scallion, salt, shrimp, and water chestnuts. Blend into a smooth paste. Shape into balls about 1 inch in diameter.

Cooking

Deep-fry the shrimp balls a few at a time in 350-degree oil until golden brown. Remove with a slotted spatula to a serving plate.

Heat the remaining ingredients over medium heat, stirring constantly until the mixture almost comes to a boil. Pour the sauce over the shrimp puffs.

Yield: 2–4 servings.

SCALLOPS WITH BLACK BEAN SAUCE

This and the next recipe call for scallops, which were not available except in dried form in western China. Freshwater shrimp were originally used, but we prefer the special sweetness of the scallops.

1 pound scallops
2 tablespoons black beans
1 leek, white part only
⅓ cup sliced water chestnuts
⅓ cup shredded bamboo shoots
2 teaspoons shredded ginger-root
2 teaspoons crushed red pepper
1 teaspoon light brown sugar

1 tablespoon white rice wine vinegar
2 teaspoons light soy sauce
2 tablespoons chicken stock
2 tablespoons peanut oil
½ teaspoon salt or to taste
1 tablespoon minced garlic
2 tablespoons water
1 teaspoon sesame oil

Preparation

Rinse and dry the scallops. Rinse and drain the black beans. Mash the black beans with the back of a spoon or the handle of a Chinese cleaver. Shred the leek and set aside with the water chestnuts, bamboo shoots, and gingerroot.

In a bowl combine the red pepper, sugar, vinegar, soy sauce, and chicken stock.

Cooking

Heat a wok or skillet over high heat until a drop of water immediately sizzles into steam. Add the peanut oil and salt. Just before the oil begins to smoke, add the black beans and garlic. When the garlic becomes pungent, add the scallops and water. Stir-fry for 2 minutes. Add the leek, water chestnuts, bamboo shoots, and gingerroot. Stir-fry for 1 minute. Add the red pepper mixture. Stir-fry for 1 minute. Turn off heat. Add the sesame oil. Stir and serve.

Yield: 3–6 servings.

SCALLOPS, HUNAN STYLE

1 pound scallops	4 dried red peppers
1 tablespoon cornstarch	1 tablespoon dark soy sauce
1 egg white	1 tablespoon white rice wine
6 Chinese black mushrooms	vinegar
6 to 8 fresh red or green hot	1 tablespoon light brown sugar
peppers	1 cup peanut oil
½ cup sliced bamboo shoots	½ teaspoon salt or to taste
10 water chestnuts	

Preparation

Rinse the scallops in cold water and drain. Place in a mixing bowl and blend in the cornstarch and egg white.

Soak the mushrooms for 30 minutes in water or until soft. Remove the hard stems and shred the mushrooms. Remove the seeds from the hot peppers and cut into 1-inch pieces. Shred the bamboo shoots and slice the water chestnuts. Add the shredded mushrooms and the dried and fresh peppers. Set aside.

In a small bowl combine the soy sauce, vinegar, and sugar.

Cooking

Heat a wok or skillet over high heat until a drop of water immediately sizzles into steam. Add the oil. Just before the oil begins to smoke, add the scallops. Stir gently for 1½ minutes but be careful not to break the scallops. Remove the scallops with a slotted spatula and drain.

Remove all but 2 tablespoons of the oil from the pan. When the pan is hot again, add the salt and then the vegetables. Stir-fry for 1 minute. Add the soy sauce mixture and mix well. Add the scallops. Mix carefully and cook for ½ to 1 minute until the sauce thickens somewhat and is scant.

Yield: 3–6 servings.

STUFFED HOT PEPPERS

The pan-frying of the peppers moderates the "fire" and highlights the more subtle flavors to be found in this vegetable.

1 pound shrimp	1 teaspoon sesame oil
5 medium Chinese black mushrooms	1 tablespoon light soy sauce
	Dash of pepper
4 scallions	2 tablespoons cornstarch
6 water chestnuts	2 tablespoons peanut oil
¼ cup roasted peanuts	5 large chili peppers
¼ pound ground pork	

Preparation

Shell and devein the shrimp. Mince the shrimp. Soak the mushrooms in water for 30 minutes or until soft. Gently squeeze the liquid out of the mushrooms, then cut off and discard the stems. Mince the mushrooms as well as the scallions, water chestnuts, and peanuts. Mix all of the ingredients together except for the peanut oil and chili peppers.

Split the chili peppers in half lengthwise. Remove the seeds and stuff with the shrimp and pork mixture.

Cooking

Heat the peanut oil over medium heat. Fry the peppers for 2½ minutes on the meat side and 1½ minutes on the pepper side or until done.

Note:

The filling may be molded into patties approximately 2½ inches in diameter and ½ inch thick. They may then be fried on each side for about 2 minutes and served by themselves.

Yield: 4–8 servings.

KAN SHAO GREEN BEANS

Kan shao means dry-cooked and is one of the distinctive techniques in Szechwan cooking. It results in crunchy vegetables with very little liquid gravy. Sliced asparagus or broccoli may be substituted.

1 pound green beans	½ teaspoon salt or to taste
1 cup peanut oil	Dash of pepper
1 tablespoon shredded ginger-root	1½ teaspoons dark soy sauce
	½ teaspoon sugar

Preparation
Snap off the ends of the green beans. Cut into two-inch lengths.

Cooking
Heat the oil in a wok or skillet. Just before the oil begins to smoke, add the green beans and fry for 2 minutes. Remove and drain the green beans.

Remove all but 2 tablespoons of oil from the pan. Reheat the pan and add the gingerroot. Stir gently for 20 seconds or until the gingerroot begins to brown. Add the green beans and the remaining ingredients. Stir-fry for 30 seconds.

Yield: 4–8 servings.

HUNAN FAMILY-STYLE EGGPLANT

2 tablespoons chili paste with garlic	¼ teaspoon salt or to taste
2 teaspoons dark soy sauce	1 pound eggplant
1 teaspoon light soy sauce	½ cup peanut oil
1 tablespoon white rice wine vinegar	1 tablespoon dry sherry
1 teaspoon sugar	1 tablespoon crushed red pepper
	¼ cup water

Preparation
In a bowl combine the chili paste, soy sauces, vinegar, sugar, and salt. Leaving the skin on, cut the eggplant into 1-inch cubes.

Cooking
Heat a wok or skillet over high heat until a drop of water immediately sizzles into steam. Maintain high heat throughout the cooking process. Add the oil. Just before the oil begins to smoke, add the eggplant, sherry, and red pepper. Stir-fry for 3 minutes or until the eggplant is slightly

brown and soft. Add the water. Cover and cook for 2 minutes or until tender. Remove the cover, add the chili-paste-and-soy-sauce mixture. Stir until the sauce has reduced slightly.

Yield: 4–8 servings.

MA PO BEAN CURD

This spicy and aromatic bean curd dish named after its creator, a famous chef's wife whose face was marred with pockmarks. Thus the name Grandmother Pockmark's bean curd. This sauce is also adapted for use with other main ingredients such as chicken, shrimp, or fish. (For example, see Slippery Chicken, p. 142.)

1 tablespoon hot bean sauce	½ cup chicken stock or water
½ pound ground pork	1 teaspoon toasted and ground
1 teaspoon dark soy sauce	Szechwan peppercorns
1½ teaspoons sugar	¼ cup minced scallions
4 bean curds	2 teaspoons cornstarch mixed
2 tablespoons peanut oil	with 1 tablespoon water
2 tablespoons minced ginger-root	1 tablespoon sesame oil
1½ tablespoons minced garlic	Chopped scallions or coriander to garnish
½ teaspoon salt	

Preparation

Mash the hot bean sauce with the handle of a Chinese knife. In a bowl combine the pork, soy sauce, sugar, and hot bean sauce. Cut each bean curd into 9 pieces.

Cooking

Heat a wok or skillet over high heat until a drop of water immediately sizzles into steam. Maintain high heat throughout the cooking process. Add the peanut oil, gingerroot, garlic, and salt. Stir for 30 seconds or until the odor of the garlic has become pungent. Add the pork mixture and stir-fry for 30 seconds. Add the chicken stock and cook for 3 minutes.

Add the bean curd pieces and stir them in with care. Cook for 2 minutes longer, stirring occasionally to avoid sticking.

Add the ground peppercorns, scallions, and cornstarch mixture. Stir for 30 seconds or until the mixture has thickened. Remove from heat and stir in the sesame oil. Garnish with either the scallions or coriander.

Yield: 3–6 servings.

SZECHWAN PICKLED CABBAGE

1 pound celery cabbage	1 teaspoon kosher salt
6 cloves garlic	4 tablespoons white rice wine
2 teaspoons Szechwan pepper-	vinegar
corns	1 tablespoon crushed red
1 quart water	pepper

Preparation

Slice the cabbage into 2-inch squares. Put into a colander and rinse with water. Peel the garlic and crush with the side of a Chinese knife. Toast the peppercorns in a skillet for 5 minutes.

Cooking

In a saucepan boil the water with the salt and vinegar. Pour into a 2-quart jar and let cool. Put the red pepper, roasted peppercorns, garlic, and cabbage in the jar. Cover and refrigerate for 2 days.

Yield: 4–8 servings.

CHENGTU WINTER MELON

6 fresh hot peppers	1 tablespoon dry sherry
2 tablespoons chili paste with	1 teaspoon sugar
garlic	¼ teaspoon salt or to taste
2 teaspoons dark soy sauce	1½ pounds winter melon
1 teaspoon light soy sauce	Oil for deep-frying
1 tablespoon white rice wine	¼ cup water
vinegar	

Preparation

Split the peppers in half lengthwise and remove the seeds. In a bowl mix together the chili paste, soy sauces, vinegar, sherry, sugar, and salt. Remove the rind from the melon and slice the meat of the melon at ⅜-inch intervals.

Cooking

Deep-fry the melon for 2½ minutes in oil heated to 375 degrees. Remove the melon with a slotted spatula.

Heat a wok or skillet over high heat. Add 2 tablespoons of the oil. Maintain high heat throughout the cooking process. Just before the oil begins to smoke, add the peppers and stir for 30 seconds. Return the melon to the pan and stir-fry for 30 seconds. Add the water and the chili paste mixture. Cook for 30 seconds. Stir until the sauce is slightly reduced.

Yield: 6–10 servings.

SZECHWAN VEGETABLE SOUP

¼ pound Szechwan preserved vegetable
¼ pound shredded pork
1 teaspoon cornstarch
½ teaspoon light soy sauce
½ cup shredded bamboo shoots
1 quart chicken stock
1 tablespoon peanut oil

Preparation
Rinse the preserved vegetable under cold water. Shred finely. Combine the pork, cornstarch, and soy sauce in a mixing bowl and mix well.

Cooking
Bring the chicken stock to a boil. Add the preserved vegetable and simmer for 1 minute. In the meantime heat a skillet or wok with the oil. Just before the oil begins to smoke, add the pork mixture and bamboo shoots. Stir-fry for 2 minutes. Add to the broth and simmer for 1 minute.

Yield: 6 servings.

SZECHWAN SESAME-FLAVORED NOODLES

Providing a delightfully different taste, these noodles are refreshing as part of a buffet or as a midnight snack.

½ pound Chinese egg noodles
2 tablespoons vegetable oil
2 scallions, finely chopped
2 tablespoons peanut butter
1 tablespoon sesame oil
1 tablespoon hot oil

Cooking
Boil the noodles until *al dente*. Rinse the noodles with cold water and drain. Heat a pan and add the vegetable oil. Place the noodles in the pan and flatten out. When they become light brown and slightly crisp, turn them over like a pancake. Repeat the process for the other side. Remove the noodles from the pan and allow them to cool. Place them in a serving bowl and sprinkle with the scallions.

Put the peanut butter in a mixing bowl and gradually add the sesame oil and hot oil until well blended. Just before serving, mix the noodles with the sauce. Serve at room temperature.

Yield: 2–4 servings.

BRAISED BEEF WITH SOUPY NOODLES

A mildly spicy stew is poured at the last minute over broad egg noodles for a hearty dish.

1 pound stew beef	1 teaspoon crushed red pepper
1 tablespoon peanut oil	¾ teaspoon salt
1 quart chicken stock	1 quart water
1 tablespoon dark soy sauce	1 pound broad egg noodles
1 tablespoon light soy sauce	
2 tablespoons light brown sugar	

Cooking

Cut the beef into 1-inch cubes. Heat a heavy pot and add the oil. Add the beef and stir for 1½ minutes until the beef has browned. Add the water and bring to a boil. Add the remaining ingredients except the noodles. Cover and simmer for 2 hours.

Boil the noodles until *al dente*. Rinse the noodles with cold water and drain. Place the noodles in a deep tureen. Pour the braised beef and broth over the noodles and serve.

Yield: 8 servings.

4

SOUTH CHINA

Kwangtung and Kwangsi

South China has a style of its own that seems both exotic and somehow foreign to other Chinese. Among other things, this attitude can be attributed to the relative lateness of the south in being absorbed into Chinese civilization.

The original inhabitants of the area were a varied group of tribes, some of whom were the ancestors of the present Thai. The first Chinese arrived in this region in 214 B.C. when the Ch'in emperor sent out an expeditionary force to occupy and Sinicize the area from the Yangtze south to Canton. These pioneers into then unknown lands were in truth little more than vagrants and other undesirables exiled by the emperor.

It was not until some centuries later that population pressures, famine, and barbarian invasions in the north drove significant numbers of Chinese southward. Because true integration into the Chinese Empire did not take place until the T'ang dynasty (A.D. 618–905), the people around Canton sometimes refer to themselves as a T'ang people. As the Chinese moved in, the original inhabitants were pushed into the hills of Kwangsi where today they are still in the majority. Kwangsi is an autonomous region under the People's Republic rather than a true province.

The focus for south China is the city of Canton in Kwangtung with its narrow, twisting streets. Throughout its history it has been a center of foreign trade. This tradition dates back to about A.D. 300 when the first Arab merchants arrived to serve as trade intermediaries between the Chinese and the Greeks in western Asia and established a small permanent colony. Early exports consisted of tea, silk, rhubarb, and porcelain. Canton was the first Chinese city to be regularly visited by Europeans beginning with the Portuguese in 1514. Later came the Spanish, Dutch, and British. In 1842 Canton became the first of the treaty ports officially open to foreign residents. Prior to that time international business could be transacted only aboard boats or in restricted warehouses.

While Canton has served as the gateway into China, it has also served as the gateway out of China. From the southern provinces have come most of the immigrants to other countries in southeast Asia, to the Americas, and to Europe. For this reason most of the Chinese food found outside China has reflected a Cantonese origin. Early immigration was mostly to Japan and other countries in southeast Asia. In the early to mid-nineteenth century Hawaii, Australia, Central and South America as well as the Indian Ocean area attracted many southern Chinese as contract laborers.

In 1849 the news of the discovery of gold in California reached China and in that year the first group of Chinese arrived in California to join the gold rush. The United States was called by them the land of the Golden Mountains. As the gold rush came to an end a new demand arose for Chinese laborers on the railroads. In the latter half of the century the promise of gold also lured Chinese to Australia. The opening of the Suez Canal in 1869 further stimulated trade between Europe and Asia, and during the 1870's Chinese began to wander westward to and through Europe.

In stature, dialect, and psychology the people of this region and the Cantonese in particular are seen as distinctive. Physically shorter and darker, they are viewed psychologically as radical and restless, able to adjust rapidly to new conditions, unlike the stolid, more conservative inhabitants of the north. There is a saying that all things new originate in Canton and one illustration is that communism found its first foothold in this region. In any event, there seems to be receptiveness to new ideas in the south and a less xenophobic attitude toward the world beyond China's borders. The generalization has frequently been made that when the capital of China was in the south, China was less introspective, more outward looking, pacifistic, and inclined to resort to diplomacy rather than warfare to achieve its ends.

The region itself is lushly tropical. Before man possessed the area most of the surface was covered with a dense tropical rain forest. Temperatures rarely drop below 40 degrees and snow is unknown except at the highest elevations. Although summers are hot and humid, temperatures seldom read as high as those in the north around Peking.

The irregular coastline backed by rolling hills has turned many inhabitants to the sea for a livelihood. As in Fukien, many live on boats. Where agriculture is possible, three harvests a year are not uncommon. Sugar competes with rice on the flat land while sweet potatoes are raised on hillsides by poorer people. Silk is also an important crop, making up one-third of China's silk production although it is inferior to that of Hangchow. Cassia, a spice gathered in the river uplands, is an important crop along with gingerroot. A wide variety of tropical fruit, including bananas, pineapples, and lychees, grow here. Like the people of Szechwan the Cantonese have worked hard to make the most of their land. Sixty-nine percent of the land under cultivation is irrigated and 14 percent laboriously terraced.

There is an old saying: "To be born in Soochow, to eat in Kwangchow (i.e., Canton), to dress in Hangchow, and to die in Leouchow." Thus a man might take advantage of the best that China has to offer. For Soochow is known for beauty, Canton for food, Hangchow for silk, and Leouchow for the wood from which coffins are made.

Many Chinese consider the Cantonese cuisine the finest in China because of its enormous variety. The Cantonese have perfected the art of stir-frying in which the ingredients are very rapidly cooked in a small amount of oil in a very hot pan. The hot oil seals in all the natural juices but great care is taken to avoid overcooking. Vegetables must remain crisp and the meat must be cooked no longer than absolutely necessary. Chicken, for example, is considered correctly cooked when the meat is done but the bones are still red inside. Since vegetables and meat are cooked together much more frequently than in other regions, the tricky matter of timing becomes all important in the success of the dish.

The flavoring of most Cantonese dishes tends to be restricted to highlighting the taste of the main ingredients with a little ginger, sugar, and a delicate soy sauce. A little cornstarch paste blends and binds the flavors together and makes a light gravy. Unfortunately, some of the inferior restaurants overdo the gravy which ends up dominating the taste and also makes one dish taste like the other. On the other hand, a change of pace can be found in dishes based on strong seasonings such as garlic, black beans, curry powder, and hot peppers. Oyster sauce with its robust quality is also from this region and is used in many dishes. Sweet-and-sour-dishes are popular and typically make use of the tropical fruits grown there such as lychee and pineapple.

In Cantonese cooking, one finds ketchup and Worcestershire sauce used with some frequency and often together in a pungent sauce. Ketchup was introduced by Americans and Worcestershire sauce by the British. Since Worcestershire sauce is primarily soy sauce and vinegar, its acceptance in China is not surprising.

Texture is greatly valued by the Cantonese. Many of the ingredients that appear in their most prized banquet dishes have little or no taste of their own, only texture. Shark's fin, fish maw, and bird's nest fall into this category and they are frequently served in a rich chicken stock. Although every region of China has its own steamed and fried pastries that are popular as a light meal or snack, the Cantonese have the greatest variety by far. And it was difficult to choose among them for inclusion as recipes in this book. Brunch in a Cantonese restaurant resembles a smorgasbord as waiters bring around to one's table a seemingly endless procession of pastries each different from the preceding ones. Perhaps the pastries best illustrate the beautifully rich diversity of the Cantonese cuisine.

FRIED CHICKEN CANTONESE

4 Chinese black mushrooms	4 slices gingerroot, the size of a
¼ pound Chinese cabbage (*bok* *choy*)	quarter
¼ cup sliced bamboo shoots	¼ teaspoon salt
2 water chestnuts	½ cup water
½ chicken, about 1½ pounds	1 teaspoon cornstarch mixed
1 tablespoon dark soy sauce	with 3 tablespoons water
2 tablespoons dry sherry	½ teaspoon sugar
4 cups peanut oil	Dash of pepper

Preparation

Soak the mushrooms in water for 30 minutes to soften. Remove the tough stems. Drain and shred. Slice the cabbage diagonally at ½-inch intervals. Cut the bamboo shoots into 1-inch squares and slice the water chestnuts finely. Dry the chicken with paper towels. Rub the skin with the soy sauce and sherry.

Cooking

Heat the oil and fry the chicken for 5 minutes on each side. Remove the chicken from the pan and let it drain on paper towels.

Heat a wok or skillet over high heat until a drop of water immediately sizzles into steam. Add 2 tablespoons oil, the gingerroot, and salt. Add the vegetables and stir-fry for ½ minute. Add the water. Cover and cook for 2 minutes. Add the cornstarch mixture, sugar, and pepper. Cook and stir for ½ minute. Chop the chicken into 1½- by 1-inch pieces and place in a serving dish. Place the vegetables on top of the chicken and serve immediately.

Yield: 2–3 servings.

DICED CHICKEN WITH WALNUTS

¼ cup shelled walnut halves	1 stalk celery
Oil for deep-frying	¼ teaspoon salt or to taste
12 snow peas	½ teaspoon dark soy sauce
½ pound boned chicken	¼ cup water
½ cup button mushrooms	1 teaspoon cornstarch mixed
½ pound Chinese cabbage (*bok* *choy*)	with 3 tablespoons water
4 water chestnuts	¼ teaspoon sugar
¼ cup sliced bamboo shoots	Dash of pepper

Preparation
Deep-fry the walnuts in the oil heated to 375 degrees for 2 minutes. Allow to cool. String the snow peas. Dice the chicken, mushrooms, cabbage, water chestnuts, bamboo shoots, snow peas, and celery into ¼-inch cubes.

Cooking
Heat a wok or skillet over high heat until a drop of water immediately sizzles into steam. Add 2 tablespoons of the oil and the salt. Just before the oil begins to smoke, add the chicken and stir-fry for 2 minutes. Add the vegetables and the soy sauce. Stir-fry for ½ minute. Add the water. Cover and cook for 2 minutes. Add the cornstarch mixture, sugar, and pepper. Stir for ½ minute or until the sauce has thickened. Place in a serving plate and garnish with walnuts.

Yield: 2–4 servings.

CHICKEN WITH OYSTER SAUCE

Despite its name, oyster sauce does not taste "fishy" or even like oysters. It is a rich sauce that has a special affinity for chicken.

½ chicken, about 1½ pounds
4 scallions
4 tablespoons oyster sauce
1 teaspoon light soy sauce
2 teaspoons dry sherry
1 teaspoon sugar
Dash of pepper
2 tablespoons peanut oil

½ teaspoon minced garlic
1 slice gingerroot, the size of a quarter
½ cup chicken stock or water
2 teaspoons cornstarch mixed with 1 tablespoon water
½ teaspoon sesame oil

Preparation
Chop the chicken into 1-inch pieces. Chop the scallions into ½-inch pieces. In a bowl combine the oyster sauce, soy sauce, sherry, sugar, and pepper.

Cooking
Heat a wok or skillet over high heat until a drop of water immediately sizzles into steam. Add the peanut oil, garlic, and gingerroot. Stir for about 30 seconds or until the odor of the garlic has become pungent. Add the chicken and stir for 3 minutes or until golden brown.

Add the oyster sauce mixture and stir to coat the chicken. Add ¼ cup of the chicken stock. Cover and lower heat to simmer. Cook for 4 minutes or until the chicken is done. Add the remaining chicken stock if necessary to keep the oyster sauce from burning. Raise heat to high and add the cornstarch mixture. Stir for 15 seconds or until the sauce has thickened. Stir in the sesame oil and scallions. Serve.

Yield: 2–3 servings.

STEAMED CHICKEN WITH VEGETABLES

8 Chinese black mushrooms	½ teaspoon sugar
½ chicken, about 1½ pounds	1 teaspoon light soy sauce
4 water chestnuts	Dash of pepper
¼ cup sliced bamboo shoots	½ teaspoon cornstarch mixed
1½ teaspoons peanut oil	with 3 tablespoons water

Preparation
Soak the mushrooms in cold water for 30 minutes to soften. Drain and slice thinly. Chop the chicken into 1-inch pieces. Slice the water chestnuts thinly.

Cooking
Combine all the ingredients in a heatproof dish. Steam over rapidly boiling water for 15 minutes.

Yield: 2–3 servings.

CANTONESE LEMON CHICKEN

This delicious marriage of chicken and lemon flavors should be compared with the quite different cold lemon chicken of the western region (see p. 138).

8 Chinese black mushrooms	1 chicken, about 3 pounds
2 lemons	Oil for deep-frying
¼ cup shredded bamboo shoots	1 tablespoon peanut oil
1 teaspoon lemon extract	½ teaspoon salt or to taste
4 tablespoons sugar	¼ cup shredded gingerroot
2 teaspoons light soy sauce	¼ cup rendered chicken fat
¼ cup chicken stock or water	2 teaspoons cornstarch mixed
2½ tablespoons dark soy sauce	with 1 tablespoon water

Preparation

Soak the mushrooms in water for 30 minutes or until they are soft. Drain and shred finely. Discard the tough stems.

Remove the skin from one of the lemons and shred it into strips the size of a matchstick. Finely grate the skin of the remaining lemon. Squeeze the juice from both lemons.

In a bowl combine the mushrooms, bamboo shoots, shredded and grated lemon skins, lemon juice, lemon extract, sugar, light soy sauce, chicken stock, and 1 tablespoon of the dark soy sauce.

Split the chicken in half. Dry with paper towels and rub with the remaining dark soy sauce. Allow the chicken to stand for 10 minutes.

Cooking

In a skillet heat the oil to 375 degrees and deep-fry the chicken for 5 minutes on each side. Cut the chicken into 1½- by 1-inch pieces and place them on a serving dish.

Heat a wok or skillet over high heat until a drop of water immediately sizzles into steam. Add the peanut oil, salt, and gingerroot. Stir for about 30 seconds or until the gingerroot browns slightly. Lower heat to medium and add the lemon sauce mixture. Stir for 2 minutes to blend the flavors.

Add the chicken fat and stir for 1 minute. Add the cornstarch mixture to thicken the gravy, stirring constantly.

Pour the sauce over the chicken in the serving dish.

Yield: 3–6 servings.

MOO GOO GAI PEEN

This dish is a standard item on Cantonese menus and admirably illustrates the Cantonese stir-fry technique.

½ pound boned chicken breast	¾ teaspoon salt
12 snow peas	¼ cup sliced bamboo shoots
½ cup button mushrooms	¼ cup water
½ pound Chinese cabbage (*bok choy*)	1 teaspoon cornstarch mixed with 3 tablespoons water
4 water chestnuts	Dash of pepper
2 tablespoons peanut oil	¼ teaspoon sugar

Preparation

Poach the chicken for 20 minutes. Allow it to cool and then slice into pieces measuring ⅛ by 1½ by 1 inch. String the snow peas. Slice the mushrooms, cabbage, and water chestnuts as thin as possible.

Cooking

Heat a skillet or wok and add the peanut oil and salt. Just before the oil begins to smoke, add all the vegetables and stir-fry for ½ minute. Add the water. Cover and cook for 2 minutes. Add the chicken, cornstarch mixture, pepper, and sugar. Stir until the sauce has thickened.

Yield: 2–4 servings.

STEAMED CHICKEN WITH TEA MELON

Tea melon is often used in steamed dishes because its piquant flavor and crunchy texture add interest to otherwise bland dishes.

½ chicken, about 1½ pounds	1½ tablespoons light soy sauce
2 ounces cellophane noodles	1 tablespoon rendered chicken
6 scallions	fat or peanut oil
½ cup shredded tea melon	1 teaspoon sesame oil
1 teaspoon salt	¼ cup water
Dash of pepper	1 tablespoon dry sherry

Preparation

Chop the chicken into 1-inch chunks. Soak the noodles in cold water for at least 30 minutes. Chop the scallions into 1-inch lengths.

Cooking

Combine all the ingredients in a heatproof bowl. Steam over rapidly boiling water for 20 minutes.

Yield: 2–3 servings.

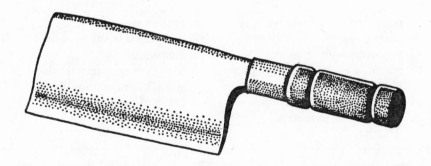

CHICKEN COOKED IN RICE

This dish is rarely found in restaurants, but is often served at home, particularly to the very young and very old who appreciate its easily digestible nature.

1½	cups raw rice	1	tablespoon peanut oil
3	cups water	¼	teaspoon sesame oil
5	Chinese black mushrooms	1	teaspoon shredded ginger-
1	ball preserved turnip		root
¾	pound boned chicken	½	teaspoon minced garlic
1	teaspoon light soy sauce	½	teaspoon pepper
2	teaspoons dark soy sauce	½	teaspoon sugar
2	teaspoons dry sherry		

Preparation

Wash the rice and put it in a pot with the water. Soak the mushrooms in water for 30 minutes or until soft. Discard the tough stems and slice the mushrooms into thin strips. Wash the excess salt from the turnip and dice. Cut the chicken into 1-inch squares.

In a bowl combine the soy sauces, sherry, peanut and sesame oils, gingerroot, garlic, pepper, and sugar. Marinate the chicken in this mixture for 15 minutes while you begin to cook the rice. Discard the marinade.

Cooking

Bring the rice and water to a boil over high heat. After the water on the rice has virtually boiled away, place the chicken and the other ingredients on top of the rice. Cover, reduce heat, and simmer until the rice and chicken are cooked, about 20 minutes. Stir thoroughly and serve.

Yield: 4 servings.

SWEET-AND-SOUR CHICKEN

½	chicken, about 1½ pounds		Oil for deep-frying
1	slice canned pineapple	¼	teaspoon salt or to taste
¼	cup red wine vinegar	1	clove crushed garlic
¼	cup sugar	¼	cup sliced carrots
½	cup water	¼	cup diced green bell pepper
1½	teaspoons dark soy sauce	2	teaspoons cornstarch mixed
	Dash of pepper		with 3 tablespoons water

Preparation

Cut the chicken into 1-inch squares. Slice the pineapple into 1-inch pieces. In a small bowl combine the vinegar, sugar, water, soy sauce, and pepper.

Cooking

Deep-fry the chicken in oil heated to 375 degrees for 5 minutes or until done. In a hot skillet or wok add 2 tablespoons of the oil and salt. Just before the oil begins to smoke, add the garlic and stir until the garlic has become pungent. Add the vinegar mixture to the pan and bring to a boil. Add the carrots, bell pepper, and pineapple. Add the cornstarch mixture. Stir until the sauce has thickened slightly. Pour the sauce over the chicken.

Yield: 2–3 servings.

GAI DING

¼ cup almonds
    Oil for deep-frying
½ pound boned chicken
½ cup button mushrooms
½ pound Chinese cabbage (*bok choy*)
4 water chestnuts
1 dozen snow peas
½ teaspoon salt or to taste

½ cup diced bamboo shoots
¼ cup diced celery
¼ cup water
½ teaspoon light soy sauce
1 teaspoon cornstarch mixed with 3 tablespoons water
    Dash of pepper
¼ teaspoon sugar

Preparation

Deep-fry the almonds in oil heated to 375 degrees for 3 minutes. Allow to cool. Dice the chicken, mushrooms, cabbage, and water chestnuts into ¼-inch cubes. String the snow peas.

Cooking

Heat a wok or a skillet over high heat until a drop of water immediately sizzles into steam. Add 2 tablespoons of the oil and salt. Add the chicken and stir-fry for 2 minutes.

Add the mushrooms, cabbage, water chestnuts, bamboo shoots, snow peas, and celery. Stir-fry for ½ minute to coat with oil. Add the water and soy sauce. Cover and cook for 2 minutes. Add the cornstarch mixture, pepper, and sugar. Stir for ½ minute or until the sauce has thickened. Top with the almonds before serving.

Yield: 2–4 servings.

CURRIED CHICKEN

Curries were introduced to China centuries ago from India and southeast Asia and are popular among the Cantonese as well as the western Chinese.

¼ cup sliced onions	½ teaspoon dark soy sauce
2 tablespoons curry powder or to taste	¼ teaspoon salt
½ pound boned chicken, sliced into 1-inch squares	1 teaspoon cornstarch mixed with 3 tablespoons water
½ cup water	½ teaspoon sugar
	Dash of pepper

Cooking
Heat a frying pan without oil over medium heat. Add the onions, then sprinkle the curry powder on top of the onions. Toast in this manner for 2 minutes. Add the chicken and stir for 1 minute but do not allow the curry powder to burn. Add the water, soy sauce, and salt. Increase heat to high and cook for 5 minutes. Stir in the cornstarch mixture, sugar, and pepper.

Yield: 2–4 servings.

CHICKEN ROLL

8 Chinese black mushrooms	1 teaspoon sugar
1 pound boned and skinned chicken breast	½ teaspoon salt
¼ pound ground pork	1 tablespoon light soy sauce
¼ cup diced water chestnuts	Dash of pepper
¼ cup diced bamboo shoots	½ teaspoon sesame oil
1 cup diced Chinese cabbage (*bok choy*)	1 egg white
2 scallions	1 tablespoon cornstarch
	1 pound lace fat
	Oil for deep-frying

Preparation
Soak the mushrooms in water for 30 minutes or until soft. Squeeze to remove the excess moisture from the mushrooms. Discard the tough stems and dice the mushrooms into cubes ¼ inch or smaller. Finely dice the chicken. Combine all the ingredients in a bowl except the egg white, cornstarch, lace fat, and oil for deep-frying. Combine the egg white and cornstarch in another small bowl.

Cut the lace fat into 6-inch squares. Place ½ cup of the chicken mixture in the center of the square of lace fat. Fold two opposite sides of the square over the mixture and then roll up the remaining lace fat around the mixture as one would wrap an egg roll. Brush the roll with the egg white and cornstarch mixture.

Cooking
Deep-fry the rolls in oil heated to 300 degrees for 15 minutes.

Yield: 4–8 servings.

BRAISED CHICKEN WITH CHINESE MUSHROOM SAUCE

This is a luscious dish for those who love Chinese black mushrooms. The double cooking of the chicken gives it a special quality.

16 Chinese black mushrooms	Oil for deep-frying
¼ cup golden needles	¾ teaspoon salt
3 scallions	1 quart water
1 slice gingerroot, the size of a half-dollar	2 teaspoons sugar
	Dash of pepper
1 tablespoon dark soy sauce	1 tablespoon dry sherry
1 chicken, about 3 pounds	2 teaspoons cornstarch mixed
1 ball preserved turnip	with 1 tablespoon water

Preparation
Soak the mushrooms in water for 30 minutes or until soft. Squeeze gently to remove excess water. Discard the tough stems and slice into ⅛-inch strips.

Pour boiling water over the golden needles in a bowl and soak for 30 minutes. Drain, discard any tough stems if present, and cut the golden needles in half. Cut the scallions thinly. Flatten the gingerroot with the side of a cleaver or broad knife blade. Rub the soy sauce into the chicken.

Open up the ball of preserved turnip and rinse it well under running water to remove the excess salt. Shred the turnip.

Cooking
In a wok or large pot heat the oil to 375 degrees. Fry the chicken for 2 minutes on each side or until the skin is golden brown. Remove the chicken and drain off the oil.

Heat a wok or pot large enough to hold the chicken over high heat until a drop of water immediately sizzles into steam. Add 2 tablespoons of the oil, ½ teaspoon of the salt, and the gingerroot. Stir to brown the gingerroot slightly. Add the mushrooms, scallions, water, sugar, pepper, turnip,

golden needles, sherry, and the remaining salt. Place the chicken on top
of this. Cover, reduce heat to medium low, and simmer for 15 minutes
more.

Remove the chicken from the pot and chop into 1-inch pieces. Place the
chicken in a serving dish. Add the cornstarch mixture to the sauce remaining in the pot. Stir for 30 seconds to thicken. Pour the sauce over the
chicken.

Yield: 3–6 servings.

CHICKEN FILLED WITH BIRD'S NEST

*This is a banquet dish which is often served as the second soup to
cleanse the palate between courses.*

1 cup bird's nest	½ teaspoon salt
1 quart water	½ teaspoon sugar
1 chicken, about 4 pounds	1 teaspoon light soy sauce
2 cups chicken stock	

Preparation

Soak the bird's nest in cold water for 3 hours. Drain. Boil in 1 quart water for 15 minutes. Remove the bird's nest and run cool water through it.
Pick out all the feathers and dirt. Bone the chicken without breaking the
skin. (See instructions below.) Stuff the bird's nest into the cavity of the
chicken. Place the chicken in a deep heatproof casserole bowl. Add the
chicken stock, salt, sugar, and soy sauce.

Cooking

Place the casserole in a steamer. Cover and steam for 3 hours. Check
the water in the steamer from time to time to make sure it has not completely boiled away. Bring the casserole to the table and serve in individual soup bowls by cutting through the chicken with the soup ladle. The
chicken should be very soft.

Yield: 4–8 servings.

HOW TO BONE A CHICKEN

With sharp scissors or a knife cut off the wing tips. Bend the wings
away from the body to break the shoulder joint. Similarly break the hip

and knee joints of the legs. Free the skin at the bottom end of the drumstick and cut through all the tendons. Pull the bone forward, at the same time drawing the skin and meat of the drumstick back with the other hand. The bone will slide out easily.

Place the chicken breast-side down. Free the skin from the spine, starting at one end and working toward the middle. Repeat from the other end. When the skin has been freed from the spine, slip your hand under the skin and free it from the rest of the back.

Turn the chicken breast-side up. The ridge of cartilage down the middle of the breast is attached to the skin and is separated last. First free the meat on either side of it from the bone, again working from both ends of the bird toward the middle. You will need to start this process with a knife but once you have separated the first inch or so of meat from the bone, it is easier and safer to continue the rest of the way using your hand. Then crush the rib cage of the chicken and using a knife carefully separate the skin from the ridge of cartilage. As you proceed down the ridge, peel the flesh and skin off the carcass as you would remove a sweater, snipping or cutting where necessary to free the last shreds of meat from the bone.

Remove the thigh bone and the single bone in the upper wing. The lower double bone in the wing is left in. Remove any other stray bones or bits of cartilage that remain. The chicken is now ready to be stuffed. The whole process should take no more than 30 minutes and will take much less time with experience.

CHICKEN STUFFED WITH GLUTINOUS RICE

The richness of the stuffing almost makes the eater forget the chicken which encases it. The effect is not unlike French terrines.

1¼ cups glutinous rice	¾ cup diced onions
1 chicken, about 4 pounds	3 tablespoons light soy sauce
2 Chinese sausages	1½ teaspoons sugar
8 Chinese black mushrooms	Dash of pepper
Oil for deep-frying	¼ cup water
1 teaspoon salt	¼ cup cornstarch
½ cup cubed bamboo shoots	1 egg, beaten
¼ cup lotus seeds	Toasted salt and pepper (see
½ cup diced water chestnuts	recipe on page 304)

Preparation

Soak the rice for at least 5 hours or overnight in water rising 3 inches above the level of the rice. Spread the rice evenly over a flat heatproof dish and steam the rice for 1 hour over boiling water. Allow the rice to cool.

Remove the gizzard and liver from the chicken and dice them. Bone the chicken, leaving the skin intact, and pat the skin dry with paper towels. (See instructions above.)

Steam the sausages over boiling water for 20 minutes. Dice when cool. Soak the mushrooms in water for 30 minutes. Remove the tough stems and dice the mushrooms.

Cooking

Heat a wok or skillet over high heat until a drop of water immediately sizzles into steam. Add 2 tablespoons of the oil and the salt. Just before the oil begins to smoke, add the sausages, giblets and liver, bamboo shoots, lotus seeds, mushrooms, water chestnuts, onions, 1 tablespoon of the soy sauce, the sugar, pepper, and water. Stir-fry for 2 minutes.

Combine these ingredients with the steamed rice and let it cool slightly. Stuff the chicken with the mixture and skewer the chicken shut. Rub the skin of the chicken with the remaining soy sauce.

Put the chicken in a heatproof bowl and steam over rapidly boiling water for 1½ hours. Remove the chicken from the steamer and let it cool.

Mix the cornstarch with the beaten egg and rub over the chicken. Heat the oil to 375 degrees. Deep-fry the chicken, basting and turning until it is golden brown. Cut into individual servings by cutting through the chicken and rice stuffing. Serve with toasted salt and pepper.

Yield: 6–10 servings.

DUCK WITH CORIANDER

4 cups coriander	2 teaspoons sugar
8 Chinese black mushrooms	1 quart water
1 duck, about 5 pounds	½ cup shredded bamboo shoots
2 tablespoons dark soy sauce	1 tablespoon cornstarch mixed
Oil for deep-frying	with ¼ cup water
2 tablespoons light soy sauce	2 tablespoons shredded Smith-
2 teaspoons salt	field ham to garnish

Preparation

Wash the coriander and discard the tough stems and roots. Soak the mushrooms in water for 30 minutes to soften. Discard the tough stems. Drain and shred. Cut through the back of the duck. Clean and pat dry.

Cooking

Rub the dark soy sauce on the duck, both inside and out. Deep-fry the duck in oil heated to 375 degrees for 10 minutes. In a wok or skillet mix the light soy sauce, salt, sugar, and water. Bring to a boil. Add the duck. Cover and simmer for 25 minutes on each side. Line a serving dish with the coriander and place the duck on top. To the remaining liquid in the pan add the mushrooms and bamboo shoots. Cook for 5 minutes. Stir in the cornstarch mixture and pour over the duck. Garnish with the ham.

Yield: 4–8 servings.

CANTONESE ROAST DUCK

This is a do-it-yourself version of a delicacy that can often be seen hanging in windows in large Chinatowns.

1 duck, about 5 pounds	2 star anise (16 sections)
1 tablespoon peanut oil	1 teaspoon dark soy sauce
1 tablespoon salt	1 teaspoon sugar
1 tablespoon minced garlic	Dash of pepper
1 tablespoon dry sherry	6 cups water
2 tablespoons five-flavor powder	2 scallions
	2 tablespoons honey

Preparation

Cut a ¼-inch hole in the neck of the duck and pump air into this hole with a bicycle pump until the duck is fully blown up. Let the air out. Clean the inside of the duck.

Cooking

Place the oil and salt in a very hot frying pan. Stir-fry the garlic for ½ minute. Add the sherry, five-flavor powder, star anise, soy sauce, sugar, pepper, and 2 cups of the water. Simmer for 15 minutes. Remove the star anise and reserve the gravy.

Cut the scallions into 1-inch pieces and place in the cavity of the duck along with the gravy. Truss the duck so that the gravy will not leak out. Pump up the duck again through the neck. Tie the duck at the neck so that the air will not leak out. Dissolve the honey in the remaining water. Pour over the duck several times to make the skin crisp. Hang the duck up in a cool, drafty place for at least three hours or overnight so that the skin dries. Place on a rack in a roasting pan. Roast for 20 minutes in an oven heated to 450 degrees. Turn the duck over. Reduce heat to 300 degrees and roast another 10 minutes.

Note: This recipe is the traditional one using a duck specially butchered in Chinatown. If using a frozen Long Island duckling, the procedure is somewhat different. Defrost the duck according to the instructions on the bag. Remove the innards from the cavity of the duck, rinse the duck under running water, and pat dry. Skewer the duck closed except for a small opening where the hose of the bicycle pump is inserted. It may take a second pair of hands to make the bird completely airtight while it is being blown up like a balloon to twice its original size. After the initial pumping up, follow the recipe as written but omit the second pumping-up operation.

Yield: 4–8 servings.

WOR SHEW OPP

The beauty of this dish lies as much in its texture as its flavor. A three-step cooking process is required, but it is well worth the effort.

1 duck, about 5 pounds
1 tablespoon plus ½ cup dark
   soy sauce
1 quart water
¼ cup five-flavor powder
2 tablespoons salt
3 tablespoons sugar

Oil for deep-frying
1 cup flour
2 teaspoons cornstarch mixed
   with 2 tablespoons water
Lettuce
2 teaspoons crushed roasted almonds to garnish

Preparation
Remove any excess fat from the cavity of the duck and split the duck down the back. Wash under running water and pat dry with paper towels. Rub the tablespoon of soy sauce into the duck.

In a large lidded pot combine the water, five-flavor powder, salt, sugar, and the remaining ½ cup soy sauce.

Cooking
Heat the oil in a wok or skillet to 375 degrees, and deep-fry the duck for 10 minutes.

Bring the mixture in the pot to a boil over high heat. Add the duck. When the mixture has come to a boil again, lower the heat to a very slow boil. Cover and cook for ½ hour.

Remove the duck from the pot and let it cool to room temperature. Reserve the cooking broth. Remove the bones from the duck except for the wings and thighs. Coat both sides with flour. Deep-fry in oil heated to 375 degrees for 3 minutes on each side. Cut into bite-size pieces.

Make a gravy by reheating 1½ cups of the broth remaining from the boiling of the duck and adding the cornstarch solution while stirring.

To serve, line a serving dish with lettuce. Place the duck on the dish. Garnish with almonds and pour the gravy over the duck.

Yield: 4–8 servings.

CHINESE FRIED SQUAB

The Chinese are uncommonly fond of squab. This recipe is quite simple to make and extraordinarily good to eat. To duplicate the beautiful dark brown skin of squabs found in restaurants your squabs must be freshly killed.

2 squabs, about 1 pound each	1 lemon
1 tablespoon dark soy sauce	1 tablespoon toasted salt and
1 teaspoon dry sherry	pepper (see recipe on page
Oil for deep-frying	304)

Preparation
Cut through the backs of the squabs and place flat in a dish. Dry with paper towels. In a bowl combine the soy sauce and sherry. Marinate the squabs in this mixture for 15 minutes.

Cooking
Heat the oil to 375 degrees and deep-fry the squabs for 2 minutes. Remove from the stove but keep the squabs in the oil for 2 minutes. Drain and cool. Deep-fry the squabs again for 2 minutes in boiling oil. Cut into bite-size pieces. Serve with lemon wedges and toasted salt and pepper.

Yield: 2–4 servings.

SQUAB WITH OYSTER SAUCE

2 squabs, about 1 pound each	1 teaspoon sugar
1 teaspoon dark soy sauce	Dash of pepper
½ teaspoon salt	1 teaspoon dry sherry
3 tablespoons peanut oil	1½ teaspoons cornstarch mixed
1½ cups water	with 3 tablespoons water
3 tablespoons oyster sauce	

Preparation

Cut through the back of the squabs and lay out flat. Dry with paper towels. Rub the soy sauce into the squabs. Brown the squabs in a very hot wok or skillet with ¼ teaspoon of the salt and 2 tablespoons of the oil. Remove from the pan and set aside.

Cooking

Heat the pan again with the remaining salt and remaining oil. Add the water, oyster sauce, sugar, pepper, and sherry. Add the squabs. Cover and cook the squabs on each side for 5 minutes. Remove the squabs and cut into 1½-inch pieces. Add the cornstarch mixture to thicken the gravy and pour over the squab pieces.

Yield: 2–4 servings.

EGG FOO YOUNG (BASIC RECIPE)

There are two types of Egg Foo Young—one is deep-fried and served with a gravy, the other is pan-fried and served without the gravy. The pan-fried version is considered more authentic and is given on page 197, but the following American restaurant version is also good and is given below.

½ cup diced onions	3 eggs
½ cup diced Chinese roast pork or Smithfield ham	Oil for frying

Preparation

Mix the onion and roast pork. Beat the eggs and stir into the pork and onions.

In a wok or skillet heat 2½ inches of oil almost to the point of smoking, about 375 degrees. Pour one-third of the egg mixture into the pan. Brown for 2 minutes. Use a ladle and splash the top of the omelet with the oil so that the top becomes firm. Flip the omelet over. Brown for 1½ minutes. Remove and drain. Repeat for the remaining mixture. Serve with gravy for Egg Foo Young.

Yield: 2–3 servings.

GRAVY FOR EGG FOO YOUNG

1 cup water
1 tablespoon peanut oil
1 teaspoon sugar
1 teaspoon salt

1 teaspoon dark soy sauce
Dash of pepper
1 teaspoon cornstarch mixed
   with 2 tablespoons water

Bring the water to a boil and add all the ingredients. Stir for ½ minute.

Yield: 2–3 servings.

CHICKEN EGG FOO YOUNG

3 eggs
½ cup diced onions

½ cup diced cooked chicken
¼ cup diced mushrooms

Mix and cook according to the Basic Recipe directions.

Yield: 2–3 servings.

SUBGUM EGG FOO YOUNG

3 eggs
¼ cup diced onions
½ cup diced Chinese roast pork

¼ cup diced green pepper
¼ cup diced button mushrooms

Mix and cook according to the Basic Recipe directions.

Yield: 2–3 servings.

SHRIMP EGG FOO YOUNG

3 eggs
½ cup diced boiled shrimp

1 cup diced onions
½ cup bean sprouts

Mix and cook according to the Basic Recipe directions.

Yield: 2–3 servings.

CANTONESE EGG FOO YOUNG

4 Chinese black mushrooms	3 eggs
4 water chestnuts	2 tablespoons peanut oil
¼ pound Chinese cabbage (*bok choy*)	½ teaspoon salt
	½ teaspoon sugar
¼ cup sliced bamboo shoots	1 teaspoon dry sherry
⅛ pound Chinese roast pork	Dash of pepper

Preparation

Soak the mushrooms in water for 30 minutes or until soft. Discard the tough stems and drain.

Dice the water chestnuts and finely shred the other solid ingredients into pieces the size of a matchstick. Beat the eggs.

Cooking

Heat a wok or skillet over high heat until a drop of water immediately sizzles into steam. Add 1 tablespoon of the oil and the salt. Just before the oil begins to smoke, add all the vegetables and the roast pork. Stir vigorously for 30 seconds. Add the sugar, sherry, and pepper. Cover and cook for 45 seconds more. Remove the vegetables and let cool. Add the beaten eggs to the vegetables and stir well.

Reheat the pan again. Add the remaining oil. Pour the egg and vegetable mixture into the pan and fry for 1 minute on each side or until the omelet has set. (If you wish you may also make smaller individual omelets.) Serve immediately on a warm platter.

Yield: 2–3 servings.

STEAMED EGGS

1¼ cups water	Dash of pepper
2 eggs	½ teaspoon peanut oil
¼ teaspoon salt	

Preparation

Boil 2 cups of water for about 3 minutes. Let it cool and then measure the 1¼ cups needed. The purpose of boiling the water is to drive out the air so that the steamed eggs will be smooth. Beat the eggs and add the water, salt, pepper, and oil. Stir lightly until the eggs are mixed with the water. Pour into a 1½-inch- or 2-inch-deep heatproof dish.

Cooking
Steam over rapidly boiling water for about 10 minutes. There is no accurate way of timing this dish. Just test it as you would test custard by sticking a chopstick into the eggs to see if the inside is still liquid. Serve with generous amounts of soy sauce.

Variation: Add ½ cup diced Chinese roast pork to the egg mixture.

Yield: 2 servings.

EGGS WITH CHINESE CHIVES AND ROAST PORK

Chinese chives look like long grass, but they are unbelievably good. They are more aromatic than scallions and sweeter than leeks.

2 cups Chinese chives	1 teaspoon salt
4 eggs	¼ pound Chinese roast pork
1 teaspoon dry sherry	2 tablespoons peanut oil
¼ teaspoon sugar	½ teaspoon minced garlic
Dash of pepper	

Preparation
Wash the chives and cut off the roots. Slice into 3-inch lengths. Beat the eggs and add the sherry, sugar, pepper, and ½ teaspoon of the salt. Shred the roast pork into slivers 1½ inches long and ⅛ inch thick, approximately the size and shape of a matchstick.

Cooking
Heat a wok or skillet over high heat until a drop of water immediately sizzles into steam. Add 1 tablespoon of the oil and the remaining salt. Just before the oil begins to smoke, add the garlic, the roast pork and the chives. Stir-fry for 30 seconds. Remove the roast pork and chives from the pan and combine them with the eggs.
Reheat the pan and add the remaining oil. Depending upon the size of your pan, you can cook all the eggs at one time or divide the egg mixture into smaller portions. Cook the eggs for 1½ minutes on each side as you would a pancake or until brown.

Yield: 2–4 servings.

PORK WITH BLACK BEANS AND BROCCOLI

½ pound boned pork	1 pound broccoli
2½ tablespoons peanut oil	2 tablespoons black beans
½ teaspoon sugar	1 tablespoon minced garlic
1 teaspoon dark soy sauce	1 teaspoon salt
½ teaspoon sesame oil	¼ cup chicken stock or water
1 tablespoon dry sherry	Dash of pepper

Preparation

Slice the pork along the grain into strips 1½ inches long, ⅛ inch wide, and ½ inch thick. In a bowl combine ½ tablespoon of the peanut oil, ¼ teaspoon of the sugar, the soy sauce, sesame oil, and sherry. Marinate the pork in this mixture. Set aside.

Wash the broccoli and slice diagonally into ½-inch thick slices. Rinse the black beans well in cold water and crush them with the handle of a cleaver or the back of a spoon. Add the garlic to the black beans.

Cooking

Heat a wok or skillet over high heat until a drop of water immediately sizzles into steam. Maintain high heat throughout the cooking process. Add 1 tablespoon of the peanut oil and ½ teaspoon of the salt, spreading the oil and salt around the pan. Just before the oil begins to smoke, add the pork and stir-fry for 2 minutes. Remove the meat from the pan to a warm dish.

Add the remaining peanut oil and the remaining salt to the still hot pan and heat for 30 seconds. Add the garlic and black beans. Stir for about 30 seconds or until the odor of the beans and garlic has become pungent. Add the broccoli and stir for 30 seconds to thoroughly coat it with the oil. Add the chicken stock, pepper, and the remaining sugar. Cover the pan and cook for 3 minutes or until the broccoli is almost done but still crisp and a bright emerald green.

Return the pork to the pan and stir well to blend. The meat should be just cooked but not pink, the broccoli tender but not limp, and the sauce scant.

Yield: 2–4 servings.

CANTONESE SWEET-AND-SOUR PORK

The Cantonese are fond of using vegetables and fruits in their sweet-and-sour dishes for added interest.

1 pound boned pork	Oil for deep-frying
¼ cup cornstarch for dredging	½ teaspoon salt
1 green bell pepper	½ teaspoon minced garlic
1 large carrot	½ cup canned pineapple
1 tablespoon dark soy sauce	chunks
¼ cup sugar	2 teaspoons cornstarch mixed
¼ cup white rice wine vinegar	with 2 tablespoons water
¾ cup water	

Preparation

Cut the pork into 1-inch cubes. Dredge the cubes in the cornstarch. Cut the pepper into 1-inch squares. Slice the carrot diagonally into ¼-inch-thick pieces. In a bowl combine the soy sauce, sugar, vinegar, and water.

Cooking

Deep-fry the pork cubes in very hot oil (375 degrees) until the cubes float. Drain the cubes well and place on a serving dish.

Heat a wok or skillet over high heat until a drop of water immediately sizzles into steam. Add 2 tablespoons of the oil, the salt, and garlic. Stir the garlic until it has become pungent. Add the pepper, pineapple, and carrot. Stir for 2 minutes or until the color of the pepper and carrot has intensified but not yet reached its peak.

Add the soy sauce mixture and stir until boiling. Immediately add the cornstarch mixture and stir until the sauce has thickened. Pour the sauce over the pork and serve immediately.

Yield: 3–6 servings.

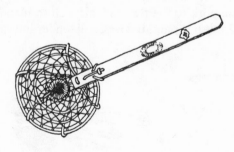

PORK WITH BITTER MELON

Bitter melon is a curiously refreshing vegetable, although something of an acquired taste. The parboiling is necessary to remove some of the bitterness and to highlight the cool aftertaste.

3 teaspoons cornstarch	1½ tablespoons black beans
2½ teaspoons light soy sauce	1 tablespoon minced garlic
¾ teaspoon sugar	½ cup chicken stock or water
1 tablespoon peanut oil	Dash of pepper
2 teaspoons dry sherry	1 teaspoon salt or to taste
¾ pound boned pork	1 tablespoon water
3 medium fresh bitter melons	

Preparation

Combine 1 teaspoon of the cornstarch with 1½ teaspoons of the soy sauce, ¼ teaspoon of the sugar, ¼ teaspoon of the oil, and the sherry to make a marinade for the pork. Slice the pork into pieces 1½ inches in length and ⅛ inch wide. Mix the pork with the marinade.

Wash the melons. Split them open and remove the seeds. Slice them very thinly and parboil them for 3 minutes.

Rinse the black beans well in cold water and crush them with the handle of a cleaver or with the back of a spoon. Combine the beans with the garlic. Set aside.

Combine the chicken stock, pepper, ½ teaspoon of the salt, the remaining sugar, and the remaining soy sauce. Set aside. Mix the remaining cornstarch with the water.

Cooking

Heat a wok or skillet over high heat until a drop of water immediately sizzles into steam. Maintain high heat throughout the cooking process. Add the remaining oil, the remaining salt, and the garlic and black beans. Stir for about 30 seconds or until the odor of the beans and garlic has become pungent. Add the pork and stir-fry for 3 minutes or until the pork is nearly done.

Add the melon and stir for 30 seconds. (A second tablespoon of oil may have to be added if the pan becomes too sticky.) Add the chicken stock mixture. Stir for a second to mix. Cover and cook for 2 minutes. Add the cornstarch mixture and stir for 15 seconds or until the gravy thickens.

Yield: 3–6 servings.

CURRIED PORK

½ pound boned pork
¼ cup sliced onions
2 tablespoons curry powder or to taste
½ cup water
¼ teaspoon salt or to taste

1 teaspoon cornstarch mixed with 3 tablespoons water
½ teaspoon dark soy sauce
½ teaspoon sugar
Dash of pepper

Preparation
Slice the pork across the grain into thin pieces.

Cooking
Using a medium flame, heat a frying pan without oil. Add the onions, then sprinkle the curry powder on top of the onions. Toast in this manner for 2 minutes. Add the pork. Stir for 3 minutes, but do not allow the curry powder to burn. Add the water and salt. Bring heat to high. Cook and stir for 4 minutes. Add the cornstarch mixture, soy sauce, sugar, and pepper. Stir.

Yield: 2–3 servings.

LETTUCE PACKAGES

This refreshing do-it-yourself-at-the-table dish is always appreciated and the recipe frequently asked for.

1 head lettuce
¼ pound bamboo shoots
12 water chestnuts
½ pound green beans
¾ cup roasted peanuts
4 tablespoons peanut oil
1 teaspoon salt
1 tablespoon minced garlic

1 pound coarsely ground pork
1 tablespoon dry sherry
¼ cup water
2 tablespoons oyster sauce
1 teaspoon sugar
1 teaspoon sesame oil
¼ cup hoisin sauce (optional)

Preparation
Remove from the head of lettuce a dozen or more of the largest and crispest leaves. Set them aside in a serving bowl. Dice the bamboo shoots, water chestnuts, and green beans into ¼-inch cubes. Mince the peanuts and set aside with the bamboo shoots and water chestnuts.

Cooking

Heat a wok or skillet over high heat until a drop of water immediately sizzles into steam. Maintain high heat throughout the cooking process. Add 2 tablespoons of the peanut oil, ½ teaspoon of the salt, and the garlic. Stir for about 30 seconds or until the odor of the garlic has become pungent. Add the pork and the sherry. Stir-fry for 1 minute or until the pork is completely gray. Remove the pork to a warm platter.

Reheat the pan. Add the remaining peanut oil and the remaining salt. Just before the oil begins to smoke, add the green beans and stir-fry for 1 minute. Add the water. Cover and cook for ½ minute.

Uncover the pan and add the bamboo shoots, water chestnuts, peanuts, oyster sauce, sugar, and the pork. Stir-fry for 1½ minutes. Just before removing the pan from the heat stir in the sesame oil.

Each guest serves himself by taking a lettuce leaf, putting about 2 tablespoons of the pork mixture in the center of the leaf, and wrapping the leaf around the filling. If desired, a little hoisin sauce may be dabbed onto the pork before wrapping. To be eaten finger fashion.

Yield: 4–8 servings.

CHINESE ROAST PORK

Because few people in China had ovens of their own, roasted meats were normally bought at the market and brought home. This is still true even among Chinese-Americans today. For readers not close to a Chinatown, here is a home-cooked version. Freeze any leftovers for use in the many recipes that specify Chinese roast pork.

2 pounds boneless pork	2 tablespoons light soy sauce
1 tablespoon brown bean sauce	¼ cup light brown sugar
2 teaspoons minced garlic	½ teaspoon five-flavor powder
½ cup chicken stock or water	1 tablespoon dry sherry
1 tablespoon salt	¼ teaspoon red food coloring

Preparation

Slice the pork with the grain into slabs about 6 inches long, 2 inches wide, and 1 inch thick. Mash the brown bean sauce with the handle of a cleaver or with the back of a spoon. Combine the beans with the remaining ingredients over low heat to partially dissolve the sugar. Place the pork in the mixture and let it marinate for 3 to 6 hours at room temperature, turning the pork from time to time.

Cooking

Place a shallow pan of water in the bottom of the oven to catch the drippings and to provide moisture during the cooking process. Preheat the oven to 450 degrees.

Hang the pork on S-shaped hooks from the top rack of the oven or place the slabs directly on the oven rack in the upper third of the oven. Roast for 15 minutes at 450 degrees and then reduce the heat to 350 degrees. Roast for an additional 15 minutes or until done, that is, when there is no sign of pink inside the meat.

The pork may also be barbecued over charcoal by first allowing the intense heat to sear the meat and then raising the grill to permit thorough cooking without burning.

The pork can be sliced thinly across the grain and served with a light soy sauce as a dip or it may be used in any one of the many recipes calling for Chinese roast pork.

Yield: 6–10 servings.

ROAST PORK WITH BEAN SPROUTS

¼ pound Chinese roast pork	3 tablespoons peanut oil
½ pound bean sprouts	¼ teaspoon salt or to taste
Dash of pepper	1 slice gingerroot, the size of a
1 teaspoon light soy sauce	quarter
¼ teaspoon sugar	1 teaspoon cornstarch mixed
3 tablespoons water	with 3 tablespoons water

Preparation

Shred the roast pork across the grain into pieces the size of a matchstick. Wash the bean sprouts and drain. Mix the pepper, soy sauce, sugar, and water.

Cooking

Heat a wok or skillet over high heat until a drop of water immediately sizzles into steam. Add 1½ tablespoons of the oil, the salt, and gingerroot. Just before the oil begins to smoke, add the bean sprouts. Stir-fry the bean sprouts for ½ minute. Cover and cook for 1 minute. Remove and set aside.

Heat and grease the pan again with the remaining oil. Stir-fry the roast pork for 1 minute. Add the bean sprouts and the soy sauce mixture. Cover and cook for 2 minutes. Add the cornstarch paste and stir for ½ minute or until the scant sauce has thickened.

Yield: 2 servings.

ROAST PORK WITH CHINESE VEGETABLES

Oil for deep-frying	½ cup diced mushrooms
¼ cup almonds	¼ cup diced bamboo shoots
½ pound Chinese roast pork	¼ cup diced celery
½ pound Chinese cabbage (*bok choy*)	¼ cup water
	1 teaspoon cornstarch mixed
4 water chestnuts	with 3 tablespoons water
12 snow peas	Dash of pepper
¼ teaspoon salt or to taste	¼ teaspoon sugar

Preparation

Heat the oil and deep-fry almonds for 3 minutes. Set the almonds aside to cool. Dice the roast pork, the cabbage, water chestnuts, and snow peas into ¼-inch cubes.

Cooking

Heat a wok or skillet over high heat until a drop of water immediately sizzles into steam. Add 2 tablespoons of the oil and the salt. Just before the oil begins to smoke, add all the vegetables. Stir-fry for ½ minute. Add the water. Cover and cook for 2 minutes.

Add the roast pork and stir. Add the cornstarch mixture, pepper, and sugar. Stir for ½ minute until the scant sauce has thickened. Place in a serving dish and garnish with the almonds.

Yield: 2–4 servings.

BARBECUED SPARERIBS

There are probably as many recipes for barbecued spareribs as there are cooks. This is a particularly good one.

1 sheet spareribs, about 4 pounds	4 tablespoons light brown sugar
1 tablespoon brown bean sauce	3 tablespoons hoisin sauce
1 tablespoon minced garlic	2 teaspoons dry sherry
4 tablespoons dark soy sauce	¼ cup chicken stock or water
	½ teaspoon salt

Preparation
Separate the ribs from one another and, if you desire, chop them into 3-inch lengths with a heavy cleaver. Combine the remaining ingredients over low heat to partially dissolve the sugar. Marinate the ribs for 4 to 6 hours in this mixture.

Cooking
Heat the oven to 375 degrees. Roast the ribs in the sauce for 15 minutes. Lower the temperature to 300 degrees and cook for 10 minutes more.

The ribs may also be cooked over a charcoal fire, allowing for an initial searing and then raising the grill to allow for a thorough but slower cooking.

Yield: 4–8 servings.

STEAMED SPARERIBS WITH BLACK BEAN SAUCE

1 pound spareribs	1 teaspoon salt
4 tablespoons black beans	1 tablespoon peanut oil
2 scallions	2 teaspoons dry sherry
2 tablespoons white rice wine vinegar	3 tablespoons sugar
1½ tablespoons minced garlic	1 teaspoon cornstarch
	¼ cup water

Preparation
With a heavy cleaver chop the spareribs into pieces 1½ inches long or have the butcher do it. Place the spareribs in a pot of boiling water for 4 minutes, rinse with cold water, and drain to remove the excess fat.

Rinse the black beans and crush with the handle of a cleaver or the back of a spoon. Cut the scallions into ¼-inch pieces. Combine all the ingredients and pour over the ribs in a heatproof dish.

Cooking
Steam for 40 minutes over rapidly boiling water. Serve immediately.

Yield: 2–3 servings.

STEAMED GROUND PORK WITH HAM

This and the other steamed ground pork dishes that follow cannot be found on restaurant menus, but they are immensely popular at home. Perhaps the reason is that steamed ground pork dishes are not especially attractive to look at even when energetically garnished. They are, however, very tasty.

4 water chestnuts	4 tablespoons chicken stock or
1 pound ground pork	water
¼ cup minced Smithfield ham	Dash of pepper
1 teaspoon cornstarch	1 teaspoon light soy sauce
½ teaspoon salt	1 tablespoon peanut oil
½ teaspoon sugar	

Preparation
Mince the water chestnuts very finely. Combine them with the rest of the ingredients in a shallow heatproof bowl or plate.

Cooking
Steam over rapidly boiling water for 15 minutes.

Yield: 2–4 servings.

STEAMED GROUND PORK WITH CHINESE SAUSAGE

2 Chinese sausages	½ teaspoon sugar
4 water chestnuts	4 tablespoons water
1 pound ground pork	Dash of pepper
1 teaspoon cornstarch	1 teaspoon light soy sauce
½ teaspoon salt	1 tablespoon peanut oil

Preparation

Mince the sausage and water chestnuts. Mix all the ingredients. Place in a heatproof dish.

Cooking

Steam over rapidly boiling water for 15 minutes.

Yield: 2–4 servings.

STEAMED GROUND PORK WITH SALTED DUCK EGG

2	water chestnuts	¼	cup water
1	pound ground pork		Dash of pepper
1	teaspoon cornstarch	½	teaspoon light soy sauce
½	teaspoon salt	1	tablespoon peanut oil
½	teaspoon sugar	1	salted duck egg

Preparation

Chop the water chestnuts finely. Mix all the ingredients with the egg white. Mash the egg yolk and place on top of the mixture.

Cooking

Steam for 15 minutes.

Yield: 2–4 servings.

STEAMED PORK WITH PRESERVED TURNIP

2	balls preserved turnip	¼	teaspoon salt
1	pound pork		Dash of pepper
½	teaspoon cornstarch	2	teaspoons peanut oil
½	teaspoon sugar	2	tablespoons water
½	teaspoon dark soy sauce		

Preparation

Rinse the preserved turnip. Cut the pork and preserved turnip into thin slices. Mix the pork, cornstarch, sugar, soy sauce, salt, pepper, and 1 teaspoon of the oil. Add the water and preserved turnip. Place in a heatproof dish.

Cooking

Steam for 15 minutes over rapidly boiling water. Spread the remaining oil over the top before serving.

Yield: 3–4 servings.

BEEF WITH ASPARAGUS AND BLACK BEANS

A delicious dish for springtime. The black beans and garlic accentuate the sweetness of fresh young asparagus.

½ pound flank steak
2½ tablespoons peanut oil
½ teaspoon sugar
¾ teaspoon dark soy sauce
½ teaspoon sesame oil
1 tablespoon dry sherry

1 pound asparagus
2 tablespoons black beans
1 tablespoon minced garlic
¾ teaspoon salt
¼ cup chicken stock or water
   Dash of pepper

Preparation

Slice the beef along the grain into long strips 1½ inches across. Then slice these strips across the grain to make thin strips ⅛ of an inch wide, ½ inch thick and 1½ inches long. Combine ½ tablespoon of the peanut oil and ¼ teaspoon of the sugar with the soy sauce, sesame oil, and sherry. Marinate the beef in this mixture and set aside.

Snap off the tough ends of the asparagus and cut the asparagus diagonally into ⅛-inch-thick slices. Rinse the black beans well in cold water and crush them with the handle of a cleaver or with the back of a spoon. Add the garlic to the black beans.

Cooking

Heat a wok or skillet over high heat until a drop of water immediately sizzles into steam. Maintain high heat throughout the cooking process. Add 1 tablespoon of the oil and ½ teaspoon of the salt. Spread the oil and salt around the pan. Just before the oil begins to smoke, add the beef and stir-fry for 1 minute or until the beef is almost done. Remove the beef from the pan to a warm dish.

Add the remaining oil and the remaining salt to the still-hot pan and heat for 30 seconds. Add the garlic and black beans. Stir for about 30 seconds or until the odor of the beans and garlic has become pungent. Add the asparagus and stir for 30 seconds to thoroughly coat it with the oil. Add the chicken stock, pepper, and the remaining sugar. Cover the pan and cook for 3 minutes or until the asparagus is almost done but still crisp and a bright emerald green.

Return the beef to the pan and stir well to blend. The meat should be just cooked, the asparagus tender but not limp, and the sauce scant.

Yield: 2–4 servings.

BEEF WITH PEPPERS, TOMATOES, AND ONIONS

A favorite of ours, this dish is robust but the many flavors are carefully balanced.

½ pound flank steak	2 tablespoons minced garlic
½ teaspoon plus 2 tablespoons peanut oil	2 onions
	2 tomatoes
½ teaspoon sugar	2 green bell peppers
1 tablespoon dry sherry	1 tablespoon dark soy sauce
1 teaspoon light soy sauce	Dash of pepper
1 tablespoon cornstarch	½ cup chicken stock or water
1 tablespoon water	1 slice gingerroot, the size of a
2 tablespoons black beans	half-dollar

Preparation

Slice the beef thinly into pieces approximately 2 by ¼ by ⅛ inch in size. Marinate the beef in a mixture of ½ teaspoon oil, ¼ teaspoon of the sugar, the sherry, light soy sauce, and 1 teaspoon of the cornstarch. Combine the remaining cornstarch with the water and set beside the pan. Soak the black beans for 15 minutes in water, drain, and mash them with the handle of a Chinese cleaver or with the back of a spoon. Add the garlic to the black beans and set aside.

Cut the onions and tomatoes into ½-inch wedges. Cut the peppers into ¾-inch squares, removing the bitter seeds and white membrane.

In a small dish combine the dark soy sauce, the remaining sugar, dash of pepper, and chicken stock.

Cooking

Heat a wok or skillet over high heat until a drop of water immediately sizzles into steam. Maintain high heat throughout the cooking process. Add 1 tablespoon of the oil. Just before the oil begins to smoke, add the gingerroot and stir briefly. Add the beef and stir-fry for 30 seconds or until it is half done. Remove from the pan.

Reheat the pan with the remaining oil. When hot add the garlic and black beans and stir until pungent, about 15 seconds. Add the onions and peppers and stir-fry for 30 seconds. Add the chicken stock mixture. Cover for 1 minute.

Return the beef to the pan and add the tomatoes. Stir for 20 seconds. Add the cornstarch mixture and stir until thickened, about 15 seconds. Remove from heat and serve immediately.

Yield: 3–4 servings.

BEEF WITH SNOW PEAS

¼ pound flank steak	¼ teaspoon salt or to taste
¼ pound snow peas	1 slice gingerroot, the size of a
Dash of pepper	quarter
½ teaspoon sugar	1 teaspoon dry sherry
1 teaspoons dark soy sauce	1 teaspoon cornstarch mixed
¼ cup water	with 3 tablespoons water
2 tablespoons peanut oil	

Preparation

Slice the beef across the grain into thin slices. String the snow peas, leaving the pods intact. Mix the pepper, sugar, soy sauce, and water.

Cooking

Heat a wok or skillet over high heat until a drop of water immediately sizzles into steam. Add the oil, salt, and gingerroot. Just before the oil begins to smoke, add the beef. Stir-fry for 1 minute, at the same time sprinkling sherry over the beef.

Add the soy-sauce-and-water mixture and the snow peas. Cover and cook for 2 minutes. Add the cornstarch mixture. Cook and stir for ½ minute.

Yield: 2 servings.

BEEF WITH VEGETABLE

This basic recipe can be varied by using broccoli, cauliflower, or any number of vegetables. Cooking time will vary somewhat depending on the vegetable. In all cases the vegetable should not be overcooked.

½ pound Chinese cabbage (*bok choy*)
¼ pound flank steak
3 tablespoons peanut oil
½ teaspoon salt
1 thin slice gingerroot, the size of a quarter

¼ cup water
1½ teaspoons dark soy sauce
1 teaspoon cornstarch mixed with 3 tablespoons water

Marinade for the beef:
1 teaspoon cornstarch
1 teaspoon light soy sauce
Dash of pepper

½ teaspoon sugar
½ teaspoon sesame oil
1 teaspoon dry sherry

Preparation
Slice the cabbage diagonally. Slice the beef across the grain into thin slices. Marinate the beef.

Cooking
Heat a wok or skillet over high heat until a drop of water immediately sizzles into steam. Add 1½ tablespoons of the oil, the salt, and gingerroot. Add the cabbage and stir-fry for 1 minute. Add the water. Cover and cook for 1 minute. Remove and set aside.

Heat and grease the pan again with the remaining oil and stir-fry the beef for 1 minute. Add the cabbage and the dark soy sauce. Stir-fry for 2 minutes. Thicken slightly with the cornstarch mixture.

Yield: 2 servings.

STEAMED BEEF WITH PRESERVED TURNIP

1 pound flank steak
2 balls preserved turnip
½ teaspoon cornstarch
½ teaspoon sugar
½ teaspoon dark soy sauce

¼ teaspoon salt or to taste
Dash of pepper
2 teaspoons peanut oil
2 tablespoons water

Preparation
Slice the beef across the grain into thin slices. Rinse the preserved turnip and slice it thinly. Mix the beef, cornstarch, sugar, soy sauce, salt, pepper, and 1 teaspoon of the oil. Add the water and preserved turnip. Place in a shallow heatproof dish and cover.

Cooking
Steam for 15 minutes over rapidly boiling water. Add the remaining oil on top before serving.

Yield: 2–4 servings.

BEEF WITH CELLOPHANE NOODLES

Cellophane noodles can be bought at Chinese groceries in dried form. They soak up a lot of water when cooking and may require more water than the recipe calls for.

¼ pound cellophane noodles	½ teaspoon salt
6 Chinese black mushrooms	1 quart water
¼ pound flank steak	½ teaspoon sugar
½ pound Chinese cabbage (*bok choy*)	½ teaspoon light soy sauce
	Dash of pepper
4 tablespoons peanut oil	

Preparation
Soak the cellophane noodles and mushrooms in separate bowls for at least 30 minutes. Drain. Discard the tough stems of the mushrooms. Shred the beef, cabbage, and mushrooms into pieces 1½ inches by ⅛ inch by ⅛ inch.

Cooking
Put 2 tablespoons of the oil and the salt in a very hot wok or skillet. Add the beef and stir-fry for 2 minutes. Add the water, sugar, soy sauce, pepper, noodles, cabbage, and mushrooms. Bring to a boil and simmer for 5 minutes.
Add the remaining oil. Cook and stir for 2 minutes.

Yield: 2 servings.

BEEF WITH BEAN CURD AND OYSTER SAUCE

¼ pound flank steak
2 bean curds
 Dash of pepper
1 tablespoon oyster sauce
½ teaspoon dark soy sauce
½ teaspoon sugar
¾ cup water

2 tablespoons peanut oil
½ teaspoon salt
1 slice gingerroot, the size of a
 quarter
1 teaspoon dry sherry
1½ teaspoons cornstarch mixed
 with 3 tablespoons water

Preparation
Slice the beef across the grain into thin slices. Cut each bean curd into 6 pieces. Mix the pepper, oyster sauce, soy sauce, sugar, and water.

Cooking
Heat a wok or skillet over high heat until a drop of water immediately sizzles into steam. Add the oil, salt, and gingerroot. Just before the oil begins to smoke, add the beef. Stir-fry for 1 minute, at the same time sprinkling the sherry over the beef

Add the bean curds and the oyster sauce mixture. Cook and stir until it comes to a boil. Add the cornstarch mixture and stir for ½ minute until the sauce has thickened.

Yield: 2 servings.

BEEF WITH PICKLED CABBAGE

Pickled cabbage is made from Chinese mustard greens. It comes in jars at Chinese grocery stores.

½ pound pickled cabbage
¼ pound flank steak
 Dash of pepper
1 teaspoon dark soy sauce
¼ cup water
4 tablespoons peanut oil
1 tablespoon sugar

½ teaspoon salt or to taste
1 slice gingerroot, the size of a
 quarter
1 teaspoon dry sherry
1 teaspoon cornstarch mixed
 with 3 tablespoons water

Preparation
Remove the cabbage from the jar and rinse thoroughly with cold water. Squeeze out the excess water. Slice the cabbage diagonally. Slice the beef across the grain into thin slices. Mix the pepper, soy sauce, and water.

Cooking

Heat a pan over medium heat without oil. Add the cabbage and toast for 5 minutes to remove excess water and to make it more crisp. Turn the heat up to high. Add 2 tablespoons of the oil and the sugar to the pan and stir-fry the cabbage for 2 minutes. Remove and set aside. Wash and dry the skillet.

Heat the skillet again over high heat until a drop of water immediately sizzles into steam. Add the remaining oil, the salt, and gingerroot. Add the beef and stir-fry for 1 minute, at the same time sprinkling sherry over the meat. Add the cabbage and the soy sauce mixture. Stir-fry for 2 minutes. Add the cornstarch mixture. Cook and stir for ½ minute.

Yield: 2 servings.

BEEF WITH CURRY

½ pound flank steak	¼ teaspoon salt
1 medium onion	1 teaspoon cornstarch mixed
4 tablespoons curry powder	with 3 tablespoons water
⅔ cup water	½ teaspoon sugar
½ teaspoon dark soy sauce	Dash of pepper

Preparation

Slice the beef across the grain thinly. Slice the onion into half rings.

Cooking

Heat a frying pan without oil over medium-high heat. Add the onion, then sprinkle the curry powder on top of the onion. Toast in this manner for 2 minutes. Add the beef and stir-fry for 2 minutes. Add the water, soy sauce, and salt and bring heat to high. Cook and stir for 3 minutes. Stir in the cornstarch mixture, sugar, and pepper.

Yield: 2 servings.

GROUND BEEF WITH VEGETABLES

6 Chinese black mushrooms	1 large clove crushed garlic
½ pound Chinese cabbage (*bok choy*)	½ pound ground beef
	¼ cup water
12 snow peas	½ teaspoon sugar
6 water chestnuts	Dash of pepper
¼ cup sliced bamboo shoots	1 teaspoon cornstarch mixed with 2 tablespoons water
Oil for deep-frying	
½ teaspoon salt or to taste	1 ounce cellophane noodles

Preparation

Soak the mushrooms in water for 30 minutes to soften. Discard the tough stems. Dice the cabbage, mushrooms, snow peas, water chestnuts, and bamboo shoots.

Cooking

Heat a wok or skillet over high heat until a drop of water immediately sizzles into steam. Add 2 tablespoons of the oil, the salt, and garlic. When the garlic becomes pungent, but before it burns, add the beef. Stir-fry for 1 minute. Add all the vegetables and the water. Cover and cook for about 3 minutes. Add the sugar and pepper. Stir in the cornstarch mixture.

Throw the cellophane noodles into a pot of oil heated to 375 degrees. Remove immediately. Garnish the dish with the cellophane noodles.

Yield: 2–3 servings.

BEEF COOKED IN RICE

This one-dish meal is particularly favored by bachelors and others eating alone. It is also popular for young infants beginning on a solid diet, in which case the water is increased by ¾ cup and the ground beef added 5 minutes earlier.

1 cup raw rice	¼ teaspoon sugar
2 cups water	Dash of pepper
¼ pound ground beef	1 teaspoon dark soy sauce
1 teaspoon dry sherry	2 slices gingerroot, the size of a quarter
1 teaspoon peanut oil	
¼ teaspoon salt	

Cooking

Wash the rice and boil until all the water has disappeared from the surface of the rice. Simmer for 15 minutes. Mix all the other ingredients and place on top of the rice in the pot. Cover and cook for an additional 5 minutes. Mix the beef with the rice.

Yield: 2–4 servings.

STEAMED FISH WITH BROWN BEAN SAUCE

The Chinese have long recognized the desirability of steaming fish. Steaming retains the sweet natural juices of the fish and moisture of the flesh. When cooking fish the Chinese always use gingerroot, garlic, or wine to remove any off flavors.

1 fish, about 1½ pounds	1 tablespoon dry sherry
1 tablespoon brown bean sauce	1 teaspoon dark soy sauce
2 scallions	¼ cup chicken stock
1 tablespoon finely shredded gingerroot	½ teaspoon sugar
	⅛ teaspoon pepper
	1 tablespoon peanut oil

Preparation

Clean and scale the fish, and remove the gills. Slash the fish diagonally on both sides and place in a heatproof dish. Mash the brown bean sauce with the handle of a cleaver or the back of a spoon. Chop the scallions into ½-inch sections. Mix all the ingredients together and pour over the fish.

Cooking

Steam over rapidly boiling water for 10 minutes or until done, that is, when the flesh flakes easily.

Yield: 2–3 servings.

RED-COOKED FISH

1 fish, about 2 pounds
¼ cup sliced bamboo shoots
4 Chinese black mushrooms
1 tablespoon shredded fresh gingerroot
2 teaspoons minced garlic
2 tablespoons dark soy sauce

2 tablespoons light soy sauce
1 tablespoon dry sherry
1 teaspoon light brown sugar
¾ cup chicken stock
1 cup peanut oil
1 tablespoon cornstarch

Preparation

Clean and scale the fish. Dry with paper towels. Soak the mushrooms in water for 30 minutes or until soft. Discard the tough stems. Slice them thinly.

Cooking

Heat the oil in a wok or skillet to 375 degrees. Fry the fish on each side for 2 minutes. Remove all but 3 tablespoons of the oil. Add all the remaining ingredients. Bring to a boil. Cover and simmer for 30 minutes, basting the fish every 10 minutes or so.

Yield: 2–4 servings.

STEAMED FISH WITH MEAT
SHREDS AND CHINESE MUSHROOMS

1 fish, about 1½ pounds
1 ounce Chinese black mushrooms
⅛ pound boned pork
2 teaspoons minced gingerroot
½ sliced scallion

1 teaspoon light soy sauce
¾ teaspoon salt
½ teaspoon cornstarch mixed with 3 tablespoons water
Dash of pepper
2 tablespoons peanut oil

Preparation

Clean and scale the fish. Soak the mushrooms for 30 minutes in water to soften. Discard the tough stems. Shred the mushrooms and pork. Place the fish in a heatproof dish. Mix together all the other ingredients except 1 tablespoon of the oil. Pour over the fish.

Cooking
Place in a steamer and steam for 18 minutes over rapidly boiling water.
Sprinkle the remaining oil over the fish before serving.

Yield: 2–3 servings.

FRIED FISH IN VEGETABLES

1 fish, about 1½ pounds	¾ teaspoon salt
8 Chinese black mushrooms	1 teaspoon shredded ginger-root
8 golden needles	
⅛ pound boned pork	1½ cups water
½ pound Chinese cabbage (*bok choy*)	1 teaspoon sugar
	1 teaspoon dark soy sauce
2 water chestnuts	1 teaspoon dry sherry
1 egg, beaten	2 teaspoons cornstarch mixed with 4 tablespoons water
5 tablespoons flour	
Oil for deep-frying	

Preparation
Clean and scale the fish. In separate bowls soak the mushrooms and golden needles in water for 30 minutes to soften. Drain. Discard the tough stems of the mushrooms. Shred the pork, mushrooms and cabbage into pieces the size of a matchstick. Mince the water chestnuts.

Mix the egg and flour and dip fish in this batter.

Cooking
Heat the oil to 375 degrees. Fry the fish for 4 minutes on each side, making sure that the fish is completely immersed in the oil. Drain on paper towels and place on a serving platter.

In a hot skillet or wok add 2 tablespoons of the oil, ½ teaspoon of the salt, and the gingerroot. Stir-fry the pork until it becomes white. Add the cabbage, mushrooms, water chestnuts and water. Cover and cook for 2 minutes.

Add the remaining salt, sugar, soy sauce, sherry, golden needles, and cornstarch mixture. Cook and stir for ½ minute. Pour over the fish.

Yield: 2–3 servings.

FISH KOW

1 pound fish fillet
3 tablespoons flour
1 teaspoon dry sherry
1 egg white
¼ pound Chinese cabbage (*bok choy*)
8 water chestnuts
12 snow peas
  Oil for deep-frying
½ teaspoon salt or to taste
1 teaspoon shredded ginger-root

1 large clove garlic
¼ cup sliced bamboo shoots
¼ cup water
½ teaspoon light soy sauce
1 teaspoon cornstarch mixed with 3 tablespoons water
¼ teaspoon sugar
½ teaspoon sesame oil
  Dash of pepper

Preparation
Cut the fish into 1-inch squares. Mix the flour, sherry, and egg white. Dip the fish into this batter. Cut the cabbage diagonally into chunks to match the fish squares in size. Slice the water chestnuts thinly. String the snow peas.

Cooking
Heat the oil to 375 degrees and deep-fry the fish for 5 minutes. To a hot skillet or wok add 2 tablespoons of the oil, the salt, and gingerroot. Brown the garlic clove. Add the cabbage, bamboo shoots, water chestnuts, and snow peas. Stir-fry for 1 minute. Add the water and soy sauce. Cover and cook for 2 minutes. Add the fish, cornstarch mixture, sugar, sesame oil, and pepper. Stir. Remove the garlic and serve.

Yield: 2–4 servings.

DEEP-FRIED FISH WITH TEA MELON

1 fish, about 2 pounds
½ teaspoon salt or to taste
1 egg, beaten
  Cornstarch to dredge fish
2 scallions
½ cup chicken stock
½ cup red wine vinegar
½ cup light brown sugar
1 tablespoon dark soy sauce

  Oil for deep-frying
1 tablespoon shredded ginger-root
¼ cup shredded tea melon
¼ cup shredded celery cabbage
¼ cup shredded bamboo shoots
1 teaspoon cornstarch mixed with 1 tablespoon water

Preparation

Clean and scale the fish. Dry with paper towels. Rub the inside and outside of the fish with the salt. Dip the fish in the beaten egg and then dredge in the cornstarch. Dice the scallions. In a bowl combine the chicken stock, vinegar, sugar, and soy sauce.

Cooking

Heat the oil to 375 degrees. Lower the fish carefully in a wire basket. Allow it to fry for 3 minutes. Remove the fish and drain it on paper towels. Allow the fish to cool for 15 minutes. Repeat the frying process, this time for 5 minutes. Remove the fish and place it on a serving platter.

Heat a wok or skillet over high heat until a drop of water immediately sizzles into steam. Add 2 tablespoons of the oil and the gingerroot. Stir for 30 seconds. Add the tea melons, cabbage, and bamboo shoots. Stir-fry for 1 minute. Add the chicken stock mixture and bring to a boil. Stir in the cornstarch mixture to thicken the sauce. Pour over the fish. Garnish with the scallions and serve.

Yield: 2–4 servings.

SWEET-AND-SOUR FISH

½ green bell pepper	1½ cups water
1 carrot	¼ cup red wine vinegar
1 ring canned pineapple	5 tablespoons sugar
1 sea bass, about 1½ pounds	1 teaspoon dark soy sauce
1 egg	Dash of pepper
5 tablespoons flour	3 teaspoons cornstarch mixed
Oil for deep-frying	with 6 tablespoons water
¾ teaspoon salt	
5 slices gingerroot, the size of a quarter	

Preparation

Shred the bell pepper, carrot, and pineapple. Clean and scale the fish. Mix the egg and flour. Dip the fish in the batter.

Cooking

Fry the fish in oil heated to 375 degrees for 4 minutes on each side. Remove the fish and place in a serving dish.

In a hot skillet or wok add 2 tablespoons of the oil, the salt, and gingerroot. Just before the oil begins to smoke, add the bell pepper, carrot, pineapple, water, vinegar, sugar, soy sauce, and pepper. Bring the mixture to a boil. Stir in the cornstarch mixture and pour over the fish. Remove the pieces of gingerroot and serve.

Note: For sweet-and-sour shrimp, substitute 1 pound cleaned shrimp for the sea bass.

Yield: 2–3 servings.

FRIED FISH FILLET WITH CHINESE VEGETABLES

1 pound fish fillet	12 snow peas
1 tablespoon cornstarch	2 tablespoons peanut oil
¾ teaspoon salt	1 large clove garlic
1 teaspoon dry sherry	¼ cup water
2 tablespoons bamboo shoots	¼ teaspoon sugar
3 water chestnuts	Dash of pepper
¼ pound Chinese cabbage (*bok choy*)	8 slices gingerroot, the size of a quarter

Preparation
Cut the fish diagonally into slices ⅛ inch thick. Mix the cornstarch, ¼ teaspoon of the salt, and sherry. Dip the fish in this mixture. Thinly slice the bamboo shoots, water chestnuts, and cabbage. String the snow peas.

Cooking
In a hot skillet or wok add 1 tablespoon of the oil and ¼ teaspoon of the salt. Brown the garlic. Stir-fry all the vegetables for 1 minute. Add the water, sugar, and pepper. Cover and cook for 2 minutes. Remove the vegetables and set aside.
Heat the pan again with the remaining oil, the remaining salt, and the gingerroot. Add the fish. Stir carefully to coat with oil. Return the vegetables to the pan and stir-fry for 1 minute. Remove the gingerroot and garlic and serve.

Yield: 2–4 servings.

FRIED FISH WITH BEAN CURD

1 fish, about 1½ pounds
1 scallion
2 bean curds
Oil for deep-frying
5 tablespoons peanut oil
1 teaspoon salt
1 teaspoon shredded ginger-root

1 cup water
1½ teaspoons cornstarch mixed with 3 tablespoons water
1 teaspoon soy sauce
1 teaspoon dry sherry
1 teaspoon sugar
Dash of pepper

Preparation
Clean and scale the fish. Slice the scallions. Cut bean curd into 8 pieces.

Cooking
Heat the oil for deep-frying and fry the bean curd until light brown. In a hot skillet or wok add 4 tablespoons of the peanut oil and ¼ teaspoon of the salt. Just before the oil begins to smoke, add the fish. Fry the fish for 4 minutes on each side. Remove the fish and set aside.

Heat the pan again with the remaining oil, the remaining salt, and the gingerroot. Add the water and bean curd. Place the fish on top and sprinkle with the scallion. Cover and cook for 4 minutes.

Remove the fish and bean curd to a serving platter. To the pan add the cornstarch mixture, soy sauce, sherry, sugar, and pepper. Stir until thickened. Pour over the fish.

Yield: 2–4 servings.

PAN-FRIED SHRIMP

Although it makes eating them more difficult, cooking shrimp in the shell makes them definitely more succulent. Try cooking this dish using first shelled and then unshelled shrimp and you will certainly taste the difference.

1 pound medium to large shrimp, unshelled
¼ cup ketchup
1 tablespoon dry sherry
¼ cup water
1 teaspoon sugar
Dash of pepper

2 or 3 scallions, sliced
1 tablespoon cornstarch mixed with 3 tablespoons water
2 tablespoons peanut oil
½ teaspoon salt or to taste
1 teaspoon minced garlic
2 teaspoons minced gingerroot

Preparation

Remove the heads and legs of the shrimp. Slit the shell to devein the shrimp, but leave the shell on. In a bowl combine the ketchup, sherry, and water. In another bowl combine the sugar, pepper, scallions, and the cornstarch mixture.

Cooking

Heat a wok or skillet over high heat until a drop of water immediately sizzles into steam. Add 1 tablespoon of the oil, ¼ teaspoon of the salt, and the garlic. Stir for 30 seconds or until the odor of the garlic becomes pungent. Add the shrimp and stir-fry for 30 seconds. Lower heat to medium and fry the shrimp on each side for 2 minutes or until pink. Remove the shrimp from the pan.

Reheat the pan. Add the remaining oil, the remaining salt, and the gingerroot. Add the ketchup mixture and bring to a boil. Return the shrimp to the pan and stir briefly to reheat them. Stir in the sugar and cornstarch mixture until the sauce has thickened, about 15 seconds.

To eat the shrimp you can either remove the shell with a knife or fork, or you can practice eating them in the Chinese manner which is to take a bite of the shrimp, shell and all, using your tongue to separate the shell from the shrimp. The shell is then removed from the mouth with chopsticks. This is not as difficult as it sounds and is well worth trying in the spirit of authenticity.

Yield: 2–4 servings.

FRIED SHRIMP

12 large shrimp	½ teaspoon dry sherry
¼ teaspoon salt	2 teaspoons cornstarch
¼ teaspoon dark soy sauce	Oil for deep-frying

Preparation

Shell and devein the shrimp, leaving the tail on. Split halfway through the back. Mix the salt, soy sauce, and sherry. Marinate the shrimp for 10 minutes. Coat with cornstarch.

Cooking

Heat the oil to 375 degrees and deep-fry the shrimp. The shrimp will float when done.

Yield: 3–6 servings.

SHRIMP WITH KETCHUP

½ pound shrimp	4 tablespoons ketchup
2 tablespoons peanut oil	1½ teaspoons sugar
½ teaspoon salt	Dash of pepper
1 tablespoon crushed garlic	1½ teaspoons cornstarch mixed
¼ cup water	with 3 tablespoons water

Preparation
Shell and devein the shrimp. Split by cutting halfway through. Boil for 2 minutes.

Cooking
In a hot skillet or wok add the oil, salt, and garlic. Just before the oil begins to smoke, add the water, ketchup, sugar, and pepper. Bring to a boil and add the cornstarch mixture. Pour over the shrimp.

Yield: 2 servings.

FRIED SHRIMP WITH CHINESE VEGETABLES

½ pound shrimp	½ teaspoon salt or to taste
½ egg white	1 large clove garlic
2 tablespoons flour	¼ cup sliced bamboo shoots
¼ pound Chinese cabbage (*bok choy*)	¼ cup water
8 water chestnuts	1 teaspoon cornstarch mixed with 3 tablespoons water
12 snow peas	¼ teaspoon sugar
Oil for deep-frying	Dash of pepper
2 tablespoons peanut oil	

Preparation
Shell and devein the shrimp. Split the back by cutting halfway through to get a fuller shrimp when fried. Mix the egg white and flour. Dip the shrimp in this batter. Cut the cabbage diagonally. Slice the water chestnuts thinly. String the snow peas.

Cooking
Heat the oil to 375 degrees and deep-fry the shrimp. They will float when done. Remove from the oil and drain.

In a hot skillet or wok add the peanut oil, salt, and garlic. Just before the oil begins to smoke, add all the vegetables and stir-fry for 1 minute.

Add the water. Cover and cook for 2 minutes. Add the shrimp, cornstarch mixture, sugar, and pepper. Stir until the scant sauce has thickened. Remove the garlic and serve.

Yield: 2 servings.

BUTTERFLY SHRIMP

12 large shrimp
12 thin slices Smithfield ham, 1½ by ½ inches
1 large onion
1 egg
4 tablespoons flour
3 slices bacon
2 tablespoons peanut oil
½ teaspoon salt

1 large clove garlic
½ cup water
¼ cup ketchup
2 tablespoons Worcestershire sauce
3 teaspoons sugar
Dash of pepper
2 teaspoons cornstarch mixed with 4 tablespoons water

Preparation

Shell and devein the shrimp. Do not detach tail. Split by cutting half-way through and flatten out. Slice the onion into half rings. Place a piece of ham on each shrimp. Mix the egg and flour. Cut each slice of bacon into 4 pieces. Dip the bacon into the batter. Place the dipped bacon over the ham and shrimp.

Cooking

Fry on the bacon side for 3 minutes in a well-greased frying pan. Turn over and fry 3 minutes more. Remove and set aside.

Stir-fry the onion for 2 minutes. Arrange the onion on a serving dish and cover with the fried shrimp.

To a hot skillet or wok add the oil, salt, and garlic. Just before the oil begins to smoke, add the water, ketchup, Worcestershire sauce, sugar, and pepper. Bring to a boil and add the cornstarch mixture. Remove the garlic. Pour the sauce over the shrimp.

Yield: 3–6 servings.

CURRIED SHRIMP

¾ pound shrimp
¼ cup sliced onion
2 tablespoons curry powder or to taste
⅔ cup water
½ teaspoon salt or to taste

1 teaspoon dry sherry
½ teaspoon dark soy sauce
1½ teaspoons cornstarch mixed with 4 tablespoons water
1 teaspoon sugar
Dash of pepper

Preparation
Shell and devein the shrimp. Split by cutting halfway through.

Cooking
Heat a frying pan without oil over medium heat. Add the onion. Sprinkle the curry powder on top of the onion. Toast in this manner for 2 minutes. Add the shrimp and stir for 3 minutes, but do not allow the curry powder to burn. Add the water, salt, sherry, and soy sauce. Raise heat to high and bring the mixture to a boil. Cover and cook for 3 minutes. Add the cornstarch mixture, sugar, and pepper. Stir until thickened.

Yield: 2 servings.

DICED SHRIMP WITH CHINESE VEGETABLES

½ pound shrimp
½ pound Chinese cabbage (*bok choy*)
8 water chestnuts
¼ cup sliced bamboo shoots
12 snow peas
4 button mushrooms
2 tablespoons peanut oil

½ teaspoon salt
1 large clove garlic
¼ cup water
½ teaspoon dark soy sauce
1½ teaspoons cornstarch mixed with 3 tablespoons water
¼ teaspoon sugar

Preparation
Shell and devein the shrimp. Dice the shrimp and vegetables.

Cooking
In a hot skillet or wok add the oil, salt, and garlic. Just before the oil begins to smoke, add the shrimp and all the vegetables. Stir-fry for ½ minute. Add the water and soy sauce. Cover and cook 2 minutes. Add the

cornstarch mixture and sugar. Stir until the sauce has thickened. Remove the garlic and serve.

Yield: 2 servings.

SHRIMP WITH LOBSTER SAUCE

As with some other recipes the name is misleading. This dish does not contain any lobster but is, rather, the sauce used for lobster Cantonese.

1 pound shrimp	1 cup chicken stock or water
2 tablespoons dry sherry	4 tablespoons vegetable oil
2 tablespoons cornstarch	½ teaspoon salt
¼ cup water	2 slices gingerroot, the size of a
2 tablespoons black beans	quarter
1 tablespoon minced garlic	½ pound ground pork
1 tablespoon dark soy sauce	1 egg, beaten
¼ teaspoon sugar	1 scallion, chopped, to garnish

Preparation

Shell and devein the shrimp. In a bowl combine the shrimp with the sherry and ½ tablespoon of the cornstarch. In another bowl mix the remaining cornstarch with ¼ cup water. Soak the black beans for 10 minutes. Drain off the water and rinse. Bruise the beans with the handle of a cleaver or the back of a spoon. Add the garlic to the black beans. Mix together the soy sauce, sugar, and chicken stock.

Cooking

Heat a wok or skillet over high heat until a drop of water immediately sizzles into steam. Maintain high heat throughout the cooking process. Add 2 tablespoons of the oil, ¼ teaspoon of the salt, and 1 slice of the gingerroot. Stir. Just before the oil begins to smoke, add the shrimp. Stir for 2 minutes or until the shrimp are definitely pinkish. Remove the shrimp from the pan.

Reheat the pan. Add the remaining oil, the remaining gingerroot, the garlic and black beans, and the remaining salt. After a few stirs add the pork and the soy sauce mixture. Bring to a boil. Cover and simmer for 2 minutes. Return the shrimp to the pan. Stir in the cornstarch mixture. Remove from heat and stir in the egg. Garnish with the scallion.

Yield: 3–5 servings.

STEAMED LOBSTER WITH SALTED EGG

1 lobster about 1¾ pounds	½ teaspoon salt
4 Chinese black mushrooms	½ teaspoon sugar
6 water chestnuts	½ teaspoon light soy sauce
1 salted duck egg	1 teaspoon dry sherry
½ pound ground pork	1 tablespoon peanut oil

Preparation
It is imperative that this dish be made with a freshly killed lobster. Have the fishmonger clean and cut up the live lobster into 8 to 10 pieces or follow the directions for chopping a lobster in the recipe for Lobster Cantonese.

Soak the mushrooms for 30 minutes or until soft in water. Drain and discard the tough stems. Mince the water chestnuts and mushrooms very finely. Break open the egg and separate the white from the yolk (which should be firm). Mix the egg white, pork, water chestnuts, mushrooms, salt, sugar, soy sauce, sherry, and oil. Spread the mixture in a heatproof dish. Slice the egg yolk into very thin pieces. Reassemble the lobster over the pork mixture.

Cooking
Place the heatproof dish in a steamer. Cover and steam over rapidly boiling water for 25 minutes.

Yield: 2–4 servings.

LOBSTER CANTONESE

1 lobster, about 1¾ pounds	¼ teaspoon salt or to taste
2 tablespoons black beans	2 slices gingerroot, the size of a
1 tablespoon minced garlic	quarter
1 tablespoon dark soy sauce	½ pound ground pork
¼ teaspoon sugar	1 egg, beaten
2 tablespoons dry sherry	1½ tablespoons cornstarch
1 cup chicken stock or water	mixed with ¼ cup water
2 tablespoons peanut oil	1 scallion, chopped, to garnish

Preparation
It is imperative that this dish be made with a freshly killed lobster. Have the fishmonger clean and cut up the live lobster into 8 to 10 pieces or

follow these directions: Chop off the tail end. Cut the tail lengthwise and then crosswise again in half. Turn the lobster over on its back. Rip off the "chest" portion with your fingers or split lengthwise in half with a Chinese knife. Remove and discard the spongy insides but not the meat. Chop off the "feelers." Chop off the large claws and split lengthwise and then again crosswise.

Soak the black beans for 10 minutes. Drain off the water and rinse. Bruise the beans with the handle of a cleaver or the back of a spoon. Add the garlic to the black beans. Mix together the soy sauce, sugar, sherry, and chicken stock.

Cooking

Heat a wok or skillet over high heat until a drop of water immediately sizzles into steam. Maintain high heat throughout the cooking process. Add the oil, salt, and gingerroot. Just before the oil begins to smoke, add the black beans and garlic. After a few stirs add the pork and the soy sauce mixture. Bring to a boil. Add the lobster. Cover and simmer for 5 minutes. Stir in the cornstarch mixture. Remove from heat and stir in the egg. Garnish with the scallion.

Yield: 2–4 servings.

ABALONE, ASPARAGUS, AND STRAW MUSHROOMS

8 medium asparagus	1½ tablespoons oyster sauce
1 tablespoon peanut oil	1 teaspoon sesame oil
½ tablespoon salt	½ teaspoon sugar
¼ cup chicken stock or water	Dash of pepper
½ cup thinly sliced canned abalone	1 teaspoon cornstarch mixed with 3 tablespoons water
1 cup straw mushrooms	

Preparation

Rinse the asparagus and snap off the tough white part at the bottom. Slice diagonally.

Cooking

Heat a wok or skillet over high heat until a drop of water immediately sizzles into steam. Add the peanut oil and salt. Add the asparagus and stir-fry for 1 minute. Add the chicken stock and cover for 1 minute.

Add the abalone, mushrooms, oyster sauce, sesame oil, sugar, and pepper. Stir-fry for 1 minute. Thicken slightly with the cornstarch mixture.

Yield: 3–4 servings.

CLAMS AND OYSTER SAUCE

2 tablespoons black beans	2 tablespoons peanut oil
24 cherrystone clams	1 teaspoon minced gingerroot
2½ tablespoons oyster sauce	1 tablespoon minced garlic
2 teaspoons sesame oil	1 cup chicken stock
1 teaspoon light soy sauce	1 tablespoon cornstarch mixed
1 teaspoon sugar	with ¼ cup water
1 tablespoon dry sherry	¼ cup chopped scallions

Preparation

Rinse the black beans, then mash them with the handle of a Chinese knife. Scrub the clamshells. In a small bowl combine the oyster sauce, sesame oil, soy sauce, sugar, and sherry.

Cooking

In a hot skillet or wok combine the peanut oil, gingerroot, garlic, and black beans. When the black beans start to smell pungent, add the clams and chicken stock. Bring to a boil. Lower heat to simmer and cover for 5 minutes. The shells will open.

Add the oyster sauce mixture. Bring heat back up to high. Stir-fry for 2 minutes. Stir in the cornstarch mixture to thicken. Garnish with the scallions.

Yield: 3–6 servings.

STIR-FRIED SPINACH

This dish is very simple to cook and goes well with chops and steaks as well as Chinese food. No water is needed because the spinach gives off sufficient water in the cooking process.

10 ounces spinach	½ teaspoon salt or to taste
2 large cloves garlic	¼ teaspoon sugar
2 tablespoons peanut oil	Dash of pepper

Preparation

Wash the spinach and discard the tough stems. Peel the garlic and mince finely.

Cooking

Heat a wok or skillet over high heat until a drop of water immediately sizzles into steam. Maintain high heat throughout the cooking process. Add the oil, salt, and garlic. Stir until the odor of the garlic has become pungent. Add the spinach. Stir. Cover for 1 minute. Uncover and add the sugar and pepper. Stir-fry for 15 seconds more or until the leaves are dark and glistening.

Yield: 2–4 servings.

SNOW PEAS AND STRAW MUSHROOMS

Snow peas are lovely and so are straw mushrooms. Add a little oyster sauce and one has a delightful dish.

6 ounces snow peas	½ teaspoon sugar
9 ounces straw mushrooms	1 tablespoon dry sherry
¼ cup water	1 tablespoon peanut oil
1 tablespoon oyster sauce	½ teaspoon salt or to taste
1 teaspoon light soy sauce	1 teaspoon sesame oil
Dash of pepper	

Preparation

String the snow peas and drain the mushrooms. In a cup mix the water, oyster sauce, soy sauce, pepper, sugar, and sherry.

Cooking

Heat a wok or skillet over high heat until a drop of water immediately sizzles into steam. Add the peanut oil and salt. Just before the oil begins to smoke, add the snow peas. Stir-fry for 30 seconds. Add the mushrooms. Stir for 1½ minutes.

Add the oyster sauce mixture. Cover for 30 seconds. Remove from heat. Stir in the sesame oil. Serve immediately.

Yield: 2–3 servings.

BRAISED CHINESE BLACK MUSHROOMS

For Chinese mushroom lovers, this is a heavenly dish. It is usually served as part of a multicourse banquet. The flavor is mellow and the texture rich and velvety.

⅓ pound Chinese black mushrooms
1 cup rendered chicken fat or
  peanut oil
2 large cloves garlic

2 star anise (16 sections)
½ teaspoon five-flavor powder
3 cups water
1 tablespoon dry sherry

Preparation
Soak the mushrooms in water for 30 minutes or until soft. Squeeze the mushrooms gently to remove any excess moisture. Discard the tough stems.

Cooking
Heat a wok or skillet over high heat until a drop of water immediately sizzles into steam. Add 1 tablespoon of the chicken fat or oil and then the garlic. Stir until pungent. Add the remaining chicken fat or oil and the rest of the ingredients. Cover the pan and simmer for 45 minutes. Discard the garlic and serve.

Yield: 8–12 servings.

BRAISED THREE MUSHROOMS

Three fungi of different textures and tastes are braised with rendered chicken fat. Very rich, but very, very good.

16 small Chinese black mushrooms
¼ cup cloud ears
9 ounces straw mushrooms
1 cup rendered chicken fat or
  peanut oil
2 large cloves garlic
2 star anise (16 sections)

1 teaspoon five-flavor powder
¼ teaspoon salt
3 cups water
1 tablespoon dry sherry
3 teaspoons sugar

Preparation
Soak the black mushrooms and cloud ears in water for 30 minutes or

until soft. Drain the straw mushrooms. Squeeze the black mushrooms gently to remove any excess moisture. Discard the tough stems.

Cooking

Heat a wok or skillet over high heat until a drop of water immediately sizzles into steam. Add 1 tablespoon of the chicken fat or oil and then the garlic. Stir until pungent. Add the remaining chicken fat or oil and the rest of the ingredients. Cover the pan and simmer for 45 minutes. Remove the garlic and star anise before serving.

Yield: 8–12 servings.

BRAISED WINTER MELON

1 dozen small Chinese black mushrooms
1 winter melon, about 1 pound
2 teaspoons cornstarch mixed with 1 tablespoon water
½ teaspoon salt
Dash of pepper

¼ teaspoon sugar
3 cups peanut oil
½ cup chicken stock
2 tablespoons oyster sauce
Shredded Smithfield ham to garnish

Preparation

Soak the mushrooms in water for 30 minutes or until soft. Squeeze gently to remove any excess water. Discard the tough stems.

Wash, peel, and seed the winter melon. Cut the flesh into pieces roughly ½ by 1½ by 1½ inches.

Combine the cornstarch mixture, salt, pepper, and sugar in a bowl and set aside.

Cooking

Heat the oil to 375 degrees. Deep-fry the melon until brown. Drain the pieces on paper towels.

Bring the chicken stock to a boil. Add the melon and mushrooms. Simmer for 10 minutes.

Add the oyster sauce and mix thoroughly. Remove the melon and mushrooms to a serving dish with a slotted spoon.

Bring the remaining liquid to a boil over high heat. Add the cornstarch mixture and stir for 30 seconds or until thickened. Pour the sauce over the melon and garnish with the ham.

Yield: 4–8 servings.

STEAMED STUFFED BEAN CURD

6 Chinese black mushrooms	3 tablespoons minced scal-
½ pound fish fillet	lions
2 tablespoons minced	1 tablespoon dry sherry
Smithfield ham	½ teaspoon salt or to taste
1 tablespoon minced ginger-	Liberal dash of pepper
root	2 teaspoons peanut oil
1 tablespoon light soy sauce	6 bean curds

Preparation

Soak the mushrooms in water until soft. Squeeze out the excess moisture and mince. Mince the fish very finely and put in a mixing bowl. Put all the ingredients except the bean curds into a mixing bowl. Mix thoroughly.

Cut the bean curds diagonally in half to make two triangles. Carefully make a pocket in each of the bean curd triangles so that the stuffing will be enclosed by the top, the bottom, and one side of the triangle when finished. Stuff the fish mixture into the pockets.

Cooking

Arrange the stuffed bean curd triangles on a lightly greased heatproof dish. Steam over rapidly boiling water for 30 minutes. Serve with light soy sauce.

Yield: 3–6 servings.

MOCK DUCK WITH SNOW PEAS

Mock duck comes canned and is made from fried gluten, safflower oil, sugar, soy sauce, and salt. It may be purchased at a Chinese grocery.

¼ pound snow peas	½ teaspoon sugar
1 tablespoon peanut oil	Dash of pepper
¼ cup chicken stock or water	
1 10-ounce can vegetarian	
mock duck meat	

Preparation

String the snow peas and rinse in a colander.

Cooking

Heat a wok or skillet over moderately high heat. Add the oil. Before the oil begins to smoke, add the snow peas. Stir-fry for 1 minute. Add the chicken stock and allow it to come to a boil. Stir for 1 minute.

Add the mock duck meat, sugar, and pepper. Stir for 1 minute or until the mock duck is heated through.

Yield: 2 servings.

CRAB SALAD

A lovely refreshing salad that can be made ahead of time.

1 cup fresh bean sprouts	2 tablespoons light soy sauce
2 cucumbers	½ teaspoon sugar
½ pound crab meat	¼ teaspoon salt or to taste
1 tablespoon sesame oil	

Preparation

Bring a pot of water to a boil. Throw the bean sprouts in for 1 minute. Drain and rinse under cold running water to stop the cooking. (If using canned bean sprouts this blanching operation is not needed.) Wash and peel the cucumbers. Shred the cucumbers into matchstick shapes. Pick over the crab meat to remove any pieces of cartilage or shell. Mix all the ingredients together. Refrigerate.

Yield: 4–8 servings.

BITTER MELON STUFFED WITH FISH

Bitter melon has a most unusual taste. It is often served in the summer because it leaves the palate with a cool aftertaste. In this dish the melons are stuffed with a fish and pork filling topped with a black bean sauce gravy.

6 Chinese black mushrooms	4 teaspoons light soy sauce
2 tablespoons black beans	½ teaspoon salt or to taste
3 bitter melons	1½ teaspoons sugar
2 tablespoons cornstarch	1 teaspoon sesame oil
Dash of pepper	1 tablespoon peanut oil
½ pound fish fillet	2 tablespoons minced garlic
2 ounces unsalted pork fat	2 tablespoons minced ginger-root
¼ cup sliced bamboo shoots	root
6 water chestnuts	2 tablespoons oyster sauce
½ pound ground pork	2 tablespoons dry sherry

Preparation

In separate bowls soak the mushrooms and the black beans for 30 minutes. Split the melons lengthwise. Seed and wash them carefully. Place the melons in boiling water for 3 minutes. Rinse with cold water to stop the cooking and dry them well. Dust the inside of each melon with a little cornstarch and pepper. Set aside.

Drain the mushrooms and discard the tough stems. Finely dice the fish, pork fat, mushrooms, bamboo shoots, and water chestnuts to correspond in size to the grains of the ground pork. Combine these ingredients in a large bowl with 1 teaspoon of the soy sauce, the salt, ½ teaspoon of the sugar, and the sesame oil. Mix very well and then stuff the melons with this mixture. Place the melons in a heatproof dish.

Prepare the sauce by draining the black beans and mashing them with the handle of a Chinese cleaver or the back of a spoon. In a bowl combine the drained black beans, peanut oil, garlic, gingerroot, oyster sauce, the remaining sugar, the remaining cornstarch, the remaining soy sauce, and the sherry. Pour the sauce over the stuffed bitter melons.

Cooking

Steam the melons over rapidly boiling water for 30 minutes. Cut each melon into 3 or 4 pieces before serving.

Yield: 6–10 servings.

EGG DROP SOUP

1 teaspoon water	½ teaspoon sugar
1 egg, beaten	3 tablespoons cornstarch
1 quart chicken stock	mixed with ½ cup water
½ teaspoon salt	

Preparation
Stir the water into the egg.

Cooking
Bring the chicken stock to a boil. Add the salt and sugar. Stir in the cornstarch mixture. Remove from heat. Pour the beaten egg into the stock extremely slowly while vigorously stirring the stock.

Yield: 5 servings.

WATERCRESS SOUP

A simple soup that can replace a vegetable, the watercress soup is always appreciated both by guests and the cook.

1 bunch watercress	½ teaspoon salt
⅛ pound boned pork	½ teaspoon sugar
1 quart chicken stock	1 egg
1 tablespoon light soy sauce	

Preparation
Wash the watercress and drain. Snip off the tougher stems. Slice the pork across the grain into thin slices.

Cooking
Bring the chicken stock to a boil. Add all the ingredients except the egg. Simmer for 7 minutes. Remove from heat. Poach the egg on top of the soup.

Yield: 6 servings.

WONTON SOUP

This substantial soup with its meaty dumplings makes a satisfying lunch.

The wonton
4 Chinese black mushrooms	Dash of pepper
½ pounds ground pork	24 pieces wonton skin
⅛ cup minced water chestnuts	1 egg, beaten
½ teaspoon light soy sauce	2 quarts water
¼ teaspoon salt or to taste	

The soup
6 cups chicken stock	
1 cup sliced Chinese cabbage (*bok choy*) or watercress	Coriander to garnish

Preparation

Soak the mushrooms in water for 30 minutes or until soft and mince finely. Mix the pork, water chestnuts, mushrooms, soy sauce, salt, and pepper in a mixing bowl. Fold into pieces of wonton skin and seal with the beaten egg (see diagram).

INSTRUCTIONS FOR FOLDING WONTON

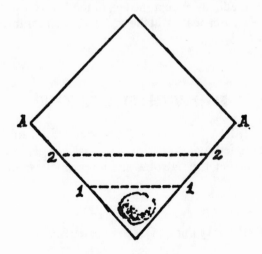

Cooking

Bring the water to a boil. Add the wonton and boil for 5 minutes. Drain in a colander. Run cold water over the wonton.

Bring the chicken stock to a boil. Add the cabbage and simmer for 1½ minutes. Add the wonton and serve. Garnish with coriander.

Yield : 6 servings.

BEAN CURD SOUP

⅛ pound boned pork	½ teaspoon salt or to taste
2 bean curds	½ teaspoon sugar
¼ pound Chinese cabbage (*bok choy*)	1 quart chicken stock
	1 egg
2 water chestnuts	
2 tablespoons sliced bamboo shoots	

Preparation

Slice the pork across the grain into thin slices. Cut the bean curds into 1-inch squares, the cabbage into 1-inch pieces, and the water chestnuts into thin slices.

Cooking

Add all the ingredients except the egg to the chicken stock. Boil for 10 minutes. Remove from heat. Add the egg and poach for three minutes.

Yield: 6 servings.

FISH WITH LETTUCE SOUP

½ pound fish fillet	1 quart chicken stock
½ head iceberg lettuce	Dash of pepper
2 slices gingerroot, the size of a quarter	¼ teaspoon sesame oil

Preparation

Slice the fish fillet very thinly. Quarter the lettuce.

Cooking

Bring the chicken stock to a boil. Add the gingerroot and lettuce. Stir to separate the lettuce leaves. When the chicken stock comes to a boil again, add the fish. Remove from heat. Add the pepper and oil. Cover for 2 minutes. Remove the gingerroot and serve.

Yield: 6 servings.

CORN SOUP

While some may scoff, this soup is authentic. The use of canned cream corn is a convenience that does not interfere with the flavor of the end result.

¼ pound boned chicken breast	½ teaspoon sugar
½ cup water	1 cup chicken stock
1 can creamed corn (16½ ounces)	1 teaspoon cornstarch mixed with 3 tablespoons water
½ teaspoon salt	1 egg white, beaten

Preparation
Mince the chicken breast, first with the sharp edge of the knife, then with the back of the knife so that it becomes very finely minced. Add the water and stir well with a fork. Remove the tendons. Drain off excess water.

Cooking
Mix the corn, salt, sugar, and chicken stock. Bring to a boil. Add the cornstarch mixture and remove from heat. Add the minced chicken and egg white. Stir for 2 minutes.

Yield: 4 servings.

MINCED CHICKEN WITH LETTUCE SOUP

¼ pound boned chicken	2 cups shredded lettuce
½ cup water	1 egg white, beaten
1 quart chicken stock	2 tablespoons minced Smithfield ham to garnish
½ teaspoon sugar	
½ teaspoon salt or to taste	

Preparation
Mince the chicken, first with the sharp edge of the knife, then with the

back of the knife so that it becomes very finely minced. Add the water and stir well with a fork. Remove the tendons. Drain off excess water.

Cooking
Bring the chicken stock to a boil. Add the sugar, salt, and lettuce. When the chicken stock begins to boil again remove from heat. Add the chicken and egg white. Stir for 2 minutes. Garnish with the ham.

Yield: 6 servings.

FUZZY MELON SOUP

Jeet qua *or fuzzy melon is a member of the squash family and is seldom served in a Chinese restaurant. It makes a wonderfully light and refreshing soup.*

½ pound fuzzy melon	1 quart chicken stock
⅛ pound boned pork	1 teaspoon light soy sauce
1 ball preserved turnip	½ teaspoon salt or to taste
(optional)	½ teaspoon sugar

Preparation
Peel the melon. Slice lengthwise first, then into 1-inch pieces. Slice the pork across the grain into thin slices. Rinse the preserved turnip in cold water and cut into 1-inch slices.

Cooking
Bring the chicken stock to a boil. Add all the ingredients and boil for 10 minutes.

Yield: 6 servings.

MUSTARD CABBAGE SOUP

½ pound Chinese mustard cabbage	½ teaspoon dry sherry
	1 quart chicken stock
¼ pound lean beef	¼ teaspoon sugar
¼ teaspoon cornstarch	½ teaspoon salt or to taste
¼ teaspoon light soy sauce	2 slices gingerroot, the size of a
⅛ teaspoon sesame oil	quarter

Preparation

Slice the cabbage across the grain into pieces about 1 inch wide. Slice the beef into thin pieces ⅛ inch wide and 1½ inches long. In a bowl, combine the cornstarch, soy sauce, oil, and sherry. Marinate the beef strips in this mixture for 15 minutes.

Cooking

Bring the chicken stock to a boil. Add the cabbage. Lower heat to medium. Cover and simmer for 10 minutes. Add the sugar, salt, gingerroot, and beef. Stir to mix and remove from heat. The meat should cook to medium.

Yield: 6 servings.

FISH MAW SOUP

Fish maw is prized for its curiously spongy texture, but it has no taste to speak of—the ultimate texture food.

¼ pound fish maw	Dash of pepper
½ pound Chinese cabbage (*bok choy*)	½ teaspoon salt or to taste
	½ teaspoon light soy sauce
¼ pound pork	2 tablespoons minced Smithfield ham to garnish
1 quart chicken stock	

Preparation

Soak the fish maw in warm water for 3 hours. Drain. Simmer for 10 minutes. Drain. Rinse thoroughly in cold water and squeeze dry. Cut into 1-inch cubes.

Cut the cabbage into 2-inch lengths, including the green parts. Cut the pork into 1-inch cubes.

Cooking

Bring the chicken stock to a boil. Add all the ingredients except the ham. Cover and simmer for 30 minutes. Garnish with the ham and serve.

Yield: 6 servings.

FISH MAW SOUP WITH WINTER MELON

¼ pound fish maw
1 ball preserved turnip
½ pound winter melon
8 cups chicken stock
½ cup sliced pork

1 teaspoon light soy sauce
Dash of pepper
½ teaspoon salt or to taste
2 tablespoons minced Smithfield ham

Preparation

Soak the fish maw in warm water for 3 hours. Drain and cut into bite-size pieces of 1-inch cubes. Unroll the preserved turnip and rinse under running water to remove the excess salt. Remove the rind from the melon and cut into 1-inch cubes.

Cooking

Bring the chicken stock to a boil over high heat. Add all the ingredients. Cover and reduce heat. Simmer for 30 minutes.

Yield: 6 servings.

WINTER MELON POND

Winter Melon Pond is served only on special occasions or at banquets. The soup is cooked right inside the melon itself and it is served with the melon as the tureen.

½ pound water chestnuts
¼ pound bamboo shoots
16 Chinese black mushrooms
½ pound boned chicken breast
½ pound boned roast duck
⅛ pound Smithfield ham
1 winter melon, about 12
pounds

1 cup lotus seeds
¾ teaspoon salt or to taste
1 teaspoon sugar
1 can straw mushrooms
Water

Preparation

Dice the water chestnuts, bamboo shoots, mushrooms, chicken, duck, and ham in ½-inch cubes. Wash the outside of the melon. Cut across the top to the melon about 2 inches below the top to make a cover. Remove all the seeds but not the flesh itself. Put all the ingredients into the melon except the ham. Pour water in up to 1 inch from the top.

Cooking

Put the whole melon on a pan so it will not tip over. Place in a large steamer or in a large soup pot with a trivet of at least 2 inches in height. For easier removal later, make a sling around the melon using several lengths of twine. Cover the melon with the top that was cut off. Steam slowly for 3 hours or until the outer skin starts to become soft. Check the pot occasionally to make sure that there is enough water in the steamer. Garnish with the ham before serving.

Yield: 10 servings.

WINTER MELON SOUP

1 pound winter melon	2 tablespoons cornstarch
2 quarts chicken stock	mixed with ¼ cup water
1 teaspoon salt or to taste	⅛ pound minced Smithfield
¾ teaspoon sugar	ham

Preparation

Remove the seeds from the winter melon. Leave the rind on the melon and cut into 3-inch squares.

Cooking

Bring the chicken stock to a boil. Add the melon and boil for 40 minutes. Remove the melon. Scoop the meat from the rind and mash. Discard the rind. Return the mashed melon to the soup. Add the salt and sugar. Bring to a boil and stir in the cornstarch mixture. Garnish with the ham.

Yield: 10 servings.

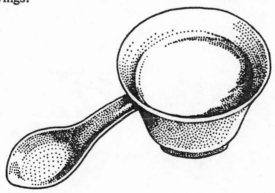

BIRD'S NEST SOUP

Bird's nest is a misnomer for this soup, because it is actually the secretions of the swallow which hold the nest together rather than the nest itself which are used. Bird's nest comes in dried form and is sold in boxes at Chinese groceries. It is another prized texture food.

1 cup bird's nest	½ teaspoon sugar
1 quart water	1 teaspoon cornstarch mixed
¼ pound boned chicken breast	with 3 tablespoons water
2 water chestnuts	1 egg white, beaten
½ cup water	2 tablespoons minced Smith-
1 quart chicken stock	field ham to garnish
½ teaspoon salt	

Preparation

Soak the bird's nest for 3 hours in cold water. Drain. Boil in 1 quart of water for 15 minutes. Drain the bird's nest and run cool water through it. Pick out all feathers and dirt. Mince the chicken, first with the sharp edge of the knife, then with the back of the knife so that it becomes very finely minced. Mince the water chestnuts. Add ½ cup water to the minced chicken and stir well with a fork. Remove the tendons. Drain the chicken to remove the excess water.

Cooking

Bring the chicken stock to a boil. Add the bird's nest, salt, sugar, and water chestnuts. Simmer for 15 minutes. Stir in the cornstarch mixture and remove from heat. Add the minced chicken. Add the egg white slowly while stirring the soup. Stir for 2 minutes. Garnish with the ham.

Yield: 6 servings.

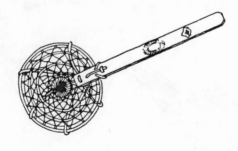

SHARK'S FIN SOUP

Shark's fin gives the soup a very interesting glutinous quality. Along with Bird's Nest Soup and Winter Melon Pond this is one of the great banquet treats.

4 ounces shark's fin (in one
   piece)
3 quarts warm water
4 slices gingerroot, the size of a
   half-dollar
2 scallions
2 quarts water
½ pound chicken breast, boned
   and skinned
1 egg white
1 tablespoon cornstarch

6 cups chicken stock
⅛ teaspoon white pepper
1 teaspoon light soy sauce
2 tablespoons soaked and
   diced Chinese black mushrooms
2 tablespoons cornstarch
   mixed with ¼ cup water
2 tablespoons finely shredded
   Smithfield ham to garnish

Preparation

Soak the shark's fin in cold water for at least 8 hours or overnight. Drain in a colander and then rinse. Wrap the shark's fin in cheesecloth and put it in a pot with 3 quarts warm water, 2 slices of the gingerroot, and 1 of the scallions. Bring to a boil. Simmer for 1½ hours. Turn off heat and allow to cool. Discard the liquid. Pick over the shark's fin to remove tough and dark pieces. Rinse the shark's fin and rewrap in cheesecloth. Put it in a pot with 2 quarts water, the remaining gingerroot, and the remaining scallion. Bring to a boil and then simmer for one hour. Drain off and discard the liquid. Rinse the shark's fin under cold water and set aside.

Shred the chicken breast into pieces 1½ inches long and ⅛ inch wide. Beat the egg white lightly. Using your fingers, blend the egg white with the chicken shreds and 1 tablespoon cornstarch.

Cooking

In a pot bring the chicken stock, shark's fin, pepper, and soy sauce to a boil. Reduce heat and simmer for 30 minutes. Add the chicken and mushrooms and cook for 5 minutes. Carefully stir in the cornstarch mixture to thicken. Serve in a tureen and garnish with the ham.

Yield: 8 servings.

ALMOND SOUP

Almond soup, a somewhat sweet creation, is usually served as the third and last soup (or dessert) of a classic Chinese banquet.

½ cup cooked rice	2 cups milk
½ cup canned almond paste	1 tablespoon sugar
2 cups water	¼ teaspoon almond extract

Preparation
In a blender, at low speed, mix the rice and almond paste. Blend until smooth. Blend the water into the mixture a little at a time. Pour into a mixing bowl. Stir in the milk.

Cooking
Cook the almond paste-milk mixture over medium heat and bring it just to the boiling point. Add the sugar and almond extract. Stir until the sugar has dissolved. Do not let the soup scorch. Serve warm.

Yield: 6-8 teacups

BASIC JOOK

What do the Chinese eat for breakfast? Well, in the south it is jook, *a bland porridge-like concoction livened up with whatever ingredients are on hand.*

1 cup raw rice	⅛ pound dried scallops or
3 quarts water	dried shrimp (optional)

Preparation
Wash the rice. Add the water and the scallops or shrimp.

Cooking
Bring to a boil. Reduce heat and simmer for 2 hours. If the *jook* is too thick, add water to thin to the consistency of oatmeal. Serve with chopped scallions and light soy sauce to season and give color to the dish.
If you happen to have a chicken carcass or cooked bones of any variety on hand, toss them in with the rice and water for additional flavor.

Yield: 6 servings.

FISH JOOK

½ pound fish fillet
2 tablespoons peanut oil
1 teaspoon salt
   Dash of pepper

1 teaspoon shredded gingerroot
2 teaspoons light soy sauce
1 tablespoon diced scallions

Preparation
   Prepare the *jook* following the Basic Jook recipe (above). Slice the fish into thin strips. Mix all of the ingredients together with the fish and then add to the hot simmering *jook*. Stir well and serve immediately.

Yield: 6 servings.

CHICKEN JOOK

½ pound boned chicken
1 teaspoon dry sherry
1 tablespoon peanut oil
½ teaspoon salt
¼ teaspoon sugar

   Dash of pepper
1 teaspoon light soy sauce
1 teaspoon shredded gingerroot

Preparation
   Prepare the *jook* following the Basic Jook recipe (above). Slice the chicken into 1½-inch squares. Mix all of the ingredients together with the chicken and then all to the hot simmering *jook*. Stir well and simmer for another 10 minutes.

Yield: 6 servings.

BEEF JOOK

½ pound ground beef
1 teaspoon dry sherry
1 teaspoon peanut oil
½ teaspoon salt
¼ teaspoon sugar

   Dash of pepper
2 teaspoons light soy sauce
1 teaspoon shredded gingerroot
½ teaspoon sesame oil

Preparation
   Prepare the *jook* following the Basic Jook recipe (above). Mix all of the

ingredients together with the beef and then add to the hot simmering *jook*. Stir well and simmer for another 5 minutes.

Yield: 6 servings.

SUBGUM FRIED RICE

1 egg
2 teaspoons dark soy sauce
¼ teaspoon sugar
   Dash of pepper
1 tablespoon peanut oil
½ teaspoon salt or to taste
¼ cup diced onions
¼ cup diced bean sprouts
2 tablespoons diced button
   mushrooms

2 tablespoons diced green bell
   pepper
⅛ cup diced tomatoes
¼ cup chicken stock or water
¼ cup diced Chinese roast pork
3 cups cooled cooked rice,
   preferably 1 day old

Preparation
Beat the egg. In a bowl combine the soy sauce, sugar, and pepper.

Cooking
Heat a wok or skillet over high heat until a drop of water immediately sizzles into steam. Add the oil and salt. Add the egg to the pan and scramble it. When the egg has cooked, break into 1-inch pieces with a spatula.

Add the vegetables and stir to coat them with the oil. Add the chicken stock. Stir for 45 seconds.

Add the pork, rice, and the soy sauce mixture. Break up the clumps of rice and stir-fry for 2 minutes.

Yield: 2–8 servings.

ROAST PORK LO MEIN

Throughout China, noodles are eaten at any time of day or night as a snack or light meal. The noodles can be boiled, pan-fried, or deep-fried. The sauce can be made separately or together with the noodles. Roast Pork Lo Mein makes an excellent lunch or midnight supper.

½ pound Chinese roast pork
1 cup bean sprouts
2 tablespoons oyster sauce
1 tablespoon light soy sauce
½ teaspoon sugar
   Dash of pepper

1 pound Chinese egg noodles
2 tablespoons peanut oil
¾ teaspoon salt
2 cups shredded Chinese cabbage (*bok choy*)
¼ cup water

Preparation
Shred the pork into pieces approximately the same size as the bean sprouts. In a small bowl combine the oyster sauce, soy sauce, sugar, and pepper.

Cooking
Bring a large pot of water to a rolling boil. Add the noodles and boil until the noodles have reached the *al dente* stage. Drain under running water to stop cooking.

Heat a wok or skillet over high heat until a drop of water immediately sizzles into steam. Add the oil and salt. Just before the oil begins to smoke, add the cabbage, bean sprouts, and the pork. Stir-fry for 2 minutes. Add the water. Add the noodles and mix with the contents of the pan. Cover and cook for 2 minutes longer. Add the oyster sauce mixture and stir to mix.

Note: ½ pound of boiled chicken breast, cooked shrimp, or roast duck may be substituted for the roast pork.

Yield: 4–6 servings.

NOODLES WITH CHINESE CHIVES AND ROAST PORK

1 pound Chinese egg noodles
½ pound Chinese chives
½ pound Chinese roast pork
3 eggs
1 teaspoon sesame oil
1 teaspoon sugar

1 tablespoon dry sherry
3 tablespoons dark soy sauce
1 tablespoon light soy sauce
¼ cup sesame seeds to garnish
1 tablespoon peanut oil
½ teaspoon salt

Preparation

Boil the noodles for 10 minutes or until they have reached the *al dente* stage. Drain in a colander under running water.

Wash the chives thoroughly. Cut off and discard the roots. Chop the chives into 2-inch pieces. Shred the pork.

Beat the eggs in a bowl and scramble them until firm over medium heat. Cut the cooked eggs into 1-inch squares.

In a small bowl combine the sesame oil, sugar, sherry, and soy sauce.

Toast the sesame seeds in a dry pan over moderate heat for 5 minutes or until the seeds are fragrant and browned slightly. Shake the pan as you are toasting the seeds to keep them from sticking to the pan and burning.

Cooking

Heat a wok or skillet over high heat until a drop of water immediately sizzles into steam. Maintain high heat throughout the cooking process. Add the peanut oil and salt. Stir. Just before the oil begins to smoke, add the chives and the pork. Stir-fry for 1½ minutes. Add the cooked noodles, eggs, and the soy sauce mixture. Mix well over high heat for 3 minutes.

Place in a serving platter and garnish with the sesame seeds.

Yield: 4–6 servings.

THREE-FLAVORED NOODLES

This dish is a favorite in Chinatown's noodle shops as a midnight snack. Hot, sweet, and tart, it is much appreciated after an evening of bridge or Mah-Jongg.

½ pound Chinese egg noodles	½ teaspoon light soy sauce
2 medium onions	1 teaspoon hoisin sauce
1 tomato	4 tablespoons curry powder
½ cup ketchup	¼ cup shedded Chinese roast
½ teaspoon salt	pork (optional)
½ teaspoon sugar	½ cup chicken stock or water
⅛ teaspoon pepper	

Preparation

Boil the noodles until they have reached the *al dente* stage. Rinse them in a colander under running water.

Cut the onions in half, then into thin slices. Cut the tomato into wedges ¼ inch thick. In a small bowl combine the ketchup, salt, sugar, pepper, soy sauce, and hoisin sauce.

Cooking

Place the onions with the curry powder on top in a wok over medium low heat. Toast the curry powder for 2 minutes or until pungent, stirring occasionally to keep the curry powder from burning.

Add the roast pork and chicken stock. Turn the heat to high and bring the liquid to a boil while stirring. Add the ketchup and hoisin mixture. Add the tomato. Stir well to mix the ingredients and blend the flavors.

To serve, pour the sauce over the noodles and blend thoroughly.

Yield: 2–4 servings.

CANTONESE EGG ROLLS

	Oil for deep-frying	8	cooked shrimp
6	tablespoons shredded bamboo shoots	½	teaspoon sugar
			Dash of pepper
3	tablespoons shredded water chestnuts	½	teaspoon salt
		4	egg roll skins
3	tablespoons shredded celery	1	egg, beaten
6	tablespoons shredded Chinese roast pork		

Cooking

Heat a wok or skillet over high heat until a drop of water immediately sizzles into steam. Add 2 tablespoons of the oil. Just before the oil begins to smoke add all the ingredients except the egg roll skins, beaten egg, and oil for deep-frying. Stir-fry for 3 minutes. Remove from heat and allow to cool.

Following the diagram on page 254, place one quarter of the mixture in the center of each egg roll skin and fold over two sides. Roll and seal the end with beaten egg. Deep-fry in the oil heated to 375 degrees until the egg rolls have turned a deep rich brown. Serve with hoisin sauce.

Yield: 4–8 servings.

EGG ROLL OR WONTON SKINS

2	cups sifted all-purpose flour	1	egg, beaten
½	teaspoon salt	2	cups water

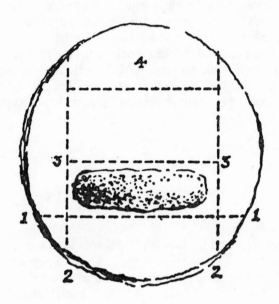

Preparation

Combine the flour and salt. Combine the egg and the water. Gradually add the flour to the water, stirring to blend well.

Cooking

Heat a lightly greased skillet over medium high heat. (Use a small skillet for wontons or a large one for egg roll skins.) Add a small amount of batter to the pan and swirl it around to coat the bottom thinly. Pour back any excess batter. Reduce heat to medium low and cook until the skin can be removed easily from the pan without tearing. It should not be allowed to brown. If this happens, lower heat to medium and the second cooking heat to low.

Repeat this process until all the skins, about one dozen, have been made. If you wish to speed things up, use 2 or 3 pans simultaneously. The skins should be stored under a damp cloth until they are filled to keep them from drying out. They may also be frozen.

Yield: 1 dozen egg roll skins.
        2 dozen wonton skins.

SHU MEI

These may be served as hors d'oeuvres or with some of the other pastries as a Chinese brunch.

½ pound ground pork	½ teaspoon salt or to taste
3 tablespoons cornstarch	2 teaspoons light soy sauce
8 water chestnuts, minced	½ teaspoon sugar
¼ cup minced bamboo shoots	1 teaspoon sesame oil
¼ cup minced Chinese roast	Dash of pepper
pork or boiled ham	1 tablespoon dry sherry

Wrapping
1 dozen wonton skins

Preparation
Mix all the ingredients together. Place a wonton on the palm of your hand. With a butter knife spread the mixture thinly and evenly over the skin. Gently stand the butterknife perpendicular at the center of the skin. Bring the skin around the knife by closing your hand gently around the blade. With your fingers pleat the skin around the filling to form an open-topped pouch. Remove the knife. Smooth the top of the filling with the butterknife. Repeat process until all of the dumplings have been filled.

Cooking
Steam for 20 minutes in a covered steamer. Serve with hoisin sauce. Leftovers, if any, may be frozen for future use.

Yield: 1 dozen dumplings.

CANTONESE STEAMED DUMPLINGS

These delicate dumplings have a wonderful, almost transparent skin. The difference in the way they are wrapped tells whether they have a shrimp or pork filling. The recipe below provides enough dough to wrap both the shrimp and the pork fillings.

1 pound wheat starch	4 cups boiling water or as
⅓ pound tapioca starch	needed
(approximately 1 cup)	Peanut oil to grease hands

Preparation

Cook the fillings for the dumplings first, and while they are cooling, prepare the wrappers according to the directions that follow.

Mix the wheat starch and tapioca starch together. Add the boiling water while stirring. The result should be a stiff, sticky, almost gelatinous-looking mixture.

Grease a board and your hands with peanut oil. As soon as you can bear the heat, knead the still very hot dough vigorously. Oil your hands as needed to keep the dough from sticking excessively to your hands. Knead 7 minutes or until the dough is quite smooth and elastic.

Divide the dough into 4 pieces. Cover 3 of them with a damp cloth to keep them from drying out. Roll the remaining piece out into a long sausage. Divide the sausage in half. Roll each sausage into a longer sausage about 1 inch thick. Cut off about 1 inch of the sausage and roll it into a ball. This ball is to be pressed into very thin round pancakes 3 or 3½ inches in diameter, depending upon the filling you are using (see Assembly section of the filling recipes).

There are four ways you can press the balls into very thin pancakes which, after steaming, seem almost translucent. The traditional method is to oil the side of a Chinese cleaver to "iron" out the ball into a circle with two or three swipes of the blade. This does take practice, but once one gets the hang of it, it is a quick way of accomplishing this task. The second way to press the pancakes is to use a tortilla press, the surface of which has been well oiled. Lest you laugh, this is a popular method in New York's Chinatown and probably other Chinatowns as well. It is a fast method that produces perfect thin circles. The third method is to use a 1-inch dowel as a rolling pin. The fourth is to use the heel of your hand.

As you finish completing the wrappers from 1 sausage of dough fill them following the directions in the Assembly section of each filling recipe. Then steam them over rapidly boiling water for 10 minutes. The dumplings may then be frozen. If you do freeze them, separate them from each other with waxed paper to keep them from sticking together. To defrost, put them in the steamer. Whether fresh or frozen, they should be served hot.

Yield: about 100 wrappers.

PORK CANTONESE STEAMED DUMPLINGS

3 large Chinese black mushrooms
3 scallions
¼ cup diced Chinese roast pork
¼ cup finely minced water
chestnuts
¼ cup finely minced bamboo
shoots
⅛ teaspoon white pepper

1 teaspoon sugar
1½ teaspoons light soy sauce
1 tablespoon peanut oil
½ teaspoon salt or to taste
2 teaspoons minced garlic
¾ pound ground pork
2 teaspoons cornstarch mixed
with 1 tablespoon water

Preparation

Soak the mushrooms in water for 30 minutes or until soft. Discard the tough stems and mince the mushrooms finely. Mince the scallions.

Set aside in a bowl the roast pork, water chestnuts, bamboo shoots, mushrooms, pepper, sugar, and soy sauce.

Cooking

Heat a wok or skillet over high heat until a drop of water immediately sizzles into steam. Maintain high heat throughout the cooking process. Add the oil, salt, and garlic. Stir for about 30 seconds or until the odor of the garlic has become pungent. Add the ground pork and stir-fry for 1½ minutes.

Add the remaining ingredients except the cornstarch mixture and scallions. Stir thoroughly. Cover and cook for 2 to 3 minutes until the pork is done.

Uncover and stir in the cornstarch mixture for 15 seconds or until the filling has thickened. Remove from heat and sprinkle with the minced scallions. Allow the mixture to come to room temperature before wrapping the dumplings.

Assembly

Take one wrapper about 3½ inches in diameter and place a heaping teaspoon of the filling in the middle of it. Make certain not to allow any of the oil to drop on the edges of the wrapper, for this makes a good seal impossible. Fold the wrapper in half and seal the edges together to form a half circle. If you wish, ruffle the edges by holding the edge between your thumb and index finger and moving them as if snapping your fingers.

Another decorative edge can be created by pinching over the edge working from right to left. Each pinch should overlap the preceding pinch slightly to create a braided effect.

Final cooking
Steam over rapidly boiling water for 10 minutes.

Yield: Enough for about 75 dumplings.

SHRIMP CANTONESE STEAMED DUMPLINGS

1 pound small shrimp (about 30 to 35 shrimp)
2 scallions
1 tablespoon dry sherry
2 teaspoons light soy sauce
½ teaspoon sugar
⅛ teaspoon white pepper

1 teaspoon sesame oil
1 tablespoon peanut oil
½ teaspoon salt or to taste
1 tablespoon minced garlic
2 teaspoons cornstarch mixed with 1 tablespoon water

Preparation
Shell and devein the shrimp. Place them in a bowl. Slice the scallions into ¼-inch lengths and add to the shrimp. Add the sherry, soy sauce, sugar, pepper, and sesame oil to the shrimp. Mix thoroughly.

Cooking
Heat a wok or skillet over high heat until a drop of water immediately sizzles into steam. Maintain high heat throughout the cooking process. Add the peanut oil, salt, and garlic. Stir for about 30 seconds or until the odor of the garlic has become pungent. Add the shrimp mixture. Stir-fry for 1 minute or until the shrimp are cooked as indicated by a pinkish color. Stir in the cornstarch mixture for 15 seconds to thicken. Allow the mixture to come to room temperature before wrapping the dumplings.

Assembly
Take one wrapper about 3 inches in diameter and place it in your left hand. Put one shrimp in the middle of the wrapper. Make a deep pleat in the right-hand side of the wrapper with the excess dough going to the inside. About ¼ of the wrapper should be taken up in this first pleat, and the wrapper should now be in the shape of a scoop. Starting from the right on the far side, make five or more small pleats until only a small hole remains. Press the pleated surface to the unpleated surface and twist the ends of this sealed section to form a Dutch cap. Care should be taken that none of the sauce from the shrimp falls on the edge of the wrapper because this will prevent a good seal. Left-handed people, of course, should reverse this process.

Final Cooking
Steam over rapidly boiling water for 10 minutes.

Yield: Enough for 30 dumplings.

CANTONESE STEAMED FILLED BUNS

Filled steamed buns are extremely good. If you find kneading dough tedious, another solution is given at the end of this recipe. It is a guiltily traded secret in America's Chinatowns. Do, however, try it from scratch if you have the time.

½ package active dry yeast	3½ cups sifted all-purpose flour
¼ cup sugar	1 tablespoon chilled lard
1 cup lukewarm water	

Preparation
   Combine the yeast, 1 tablespoon of the sugar, and ¼ cup of the lukewarm water. Set aside.
   In a large bowl stir together the flour and the remaining sugar. Add the lard and blend well. Slowly add the yeast mixture to the flour, stirring well. Then add the remaining lukewarm water, blending well. The resulting dough will be stiff and slightly sticky.
   Turn the dough out on a lightly floured surface and knead for 5 minutes or until the dough becomes smooth and elastic. If the dough sticks to the board, give the board another light dusting of flour. During this exercise it is helpful to rub a little peanut oil into one's hands to keep the dough from sticking too badly.
   Roll the dough into a ball and put it in a clean bowl. Cover the bowl with a warm, slightly damp dish towel and place it to rise in a warm place away from drafts for 1½ to 2 hours.
   If you are planning to fill the buns, begin preparing the filling at this time.
   When the dough has doubled in bulk, punch it down with your fist to deflate it. Re-cover the bowl with the towel and set it aside to rise for another ½ hour.
   When the dough has again doubled in size, remove it to the lightly floured board and knead it some more. Roll the dough into a long, sausagelike roll about 2 inches in diameter. With a knife, slice the roll to obtain enough dough to make little balls about 2 inches in diameter.
   To fill the buns, take a ball of dough and flatten it between the palms of

your hands. Place a heaping teaspoon of filling (see below) in the center and then gather up the edges of the dough to meet at the top like a pouch. Twist the top of the bun to seal it. Place each bun on a 2-inch square of waxed paper and set it aside to rise for ½ hour.

Cooking
    Steam the buns for 15 minutes over rapidly boiling water. Do not crowd the steamer for the buns will expand slightly. Serve hot.

    Note: If time is short, a reasonable although not perfect facsimile of this dough can be devised by using frozen Parkerhouse rolls, following the instructions on the bag, and steaming them rather than baking them. The main difference will be that the texture of the frozen rolls will not be as fine as the ones made from scratch.

Yield: About 20 buns.

ROAST PORK FILLING FOR STEAMED BUNS

½ pound Chinese roast pork
1 tablespoon brown bean
  sauce
3 tablespoons sugar
2 tablespoons light soy sauce
½ teaspoon red bean curd
  (optional)

2 tablespoons peanut oil
½ teaspoon salt or to taste
1 tablespoon minced garlic
4 tablespoons chopped scallions
2 teaspoons cornstarch mixed
  with ¼ cup water

Preparation
    Dice the pork into ¼-inch cubes. Mash the brown bean sauce. Mix together the brown bean sauce, sugar, soy sauce, and red bean curd. Set aside.

Cooking
    Heat a wok or skillet over high heat until a drop of water immediately sizzles into steam. Maintain high heat throughout the cooking process. Add the oil and salt to the pan and spread around. Just before the oil begins to smoke, add the roast pork and stir for 30 seconds. Add the garlic and scallions and stir-fry for 15 seconds or until the odor of the garlic becomes pungent. Add the brown bean sauce mixture and stir briefly. Add the cornstarch mixture and stir until thickened. Remove from heat and let the mixture cool to room temperature before filling the buns.

Yield: Filling for 20 buns.

CHICKEN FILLING FOR STEAMED BUNS

½ pound boned chicken breast
1 egg white
2 tablespoons minced water chestnuts
2 tablespoons minced bamboo shoots
2 tablespoons chopped scallions

1 tablespoon sesame oil
1 teaspoon sugar
1 tablespoon light soy sauce
2 tablespoons dry sherry
1 tablespoon peanut oil
½ teaspoon salt

Preparation

Mince the chicken finely and mix with the egg white. Combine the water chestnuts, bamboo shoots, and scallions. Set aside. Combine the sesame oil, sugar, soy sauce, and sherry. Set aside.

Cooking

Heat a wok or skillet over high heat until a drop of water immediately sizzles into steam. Maintain high heat throughout the cooking process. Add the peanut oil and salt to the pan and spread around. Just before the oil begins to smoke, add the chicken and stir-fry for one minute. Add the vegetables and stir for a second before adding the sesame oil mixture. Stir-fry for 2 minutes. Remove from heat and let the mixture cool to room temperature before filling the buns.

Yield: Filling for 20 buns.

SESAME FILLING FOR STEAMED BUNS

In China this filling would be made with sesame paste. The combination of peanut butter and sesame seeds is virtually identical in taste and a lot easier to find.

2 tablespoons sesame paste or smooth peanut butter
1 tablespoon sesame seeds, untoasted

1 tablespoon sugar
2 teaspoons peanut oil

Preparation

Mix all the ingredients together quite thoroughly.

Yield: Filling for 6-8 buns.

CURRIED PORK FILLING FOR BUNS

This bun is baked rather than steamed—an anomaly.

1 medium onion	1½ teaspoons light soy sauce
1 teaspoon dry sherry	2 tablespoons curry powder
1 teaspoon sugar	½ pound ground pork
2 tablespoons water	

Preparation
Dice the onion into ¼-inch cubes. Combine the sherry, sugar, water, and soy sauce.

Cooking
Over medium heat toast the diced onion in a dry pan for 2 minutes. Add the curry powder and stir until the smell of the curry powder has become pungent. Add the pork and stir-fry for 2 minutes. Add the soy sauce mixture and stir well for ½ minute. Remove from heat and let the mixture cool to room temperature before filling the buns.

Fill the buns as described in the recipe for Steamed Buns but do not steam them. Instead, bake them in a 425-degree oven for 10 minutes or until nicely browned.

Yield: Filling for 20 buns.

STEAMED ROLLS

These rolls are easily made by following the recipe for Cantonese Filled Buns until you reach the point of filling the buns. At this step, take one of the balls of dough and flatten it between the palms of your hands. Brush the top lightly with sesame oil and fold it in half with the oiled side together. Allow the rolls to rise for 30 minutes and then steam over rapidly boiling water for 10 or 15 minutes. Serve the buns hot with Szechwan Duck or Mongolian Hot Pot.

CHINESE COOKING AT HOME

THIS and the following section were written with both the beginning and the advanced cook in mind. They offer guidance on equipment and cooking utensils, information on menu planning, cooking techniques, serving a meal in a correct Chinese manner, and a detailed list of ingredients used in Chinese cooking including substitutions and equivalents.

The average American kitchen, with its many gadgets and utensils, is well suited for Chinese cooking. However, a few comments may help in successfully translating Chinese cooking to American kitchens.

The Stove

In Chinese cooking intense heat is required for stir-frying. Unfortunately, burners on kitchen ranges seem to be getting smaller every year and many of the newer stoves do not seem to give off as much heat as they should. Although there is not much one can do about an electric stove whose "high" should be higher, with a gas stove one can investigate the possibility that the gas line into the stove can be opened wider. Your local gas company can tell you whether this is possible. A gas range is preferred for Chinese cooking because heat recovery is more rapid after ingredients have been added to the pan and because of the speed with which one can adjust cooking temperatures when needed.

Pots and Pans

While the wok is the basic cooking vessel in China, it is not essential to successful Chinese cooking. In fact, a wok cannot be used successfully on an electric stove because its rounded bottom only barely touches the hot coils and cannot be heated to a high enough temperature. An alternative to a wok in such a case would be a 12-inch skillet, preferably the cast-iron variety Grandmother used and loved. Cast iron is preferred to the thinner stainless steel and aluminum skillets because of its ability to withstand very high heat without developing annoying hot spots. Also, when well seasoned it develops the nonstick quality of Teflon but without Teflon's vulnerability to high temperatures.

If you would like to experiment with a wok on a gas range, woks are now sold in most department stores and gourmet shops as well as in Chinese groceries and gift stores. They generally cost no more than a good saucepan and are fun to use.

Woks come in a variety of sizes from about one foot across to about three feet in diameter. A 12- or 14-inch wok would be the most useful size for most of the recipes in this book. Woks are made in a variety of metals including stainless steel, aluminum, and iron. The iron variety is preferred for the same reasons that we also recommend cast-iron skillets. The wok comes with a high cover and a ring that supports the wok on top of the stove. Some rings do not have enough holes to allow sufficient oxygen to feed the hot flame. In such cases it is advisable to cut additional holes or enlarge the existing holes with a pair of metal cutters. Electric woks are also on the market, and although we have heard of a few skilled cooks mastering them, they generally create more problems than they solve, for they do not provide the instantaneous control of a gas stove and one cannot remove the pan from the slow dying heat source as one can when using a skillet on an electric stove.

To season a new iron wok or skillet, wash it well, dry it, and then rub the surfaces well with peanut or other vegetable oil. Put the pan over medium heat until the oil begins to smoke. Repeat this process one or two times more and the pan will be sufficiently well seasoned to cook with. After each use, wash the pan, rinse, and then put it over moderate heat to dry thoroughly. As time goes on, the pan will darken from gray to black and its nonstick characteristics will become more pronounced. Unfortunately, cast iron rusts if one is not careful, although as the pan becomes increasingly well seasoned this is less and less of a problem. If the pan develops rusty spots, use steel wool to remove them, and then re-season the pan as you would a new one. This is the only time when one should use steel wool or any strong abrasive on a seasoned surface. Should any food stick to its surface, soak the pan for a few minutes and the food will come off easily.

The one item that most kitchens lack and which must be either purchased or improvised for Chinese cooking is a steamer. Basically all you need is something that will hold a heatproof dish over boiling water. If you have a wok, you might want to buy one or two bamboo or aluminum steamers with a lid from a Chinese grocery or hardware store. You might also prefer to improvise by wedging a pair of chopsticks into the wok to keep the dish above the boiling water and using the high wok cover as a lid. A round cake rack in a wok provides an even more secure way to support the dish.

If you don't have a wok, complete aluminum steamers in varying sizes can be purchased in Chinese hardware stores. These, unfortunately, are rather expensive, and unless you plan to do a great deal of steaming are probably not worth buying. On the other hand, just about everybody has a spaghetti pot with a lid that can serve as a makeshift steamer by the addition of something to raise the dish above the boiling water. This can be a tin can with both the top and bottom removed, a French vegetable steamer, an inverted custard cup—almost anything will do.

Knives

The careful cutting, slicing, and chopping of ingredients is one of the most distinctive elements of Chinese cooking.. Unlike other cuisines, where most of the time consumed is in the cooking of a dish, much of Chinese food preparation is based on the careful and often lengthy assembling and cutting of ingredients followed by a relatively brief cooking period. If you are going to do much Chinese cooking at all, it is important that you have razor-sharp knives that will cut evenly without mashing the food and with a minimum of effort on your part. One way to test the sharpness of your knives is on a naturally ripe tomato; if you can rest the blade of your knife on the tomato and little more than the weight of the knife will cut through the skin, then your knife is as sharp as it should be.

Knives made of carbon steel are the best if you want a really sharp edge, for they sharpen quite readily, unlike stainless steel which is almost impossible to sharpen satisfactorily. Carbon steel is also much more rigid than stainless steel so that the knife is easier to control when cutting precisely. The only disadvantage is that carbon steel rusts very easily and such knives must be dried immediately after being used, but this is a small price to pay for superb service.

The versatility of the rectangular Chinese cleaver is remarkable. It is truly the equivalent of a drawer full of knives and despite its unwiedy appearance can perform just about any cutting chore. We use ou. cleaver constantly. Its broad side is perfect for hammering veal scallops to the appropriate thinness. Its rigidity makes it the perfect instrument for the precision slicing required, for example, in preparing *pommes de terre soufflés*. The handle serves as a pestle, the blunt top as a meat tenderizer. Once in a long while a small paring knife is needed, for example, to core an apple, but that is the only other cutting instrument we use. A medium-size French chef's knife is almost as versatile as the cleaver, although it lacks the broad blade to carry the ingredients to the pan and a few other features which endear the cleaver to the Chinese cook. If you have a French chef's knife by all means sharpen it up and use it. If you don't have one, consider buying a Chinese cleaver in carbon steel, not stainless. They can be bought in department stores, Chinese groceries, and just about anywhere cooking utensils are sold.

The best instrument to sharpen your cleaver or chef's knife is a honing stone that can be purchased at hardware stores which stock them for sharpening tools. They are generally about two inches wide and six inches long. They have a coarse side and a fine side. Bring the stone home; take out your knives to be sharpened. Moisten the stone with water, hold the knife almost parallel to the stone and rub it back and forth several times. Turn the knife over and repeat on the other side. Repeat the procedure until the edge is sharp, moistening the stone when it dries out. It may take as long as five minutes to get an acceptable edge on a really dull knife. Once it is razor-sharp, give the edge a brief brush-up on the fine side of the honing stone every now and then to maintain the edge. Chefs in Chinese restaurants habitually hone their knives at off moments. It is a good habit to develop.

Methods of Cutting
The Chinese use several different methods of cutting up meats and vegetables. In the recipes you will find that if the meat for a particular dish is to be sliced into long strips, then the vegetables will also be of the same shape. If you are using a Chinese cleaver, you should grip the top with the thumb and index finger while the rest of the fingers wrap themselves comfortably around the handle. This grip gives excellent control of the knife.

(1) Slicing
Straight slicing is normally used for meats and vegetables such as mushrooms, scallions, and other fleshy and fibrous vegetables. Meat is always cut against the grain; i.e., at right angles to the direction of the fibers, and usually into pieces ⅛ inch thick. If this degree of thinness is difficult to achieve with meat, try partially freezing it.

Diagonal slicing is used for slicing vegetables such as Chinese cabbage and other stalklike vegetables so that a larger area will be exposed to the heat in cooking and in absorbing flavors. Generally the slices are ⅛ inch thick by ½ inch by 1½ inches.

Rolling slicing is an optional way of cutting cylindrical vegetables. First, you cut the vegetable diagonally. Then you give the vegetable a quarter turn and make another diagonal cut which slightly overlaps the surface exposed by the last cut. Continue turning and slicing until the vegetable has been reduced to small faceted pieces.

(2) Shredding
This term usually applies to the cutting of gingerroot although one also comes across the term in the slicing of meat. For gingerroot this means careful slicing into long thin pieces no larger than a matchstick and the more narrowly cut the better. For meat or scallions a little more leeway is allowed, but the matchstick analogy still obtains. It is almost impossible to match these specifications unless the meat is half frozen.

(3) Dicing

The meat or vegetable is cut into little cubes varying from ½ to ⅛ inch depending on the dish.

(4) Chopping, Grinding, and Mincing

Chopping is little more than very fine dicing with the end result resembling hamburger. Indeed, for meat you can use a meat grinder and for vegetables you can use an electric blender. The Chinese, however, feel that ground meat has a very different texture from meat that has been chopped up by hand using two cleavers at the same time to expedite matters. We agree that there is a difference, but feel that in all but a few cases the convenience of ground meat outweighs the noticeably smoother texture achieved by hand chopping. However, we suggest that you try hand chopping at least once. Mincing is little more than very fine chopping.

Organization

Since Chinese cooking is often "quick cooking," good organization is essential. A difference in one or two minutes in cooking time may mean that your food will come out overcooked, soft, soggy, and tasteless. You will realize how fast the seconds tick away as your dish is cooking when you suddenly discover that one of your ingredients has not been cut yet or as you try to find the bottle opener for the soy sauce.

After you have finished preparing the meat and vegetables, place in one dish all the ingredients that will be added to the pan at the same time. It is also helpful to arrange all your ingredients near the stove in the order in which they go into the pan. A final review of the list of ingredients will insure that nothing is left out.

Stir-frying

Many Chinese dishes are prepared by methods common to Western cooking, such as deep-frying, sautéing, poaching, and roasting, and it is not necessary for us to go into a lengthy description of them. However, the techniques involved in stir-frying—particularly meat with vegetable dishes—are quite unlike anything found in the Western world.

In stir-frying the most important thing to remember is that the pan must be very, very hot throughout the cooking process unless the recipe specifically directs otherwise. When ingredients are added there should always be loud crackling, hissing, popping, and a great poof of steam. It takes a while for the Western cook not to be alarmed by all this noise and steam and to realize that the more noise and steam there is, the more likely the dish will possess the highly desirable quality the Chinese call *wok hai* or "flavor of the wok." The Western cook must also guard against the premature addition of liquids or other ingredients to lower the temperature of the pan until it is time to do so. Only the beginning of demonstrable burning should hasten the adding of liquid. Above all, resist any impulse to turn down the heat. In desperation, it is better to remove the pan completely from the heat until it has cooled to an acceptable level and then return it to the still high heat source.

The basic process for stir-frying meats and vegetables is really quite simple and logical. First the pan is heated until it is quite hot, and then the oil is added along with any ingredients, usually salt, garlic, or gingerroot which will flavor the oil. Stir the seasonings to brown them in the hot oil until the oil is just about to start smoking or, in the case of the garlic, until its odor has become pungent. At this point the meat should be added and tossed rapidly in the hot oil to seal in the juices. The meat is always cooked before the vegetables because the moisture in the vegetables would remain in the pan and toughen the meat. If the meat sticks to the pan, add a little more oil, letting it flow down the sides of the wok or pouring it directly onto the hot metal on the bottom of a skillet so that the fresh oil has been warmed when it hits the meat. If liquid seasoning is to be added to the meat, it should be done only after the meat is almost half cooked, for if it is added before then, the meat will toughen. When the meat is almost completely cooked, it is removed to a warm dish.

If needed, more oil is then added to the pan and heated along with any seasonings for the oil. When the oil has just about reached the point of smoking, begin to add the vegetables starting with the toughest ones which will take the longest to cook, for example, onions, Chinese cabbage, or celery. Stir them well to coat them with oil. After 15 seconds or so, add chicken stock or water if needed to keep them from burning, cover them, and let them steam. Some vegetables like spinach actually contain so much water that the addition of water or chicken stock is unnecessary. When the vegetables are almost done, the cover is removed, the meat is returned to the pan, stirred, and any remaining seasoning is added. If there is any sauce to be thickened, a well-mixed solution of cornstarch and water should be added to the pan and stirred until the sauce has thickened to the desired degree.

Green vegetables are cooked correctly when they have reached their height of color and have not yet begun to yellow. They should be definitely crisp but not raw to the taste.

Basic Vegetables

Although we have included many vegetable recipes in this book, each has been chosen for being in some way unusual. The following is a basic recipe for stir-frying most vegetables as an accompaniment to a more elaborate meat dish. It cannot be classified northern, southern, eastern, or western—only Chinese. It works well for thinly sliced broccoli, asparagus, carrots, celery, or any stalky vegetable. It also works well with cut green beans and bean sprouts.

STIR-FRIED CHINESE CABBAGE

1 pound Chinese cabbage (*bok choy*)	¼ cup chicken stock
	¼ teaspoon sugar
2 tablespoons peanut oil	Dash of pepper
½ teaspoon salt or to taste	
1 slice gingerroot, the size of a quarter	

Wash the cabbage. Slice diagonally. Heat a wok or skillet over high heat until a drop of water immediately sizzles into steam. Add oil, salt, and gingerroot. Stir for 30 seconds. Add the cabbage and stir-fry for 1 minute. Add the chicken stock, sugar, and pepper. Cover for 1½ minutes. Uncover and stir-fry for 15 seconds.

Yield: 4–6 servings.

BOILED RICE

Rice is the staff of life for all in China. It is not difficult to make using this method. If you like softer rice add a bit more water.

Measure ½ cup long-grain rice for each person. Wash the rice by rinsing and rubbing it between the palms until the water remains clear. Drain. In a pot add 1½ cups water for each cup of rice. Bring to a boil. Boil about five minutes until most of the visible water has evaporated and you can see air holes on top of the rice. Cover and simmer over low heat for 20 minutes.

RICE CRUSTS

Follow the preceding recipe for boiled rice, but use at least 2 cups of raw rice. Instead of simmering for 20 minutes, add an additional 15 minutes which will create a crust on the bottom of the pot. Serve the boiled rice. Allow the crust to cool and break it into 2-inch pieces. They will keep for weeks in a plastic bag kept in a cool spot. Just before serving, deep-fry the rice crusts in vegetable oil heated to 375 degrees for 3 to 5 minutes until they are golden brown. Drain the excess oil from the rice crusts on paper towels or in a colander. Bring to the table at once. Pour the soup or other dish that it is to be served with over the rice crusts.

Tea

Among the Chinese, tea is drunk at all times of the day. No social call or business meeting begins without the host serving tea. It is said that there is a kind of tea for every season of the year and every mood. In summer green teas are raised in the mountains, and flower teas are preferred, while in winter the heavier black teas are used. It is said that jasmine tea enhances the pleasure of reading poetry, while oolong stimulates conversation with new friends. A light green tea such as Silver Needles complements the pleasure of renewing old friendships.

To enjoy tea in the Chinese manner, a few simple rules must be followed. It must be remembered that tea is a very delicate herb. Exposure

NAME	PROVINCE	TYPE	SERVED
Black Dragon	Canton	Black	Served with the evening meal
Clear Distance	Canton	Black	For late at night
*Chrysanthe-mum	Chekiang	Dragon Well and Flowers	Mix with rock sugar and drink with Chinese pastry after meals
Cloud Mist	Kiangsi	Green	Serve in afternoon or teatime
Dragon Beard	Canton	Green	Pastime drink, afternoon, listening to music
*Dragon Well	Chinkiang	Green	Among the finest green teas, serve day and night
*Eyebrows of Longevity	Canton	Green	Serve in the garden on a spring afternoon
Fragrant Petals	Chinkiang	Green	Serve at home when entertaining relatives or close friends
*Hung Cha	Fukien	Black	Tea "served" at the Boston Tea Party. Most common at teahouses in China, restaurants in America
Iron Kuan Yin	Fukien	Black	Served as fine brandy. Produced by Buddhist monks
Iron Lo Han	Fukien	Black	
*Jasmine	Taiwan	Oolong and Flowers	For reading poetry with your love
*Keemun	Kiangsu	Black	Playing chess
*Lo Cha	Taiwan	Oolong	Conversation
*Lychee	Taiwan	Oolong and Lychee Flowers	Served to renew friendship
Ning Chow	Canton	Black	To begin the day, before breakfast
*Silver Needle	Canton	Green	Ideal for banquets
Su Tang	Fukien	Black	For a winter evening
Water Nymph	Canton	Green	Light tea, midmorning
Woo Lung	Chekiang	Black	Most popular at public teahouses, with talk of the day
Wu-I	Yunnan	Black	To cure a cold

to air will cause it to lose its flavor. Therefore it must be kept in a container with a tight lid. It is at its best when freshly opened and should not be kept indefinitely.

The pot and cups should be used only for brewing tea. These implements must be thoroughly clean but never washed with soap. A low round ceramic pot should be used. A metal pot might distort the flavor, and a tall pot allows too small an area of tea leaves to be exposed to the water and the tea will not steep properly. Both the pot and cups should be scalded before the tea is brewed.

The proper amount of tea depends on the kind of tea used and must be determined by trial and error. Since the Chinese prefer a pale golden infusion with subtle favor, only one heaping teaspoon of tea for each pot is used in brewing most popular teas. The water should be freshly drawn and poured on the tea leaves just at the moment it reaches a rolling boil. Boiling for a longer time will drive too much oxygen out of the water and the tea will have a flat taste. The tea should steep from 3 to 5 minutes.

Once the first pot of tea is drunk, add a few new leaves and brew a second pot. Experts consider the second infusion to be superior to the first.

Although it is impossible to list every variety of Chinese tea, this list includes some of the most popular. At present some of these are in short supply, but those starred are generally available. With each tea is listed a pastime which, according to custom, the tea will enhance.

Menu Planning

Planning a Chinese menu is quite different from planning a Western one. First of all there is no main dish. Instead there are series of dishes which roughly correspond to the number of people at the table. The portions at a Chinese restaurant normally require a one-to-one ratio. The size of portions in this book would approximate one dish for every one and a half persons. When an unexpected guest joins the family for dinner, a whole new dish is prepared instead of trying to stretch the prepared dinner to include an additional mouth. In this respect Chinese meals are similar to a buffet. Each person serves himself, taking what he wants and leaving what he doesn't care for.

Because of the number of dishes involved in preparing a Chinese meal, we would not recommend that the beginning Chinese cook start off by trying to cook a full Chinese meal. Instead we would recommend preparing one Chinese dish and filling in with more familiar non-Chinese dishes until a repertoire of recipes has been mastered that can be comfortably put together to make a complete meal.

Once the number of dishes to be served has been determined, the fun of putting together a menu begins. The central idea is variety and contrast, in other words, to put together an interesting meal full of complementary surprises. Try to avoid using the same meat or vegetable in two dishes. Look for a variety of tastes: sweet, sour, hot, bitter, and salty are the five classic Chinese flavors, but consider the need for a bland or refreshing dish between two strongly flavored ones. Be aware of texture: contrast the smoothness of bean curd with the crispness of stir-fried vegetables, for example. Akin to texture, try to avoid having more than one dish that is shredded, cut in chunks, or sliced.

For practical as well as aesthetic reasons, it is wise to vary your method of cooking. Try to avoid more than two stir-fried dishes for any single meal. Stir-fried dishes require last-minute attention and must be served immediately if their special character is to be preserved. Try adding a deep-fried dish which can be prepared some time in advance and kept warm in the oven or warmed up by a hot sauce poured over it, as in most sweet-and-sour dishes. Consider the virtues of some of the longer-cooking braised dishes which can cook happily away with a minimum of attention and can even be reheated. For this reason we find it hard to resist adding a red-cooked roast to a menu for any large dinner party. And don't forget soups, which may be properly served at any time during the meal. Look for dishes that can be steamed, for they do not require attention while they are cooking and generally are not harmed if they are slightly overcooked. There are also many excellent cold dishes that are served at room temperature.

Perhaps most important, take into account the number of burners on your stove. If you have four, like most people, save one for rice unless you have an electric rice maker, an excellent invention that not only saves a burner for other use but has the added virtue of cooking the rice with no effort on your part save pushing down the "on" button about a half hour before dinner. If the three remaining burners are inadequate to your needs, think of cold dishes, or dishes that can be cooked in electric fry pans, electric Dutch ovens, electric deep fryers, or any other appliance.

If you are cooking for a large group or prefer to serve fewer dishes by doubling up on the amount, do keep in mind that really no more than one pound of meat with vegetables can be successfully stir-fried in one wok or average-sized skillet at any one time. It should also be kept in mind that doubling any recipe does not automatically mean doubling the salt, in particular, and other herbs and spices as well. Start with the basic recipe and add "to taste."

Suggested Menus

The following are menus for dinner parties we have given which illustrate some of the principles of menu planning.

1. DINNER FOR 6

Watercress Soup (southern)
Yunnan Lamb with Curry and Black Beans (western)
Fukienese Scallion Beaded "Spareribs" (eastern)
Lemon Chicken (western)
Roast Pork with Chinese Vegetables (southern)
Boiled Rice

This dinner was given in the summer, so there was a desire to keep it somewhat light. Only two of the dishes, the lamb and the roast pork, had to be stir-fried at the last minute. The "spare ribs" were deep-fried ahead of time and kept warm in the oven, and the sauce was reheated on a back burner.

The Lemon Chicken was chosen because of its refreshing citrus taste and light tang from the hot peppers. It balanced the Yunnan Lamb with Curry and Black Beans which was considerably more robust. The Scallion Beaded "Spareribs" added a very subtle sweet-and-sour flavor. A stronger sweet-and-sour taste would have made the meal appear heavier than we wanted. The Roast Pork with Chinese Vegetables provided the major vegetable dish.

The menu played up a subtle range of sour, hot, and salty tastes. The sour tastes ranged from lemon to red wine vinegar, the hot tastes from hot green peppers to curry, the salty tastes from black beans to a hint of light soy sauce. The mixture of textures in this meal could have been improved by substituting Diced Roast Pork with Chinese Vegetables or Lettuce Packages for the Roast Pork with Chinese Vegetables. As it turned out, the lamb was sliced, the "spareribs" served in chunks, the chicken was shredded. A diced or minced dish would have added one more dimension.

2. A DINNER OF "ROLLS"

There are many people who just love dough-filled or batter-filled dishes. This dinner was planned for such people at an informal occasion where the guests were asked to put on an apron and help prepare the dinner.

Cantonese Egg Rolls (southern)
Shanghai Spring Rolls (eastern)
Peking Pork Rolls (northern)
Steamed Jao-tze with Lamb Filling (northern)
Curried Pork Rolls (western)

Each filling was quite different and each of the wrappers had a different texture which adds to the interest of the meal. There is a lot of chopping and preparing for this meal. But it is great fun if you have a large kitchen for an evening of continuous cooking, talking, and eating.

3. COLD SUMMER SUPPER FOR 6

Asparagus Salad (eastern)
Barbecue Spareribs (southern)
Pon Pon Chicken (western)
Mandarin Noodles (northern)

Everything can be made ahead of time except for the spareribs which were reheated for a few minutes under the broiler. In fact, we took this dinner to a friend's house for a pool-side picnic.

4. DINNER FOR 6

Shark's Fin Soup (southern)
Chicken Filled with Glutinous Rice (southern)
Abalone, Crab Meat, and Miniature Corn (southern)
Thrice-Cooked Pork (northern)
Asparagus Salad (northern)
Boiled Rice

This dinner was given for people who really appreciated Chinese cooking. Shark's fin is very expensive and the soup took a great deal of advance preparation. The Chicken Filled with Glutinous Rice also requires advance preparation, the deboning of a chicken, and a good deal of trouble, but it is well worth the effort. Only one dish required last-minute stir-frying.

5. FUKIENESE DINNER FOR 6

Fukienese Dumplings in Soup
Abalone with Miniature Corn and Straw Mushrooms
Braised Chicken in Red Wine Paste
Fukienese Pork with Scallion Sauce
Fukienese Crab Rolls
Boiled Rice

As noted elsewhere in this book, Fukienese cooking is very delicate in its seasonings. Seafood is plentiful and red wine sediment paste is a specialty of the region.

6. SHANGHAI DINNER FOR 6

Shanghai Spring Rolls
Sizzling Rice Soup
Lion's Head
Ten Varieties Dish
Rock Sugar Chicken
Boiled Rice

7. NORTHERN DINNER FOR 6

Mandarin Cucumber Soup
Stir-Fried Lamb and Leeks
Ju Ling Chicken
Shrimp with Hoisin Sauce
Creamed Chinese Cabbage
Boiled Rice

8. WESTERN DINNER FOR 6

Kung Pao Chicken
Hunan Lamb
Shrimp Puff in Ginger Sauce
Hunan Family-Style Eggplant
Boiled Rice

9. SOUTHERN DINNER FOR 6

Watercress Soup
Braised Chicken in Chinese Mushroom Sauce
Lettuce Packages
Sweet-and-Sour Fish
Beef with Asparagus
Boiled Rice

Larger and More Formal Dinners or Banquets

BANQUET DINNER FOR 10

Appetizers
Tea Eggs (northern)
Red-Cooked Chicken Livers (eastern)
Shrimp Toast (eastern)

Main courses
Watercress Soup (southern)
Drunken Chicken (northern)
Sweet-and-Sour Fish (southern)
Potato Duck (northern)
Crab Salad (southern)
Spicy Ground Pork and Bean Curd (western)
Boiled Rice

Dessert
Canned Lychees and Loquats
Tea

This banquet dinner requires very little last-minute preparation. The appetizers were served with cocktails, which is the way we normally do it even though it is not traditional. After the soup was served and the soup bowls cleared away, we served the Drunken Chicken and the Sweet-and-Sour Fish. To make the fish dish easy and quick to serve, the fish was deep-fried ahead of time and kept warm in the oven. The sweet-and-sour sauce was prepared and kept in a small pot, ready to be reheated. Just before serving, the fish was placed on a serving plate and the heated sauce poured over it. ____

After these dishes were consumed, we brought out the Potato Duck and the Cucumber Salad. About halfway through, and before everyone was too full to eat any more, the Spicy Ground Pork and Bean Curd and Boiled Rice were brought to the table. At this point, not many people had room for rice.

At banquets like this we place copies of the entire menu at the table so that our guests will pace themselves accordingly.

CLASSIC CHINESE BANQUET
The classic Chinese banquet, which is basically Cantonese, consisting of 12 to 15 dishes, also features three soups. Except for the appetizers, each of the dishes is served separately. The meal lasts two to three hours.

Appetizers
Sweet-and-Sour Spareribs (southern)
Diced Shrimp with Chinese Vegetables (southern)
Red-cooked Chicken Livers (eastern)

Main courses
First soup: Shark's Fin Soup (southern)
Chicken with Ham and Broccoli (eastern)
Deep-Fried Squab (southern)
Braised Chinese Black Mushrooms (southern)

Second soup: Chicken Filled With Bird's Nest (southern)
Fried Fish Fillet with Chinese Vegetables (southern)
Crab or Lobster Roll (eastern)
Duck with Coriander (southern)
Yangchow Fried Rice (eastern)
Third soup: Almond Soup (southern)

SNACKS AND MIDNIGHT SNACKS

In China the affluent were very fond of snacks and particularly midnight snacks following an evening of talk or Mah-Jongg. The American equivalent, of course, is a midnight snack after bridge. We have found noodles to be a real hit for such purposes. Only one course is served and everything is prepared ahead of time except for the last-minute stir-frying. Dumplings are also very good, although these require a bit more preparation.

Chinese Eccentricities and Miscellaneous Concerns

Many will read the section above and ask: "But what about desserts?" The answer is that there are very few. If you wish to be completely authentic, you will end your dinner without dessert or at the most with a bowl of Chinese fruits, for example, loquats, logans, lychees, mandarin oranges, peaches. Sweet dishes are sometimes served either between courses in much the way that the sherbet refreshes the mouth between courses of an English banquet or else they are served as a snack between meals. We have, however, included a few desserts, namely, Peking Dust Glazed Apples and Almond Soup.

As to what should be served as a beverage with the meal, that is problematic. Traditionally, rice wine was served with any important meal. On the other hand, tea was served with most meals, although in some parts of China clear soups serve the same purpose. Since rice wine does not travel well and is not easy to find, we would suggest that you substitute either a chablis or a claret if you are interested in a wine with dinner. Beer is also remarkably good with Chinese food. In the United States at Chinese banquets, a bottle of whiskey is frequently set out on the table. This whiskey is traditionally drunk neat without water, soda, or ice, and we sometimes wonder how people survive to the end of the banquet. In point of fact, anything of your choosing may be served as long as it fulfills the primary function of cleansing the palate between courses and leaving a minimum of aftertaste to interfere in the appreciation of the course to come.

Serving Chinese

An informal Chinese table setting usually consists of a pair of chopsticks, a bowl for soup and rice, a saucer for soy sauce, a porcelain spoon, and a tiny teacup. Soup is usually served first and then the empty soup bowls are filled with rice. Serving spoons are never used in the traditional Chinese table setting. All the dishes are placed in the center of the table where everyone can reach them to serve themselves. The Chinese prefer round tables because it makes it easier for each one to reach for everything on the table. If you are using a long table it may be necessary to divide your portions in half and put them on both ends of the table so that they can be easily reached.

So far as etiquette is concerned you are supposed to eat only those pieces which are facing you, and you do not reach for anything which you already have in your bowl until you have finished it. When eating rice it is proper and necessary to hold the bowl up to your mouth with your left hand while you shovel the rice in with the chopsticks with your right hand.

How to Hold Chopsticks

In holding chopsticks it is very important to know the different functions of the upper and lower chopsticks. The lower chopstick is the stationary one and is held at the base between the thumb and index finger (A) and the first knuckle of the ring finger (B). The upper chopstick acts as a fulcrum (C). The tips of the thumb, index finger, and middle finger hold the chopstick farther down on the other end (D) like a pencil. Be sure that the chopsticks are even so that the two ends will meet. When picking up a piece of food the middle finger pushes upward at (D) so that the tips of the chopsticks are opened in order to fit a piece of food between the tips. Then the index finger pushes down at (D) so that the tip of the upper chopstick pinches the food against the fixed chopstick.

HOW TO HOLD CHOPSTICKS

INGREDIENTS FOR CHINESE COOKING

Shopping for Ingredients

It used to be that the most difficult part of Chinese cooking was tracking down the ingredients. It was not that the writers of cookbooks did not try very hard to substitute hard-to-find ingredients for items that could not be found at the supermarket or to avoid strange ingredients. It was simply that outside of a few major Chinatowns such as those in New York and San Francisco these ingredients simply could not be found. Even in New York or San Francisco one could run into difficulty finding ingredients used predominantly in non-Cantonese cooking since most of the customers in these shops were Cantonese.

Fortunately, the situation has changed considerably and for the better. More Chinese markets have opened, many of them outside the traditional confines of Chinatowns, and they are stocking a wider variety of goods. The reasons would appear to be several: a new influx of immigrants from different parts of China, the resumption of trade with the People's Republic of China, and most of all a dramatic growth of interest in Chinese cooking on the part of the American public, not only to eat in restaurants but to prepare at home.

For all our talk about improvements in Chinese grocery stores, we should mention those ingredients for Chinese cooking that are available in the American supermarket. Our supermarket, in fact, provides us with most of the ingredients we need to prepare the recipes in this book. For example, we can find there on a regular to sporadic basis: water chestnuts, bamboo shoots, fresh and canned bean sprouts, celery cabbage, Chinese cabbage, sweet and hot peppers, gingerroot, scallions, leeks, garlic, frozen snow peas, long-grain rice, cooking fats and oils, many spices and dried herbs, as well as most of the meat, poultry, and seafood. About the only important ingredient we do not buy at the supermarket is soy sauce since the American and even the imported brands sold there are too salty, watery, and unflavorful to be used for cooking. But if domestic soy sauce is the only kind available, cut down the amount of salt in the recipes and use a richer chicken stock where water or stock is called for.

Nonetheless, anyone seriously interested in Chinese cooking will have to find a Chinese market sooner or later. This is not as difficult as it may sound and it will not mean that you have to replenish your Chinese larder very often, for most of the ingredients you will be buying there will keep for some time, if not indefinitely, either in the refrigerator or on the shelf. A basic Chinese shopping list of such ingredients would include light soy sauce, dark soy sauce, sesame oil, dried hot peppers, brown bean sauce, black beans, hoisin sauce, oyster sauce, gingerroot, five-flavor powder, star anise, Chinese black mushrooms, and Szechwan peppercorns. Even if you live in the country, the chances are that you will be able to find a Chinese market in whatever medium-to-large city you visit from time to time where you can stock up on canned and dried goods. The markets are often open on Saturday evenings and Sundays when other stores are closed. Indeed, these days are often the busiest of the week and their stock is usually at its best at this time.

There are several ways of tracking down a Chinese market by using the Yellow Pages of the telephone directory. If you think there might be a Chinatown someplace in your particular city, check the restaurant listings in the Yellow Pages. If you find a number of Chinese restaurants located on the same street, chances are that there is a Chinatown, perhaps only a block or two long, but at least one Chinese grocery is likely to be found there. A second more precise way is to check the Yellow Pages under "Oriental goods" where art galleries and gift shops are listed along with Oriental grocers. The problem with this method is that not all of the Oriental groceries are necessarily listed under this heading and not all of the Oriental groceries will carry a full line of Chinese ingredients. A third approach is to hunt for likely sounding names under "groceries" and then call the place to find out if it is really what the name would seem to indicate. Do not overlook health food stores and gourmet shops as a source of some unusual ingredients. Neighborhoods surrounding large universities seem to attract stores carrying Oriental foodstuffs, so keep your eyes open if you are in such an area. Finally, if all else fails, on page 306 is a list of Chinese groceries that accept mail orders.

Any problem you run into will most likely be related to language difference. For this reason we have given the Cantonese name for all ingredients that you would be likely to ask for in a Chinese market. Cantonese is the most widely spoken Chinese dialect in the United States and the shopkeeper will be familiar with the Cantonese names for various items even if the English name has him scratching his head. In some cases, we have also given more than one English name for an ingredient, since labels vary from brand to brand. But when in doubt ask the shopkeeper.

A word should be said about shopkeepers, however. Their English is not always the best, but somebody in the store, another clerk or even another customer, can usually help you out. On the other hand, they work hard to keep their regular customers, and if they get to know you as one, don't be surprised if they offer to "special order" some item for you that they ordinarily do not stock.

Meats

In our recipes, we have been deliberately vague about the appropriate cuts of meat since you will be guided by availability, price, and other considerations, but we can provide a few guidelines and tips on what to buy.

PORK

Just about any meaty cut will do. Boneless fresh hams are expensive, but certainly have their merits in their ease of handling. Our next choice would be the butt half of a fresh ham which provides a great deal of meat with a minimum of bone. It is also an uncomplicated job to remove the large leg muscles from the bone intact. This job is more difficult when you attack a pork shoulder or fresh picnic ham. Pork loin is fairly easy to bone, but it is a considerably more expensive cut.

BEEF

It is a bit silly to use tender cuts of beef for Chinese cooking since nearly all recipes call for thin slices across the grain and marinating. Also the marbling that makes prime meats tender interferes with the even slicing which is so important to Chinese cooking. The easiest cut to handle is flank steak which is lean and boneless and has a well-defined grain. Unfortunately, it has become woefully overpriced. Chuck and round steak are less expensive, but will result in more waste in the form of fat and bones.

CHICKEN AND DUCK

The Chinese are very fussy about chicken. Thrifty though they be in other ways, they think nothing of paying a premium for freshly killed chicken and prefer if possible that it be a pullet that has not laid an egg. For freshly killed chicken, try either a Chinese or a kosher butcher. Italian markets also sometimes have freshly killed fowl. If you cannot locate a pullet that has not laid an egg, a roasting chicken would be your next choice and after that a fryer.

As to duck, unless you have a poultry farmer for a friend or have access to a genuine farmer's market, it is unlikely you are going to find any duck other than the frozen Long Island ducklings. This is not disastrous since Long Island ducks are the descendants of a prized breed of Chinese duck. The only problem with these frozen ducklings is that they are sometimes quite difficult to seal up when you want to put a sauce inside them or pump them full of air as in the case of Peking Duck. Even so, difficult though it may be, we have never come upon a duck that could not be sealed if we tried long enough.

Fish

The most important criterion for fish is that it be absolutely fresh with clear eyes, red gills, and no strong fishy odor. The Chinese prefer firm, meaty, unoily, white-fleshed fish with a minimum of bones. Of American fishes, sea bass is the first choice. After that would come such fish as porgy, cod, scrod, pike, striped bass, butterfish, snapper, and carp. Although pompano and bluefish have dark flesh, they are otherwise desirable. A consultation with your fishmonger will help you choose an acceptable fish if you let him know how you plan to cook it. When cooking a whole fish, the Chinese prefer to keep the head and tail on. If you are squeamish, this is not essential, although some of the juices will be lost by removing them. If you do decide to serve the fish whole, have the fish cleaned, scaled, the fins and gills removed. By all means, when eating your whole fish don't overlook the fish's cheek which yields a tasty morsel.

List of Ingredients

In the following alphabetical listing, you will find descriptions of all the ingredients needed in the recipes in this book. The list includes vegetables as well as herbs, spices, and other exotica. Substitutions are given where advisable.

ABALONE (BAUYU)

The flesh of this mollusk can be found canned in most Chinese and Japanese groceries. Canned abalone is already cooked so that it needs nothing more than warming in most dishes. In fact, overcooking will only make it tough. Very thinly sliced it makes a useful hors d'oeuvre or constituent of a cold platter.

BAMBOO SHOOTS (JOOK SOON)

One of the most versatile Chinese plants, bamboo is cultivated throughout the southern half of China. It is valued not only for the edible shoots of many of the species, but also as an important source of timber (actually it is a grass) used for houses, bridges, furniture. rope, and paper.

The ivory-colored shoots of this plant can be found canned in Oriental food stores and, occasionally, in supermarkets in this country. The shoots are canned either whole or thinly sliced. Once the can is opened, the bamboo shoots should be refrigerated in a jar filled with water. If the water is changed every few days, the shoots will last for a month.

BEAN CURD (DOW FOO)

These white custard-like squares are sold fresh and by the piece at Chinese and Japanese markets. Their flavor is very bland and their texture smooth. High in protein, they are sometimes referred to as the poor man's meat. Stored in water in the refrigerator, bean curd will last a week and sometimes longer if the water is changed regularly.

BEAN SPROUTS (NGAH CHOY)

These delicate white sprouts of mung beans (*look dow*) can be found fresh in Oriental markets and some health food stores, but they should not be confused with the larger, coarser soy bean sprouts.

The fresher sprouts will keep for a few days in a bag in the refrigerator. The canned variety should be transferred to a glass jar after being opened. Fill the jar with water, cover, and store in the refrigerator for up to two weeks, changing the water every few days. The canned sprouts last longer because they have been blanched. As a consequence they lack the crispness of fresh sprouts.

Bean sprouts may also be raised at home from dried mung beans that can be found in Oriental or health food stores. To cultivate your very own sprouts, soak a handful of the beans in warm water at least overnight. Spread a linen dish towel over a rack in a roasting pan. Rinse the beans well under running water and then sprinkle them in a single layer across the dish towel. Cover the beans with another linen dish towel. Pour one or two cups of warm water over the towel to moisten the beans thoroughly. Place the pan in a dark place to keep the sprouts white. Water the towel as needed to keep it moist, discarding any accumulated water in the bottom of the pan each time. At the end of about five days the sprouts should be three inches long and ready to eat.

Before being used the sprouts should be rinsed well in a sink of water. For aesthetic reasons the little green caps are usually removed. If one is a perfectionist, the little dark roots should be snipped off too.

BIRD'S NEST (YIN WAW)

A great delicacy, bird's nest is really the dried salival secretion of a small swallow, used to line its nest. It is sold in boxes usually of four or six ounces. There are several grades, the most expensive being a whole intact nest. The nest grade comes in chips that are sometimes poetically called "dragon's teeth." Least desirable are ground-up bird's nest fragments. Sold in Chinese groceries only, bird's nest will keep indefinitely in the pantry.

BITTER MELON (FOO QUA)

A favorite of the Cantonese, who relish its cool, bitter flavor, this vegetable roughly resembles a cucumber in size and shape but has a dark green alligator-like skin. It is also known as a balsam pear. It will keep in the vegetable crisper of the refrigerator for up to a week. Before cooking, the seeds should be removed and the melon simmered for about three minutes to reduce the bitterness. There is no substitute for this unique vegetable.

BLACK BEANS   (DOW SEE)

A favorite ingredient of ours with a strong affinity for garlic, black beans are sold in one-pound cans or plastic bags of varying sizes in Chinese stores. Sometimes called fermented black beans to differentiate them from a less commonly used dried black bean, these soft beans have a salty, pungent odor. They need to be soaked or thoroughly rinsed under running water before they are used. Bruising them with the handle of a cleaver or the back of a spoon releases their flavor. They should be stored in an airtight container either in a cool pantry or in the refrigerator and should last indefinitely.

BROWN BEAN SAUCE   (MEIN SEE)

Called "miso" by the Japanese, this full-bodied salty sauce can be found in one-pound tins in Chinese and Japanese markets. The brown beans should be bruised with the handle of a cleaver or with the back of a spoon to release the flavors before being added to other ingredients in a dish. If placed in a glass jar in the refrigerator, this sauce will keep for months.

BROWN SUGAR

See sugar.

CELERY CABBAGE   (SIU CHOY)

Called Tientsin cabbage in the north of China where it originated, this vegetable is distinguished for its broad, tightly packed leaves and pale yellow-white color tinged around the edges with pale green. Its first cousin can be found in many supermarkets. The true item is found in Oriental groceries. It will keep for at least a week in the vegetable section of your refrigerator.

CELLOPHANE NOODLES   (FUN SEE)

Thin, dried white noodles made of mung bean flour, cellophane noodles become transparent when soaked in warm water and are thus true to their name. When used in a stir-fried dish, they have a blotterlike capacity for soaking up water, so care must be taken to add more liquid if necessary. They have no flavor of their own but absorb surrounding flavors. Unfortunately, if overcooked or reheated, the noodles become shapeless and mushy. Deep-fried, these noodles turn chalk white and very crisp, making an excellent garnish, perhaps most effectively used against the red shell of a lobster.

CHICKEN STOCK

From a nutritional, economic, and culinary standpoint, we should all have a stockpot simmering away on the back burner; however, most of us do not make a stock or only rarely, since the soup section of our supermarkets offer great convenience in a can. Unfortunately, canned chicken broth is highly variable and it is worth trying several brands before settling on a preferred one.

CHILI PASTE WITH GARLIC

Sometimes called Szechwan paste, this sauce is found in six-ounce jars in Chinese markets. There is really no substitute for it. But in desperation you may add 1 teaspoon of crushed red pepper for each tablespoon of the paste and increase the garlic called for by about 1 teaspoon. If refrigerated after opening, this paste will keep indefinitely.

CHINESE BLACK MUSHROOMS   (DUNG GOO)

These come dried and must be soaked for 15 to 30 minutes. The Japanese call them "shiitake." They are highly prized in Chinese cooking and are relatively expensive. In China, the best ones come from the south where they are extensively used. There is no substitute for these mushrooms.

CHINESE BROCCOLI   (GUY LON)

This vegetable is not always available in Chinese markets, but it is worth watching for. The flavor is definitely sweeter and more subtle than conventional broccoli. It is similar in color to supermarket broccoli but its stalks are thinner, the tips are leafier, and it sometimes has little yellow flowers, which should be removed before slicing. It will keep for about a week in the vegetable crisper of the refrigerator.

CHINESE CABBAGE   (BOK CHOY)

Some supermarkets stock this vegetable as do Chinese groceries. It has long white stalks and dark green leaves with little yellow flowers which are removed before slicing. There is also a smaller more delicate version called *choy sum. Choy sum* is more expensive than *bok choy.* Both the leaves and the stems can be used although the tender leaves are always added at the end of the cooking process. Although substitutions are not recommended for this fairly common vegetable, blanched celery can be substituted in stir-fry dishes where the crunchiness of the stem is desired and either celery cabbage or iceberg lettuce for the leaves. *Bok choy* keeps for about a week in the crisper section of a refrigerator.

CHINESE CHIVES   (GOW CHOY)

Sometimes confusingly labeled scallions in Chinese groceries, the long leaves of this vegetable look like a cross between those of chives and scallions, but the Chinese chives lack the bulb of the scallion. The taste of these chives is distinctive and pungent. There is no acceptable substitute. Chives need a careful washing to remove the grit around the base of the roots. They will keep for about a week in the crisper section of a refrigerator.

CHINESE EGG NOODLES   (DON MEIN)

These long thin noodles can be found both fresh and dried in Chinese markets. They are somewhat more rubbery than spaghetti and take a bit longer to cook. Legend has it that noodles were introduced to Europe by Marco Polo on his return from China in the thirteenth century. However, recent evidence indicates that the noodle may have wiggled its way to India by the eleventh century where seafaring Arab merchants discovered its delights and brought it to the Mediterranean world.

CHINESE MUSTARD   (GAI LAT)

Also called English mustard, this condiment can be found in dried or paste form in many supermarkets and gourmet stores as well as in Chinese groceries. It is less expensive to make your own paste from the dried English mustard. To do this you simply add some boiling water to some English dried mustard to make a thin paste. Sprinkle the paste with a little salt and let it stand for at least twenty minutes. As it cools, it will thicken slightly.

CHINESE MUSTARD CABBAGE   (GUY CHOY)

Guy choy resembles Chinese cabbage but is smaller, and both the stems and the leaves are a dark green. It has a bittersweet taste and is often used in soups and occasionally in stir-fried dishes. Supermarket mustard greens are an acceptable substitute.

CHINESE ROAST PORK   (CHAR SHEW)

Sometimes called Cantonese roast pork, *char shew* can be bought by the pound in Chinese markets or it can be made at home according to the recipe on page 203. If you live near a large Chinatown, it is worth shopping around until you find a source of roast pork that you particularly like, since the flavor varies considerably from store to store. In making roast pork the Chinese use special ovens which give the meat a character that cannot be achieved in conventional ovens. However, the homemade version is almost as good as the Chinese version and is certainly worth making if a Chinatown is not nearby. *Char shew* can be used as an ingredient in more complex dishes, or it is delicious as is, thinly sliced with a small saucer of soy sauce for a dip.

CHINESE SAUSAGE (LOP CHONG)

Although Chinese sausage is sometimes called Cantonese sausage, there are actually two types of sausage, pork and duck's liver with pork. Both need to be steamed for about fifteen minutes before being eaten. One classic and simple way of steaming them is to put them on top of a pot of rice once the excess water has boiled off. The sausages are thus cooked and also delicately flavor the rice.

CINNAMON

The cinnamon used in China is actually the bark of the cassia tree rather than that of the true cinnamon tree. If truth be known, they are first cousins, the Chinese variety being somewhat less refined than its Indian and Malaysian relative. The recipes in this book are based on the cinnamon stick found in supermarkets.

CLOUD EARS (WUN YE)

Also known as woods' ears and trees' ears, this dried fungus expands five or six times its size on soaking in warm water. It has a delicate taste and a wonderful crunchy quality. Like any dried ingredient, it keeps indefinitely on the pantry shelf. If you have a choice between a larger variety and a smaller one, choose the smaller. There is no substitute for cloud ears.

CORIANDER (YUEN SAI)

This pungent fresh herb is also known as Chinese parsley, in Italian markets as *cilantro*, and in Spanish markets as *culantro*. It resembles regular parsely in appearance but has quite a different flavor. It is used primarily as a garnish. If you have trouble finding coriander, either substitute chopped scallions or try growing some of your own. To do this, you need seeds from a garden supply house or from the spice rack of your supermarket. Before planting them, crush the seeds gently between the palms of your hands. After planting them, keep the soil moist. They germinate in about two weeks. Unfortunately this herb has a taproot and so is not amenable to being grown in a container. Fresh coriander can be kept for about a week in the vegetable compartment of a refrigerator.

CORNSTARCH

In China the favored thickener is lotus root flour. However, this flour is difficult and expensive to obtain in this country and cornstarch has become the universally accepted substitute. Wheat flour is not acceptable for it clouds the sauce. Arrowroot can be used but it is expensive and sauces made from it cannot be reheated or held for any length of time.

When used as a thickener cornstarch is always mixed with water, so that when it is added to the sauce lumps will be avoided. Cornstarch settles very quickly in water so that it must be stirred again just before it is added to the pan.

The amount of cornstarch needed to thicken a given sauce is a highly variable matter and reflects the amount of moisture given off by the ingredients, the intensity of the flame which affects the rate of evaporation and the time needed to cook the dish. The amount of cornstarch we have given in the recipes is simply the amount that has worked for us and our ingredients. We have tried to note whether the gravy should be thick or only lightly thickened, and this should serve as your guide. When in doubt use less cornstarch, for "gooey gravies" all the time is the sign of a bad cook.

Foods to be deep-fried are often dredged in cornstarch to seal in the juices and insure a nice brown crust. Cornstarch is also mixed into ground meat dishes to act as a binder and to hold in the juices.

CRUSHED RED PEPPER

These flakes are finely minced dried red peppers with the seeds included. They are widely used in western Chinese cooking and can be found on most supermarket spice shelves. Substitutes are numerous: cayenne, Tabasco, fresh hot peppers with the seeds removed, and whole dried red peppers. If using cayenne or Tabasco, start with ¼ teaspoon for each dish and add on to taste. If using fresh hot peppers, you will need to use twice the amount specified in the recipe. Store the flakes as you would any spice.

CURRY POWDER   (GAR LAY)

This powder was introduced from India centuries ago and is a popular seasoning in the south and west where it is said to help perspiration in a hot humid climate. The hot Madras-style curry powder is preferred, and it is the one most frequently found on the shelves of Chinese markets. The usual supermarket variety cannot match the Madras style in hotness and richness of flavor. Store curry powder as you would any spice.

DARK SOY SAUCE   (SEE AU)
See Soy Sauces.

DRIED BEAN CURD   (TIEM JOOK)
This dried soy milk sediment comes in thick shiny sheets.

DRIED BEAN CURD SHEETS
Packaged in a large envelope, these fragile semicircles when sprinkled with water become a soft pliable wrapper for foods to be deep-fried. The dampened pieces can be overlapped if necessary to make a larger wrapper. They will keep for several months in the pantry.

DRIED LOTUS NUTS   (LIEN GEE)
Sold by weight in Chinese markets. No substitute.

DRIED SCALLOPS   (GONG YU GEE)
Small cylinders about one inch in diameter, dried scallops are used in *jook* and other long-cooking dishes. They are available in Chinese markets and will keep indefinitely on your pantry shelf.

DRIED RED PEPPERS
May be found in Chinese groceries. Substitute ½ teaspoon crushed red peppers for every red pepper called for in the recipe. They will keep indefinitely on the pantry shelf.

DRIED SHRIMP   (HAR MEI)
These tiny salty shrimp may be bought in Chinese or Japanese stores. They are occasionally used in stir-fried dishes, in which case they have to be soaked first. More often they are used in soups, *jook*, and other long-simmering dishes and do not need the initial soaking.

DRY SHERRY
In China rice wine rather than grape wine is used both as a beverage and for cooking. Unfortunately rice wine does not travel well and is difficult to find in the United States. Dry sherry is the best substitute for rice wine. So-called cooking sherry is not recommended because the seasonings added to it will throw off the flavorings in the recipes. In China as elsewhere wine is valued not only for its flavor but also for its tenderizing qualities and ability to deodorize fish. Rice wine is used throughout China but in the north, *kaoliang*, a grain-based liquor, is sometimes used instead.

EGGPLANT

Chinese eggplant is the size of a cucumber and has a white skin. Our purple variety is an excellent substitute.

EGG ROLL SKIN   (CHUEN GUEN PAY)

See Wonton skin

FISH MAW   (YU TOE)

Used in soups and occasionally in stir-fried dishes, fish maw is prized for its texture and lack of fishy taste. It is the dried and deep-fried stomach lining of fish and comes in large curved pieces. It needs to be soaked before being used. It can be bought in Oriental food stores. There is no substitute and it should be omitted from the recipe if it cannot be found. Like all dried foods it is not perishable, but after several months it may become rancid.

FIVE-FLAVOR POWDER   (HEUNG NEW FUN)

Sometimes called five-fragrance spice powder, this is made up of Szechwan peppercorns, star anise, fennel seeds, cinnamon, and cloves. While one can make this spice at home, two of the ingredients must be bought at a Chinese market anyway so the prepackaged version is recommended. Since five-flavor powder is quite powerful, it is rare to use more than ½ teaspoon in any given dish. It should be stored as one would any other spice in the pantry.

FRESH HOT PEPPERS, RED OR GREEN   (SUN SEEN LOT CHEEL)

Chinese hot peppers are only about three or four inches long and very hot, hotter in fact than the larger chili peppers which are frequently stuffed. The seeds must be removed before they are cooked but take care not to touch your eyes without washing your hands first during this process. Caustic is the only word for the juice of these uncooked peppers. If hot peppers make your hands burn, apply fresh cream.

These peppers may be found in Chinese, Italian, and Spanish groceries. They last about two weeks in the vegetable compartment of the refrigerator and, if need be, frozen, although they lose their crispness. A half-teaspoon of crushed red pepper which can be found on supermarket spice racks may be substituted for every four fresh red peppers.

FUZZY MELON   (JEET QUA)

Sometimes called hairy melon or summer melon, this vegetable is about the size and shape of a cucumber except that as the name implies it has hairs all over the skin. It is a very nice melon that has a slightly more delicate flavor than cucumber and does not have as many seeds. It will keep in the refrigerator for about two weeks and should be peeled before cooking. Zucchini as well as cucumbers are perfectly acceptable substitutes.

GARLIC   (SUEN JEE)

An important ingredient in Chinese cooking, garlic is used with discretion in the south and east of China and with at times wild enthusiasm in the north and west. Garlic can be bought at the supermarket or at an Oriental grocery. We suggust you buy your garlic at the latter establishment because the heads are generally quite a bit larger than their boxed cousins in the supermarket and thus easier to peel and handle. We have tried where possible to avoid using the clove as the unit of measure in our recipes because of the considerable variation in size among garlic cloves. Where we have been forced to use the term clove we are referring to a big fat one about the size of the end joint of your little finger.

Garlic can be stored for many months in a cool dry place as you would onions or potatoes. To peel garlic, give the clove a good whack with a flat object like the wide blade of a Chinese cleaver. This will loosen the skin and make peeling a much easier operation.

For fun, plant a clove of garlic in a little pot and place it on your kitchen windowsill. Keep the soil moist but not soggy and in about two weeks it will send up green leaves which can be chopped up and used as a garnish for your salads or Chinese dishes.

GIN

Gin is used as a substitute for the northern grain-based liquor *kaoliang* that is not yet widely available in this country.

GINGERROOT   (SANG GUENG)

Fresh gingerroot is one of the most important ingredients in Chinese cooking. It is used to flavor the oil in the pan when stir-frying. It is shredded and used to deodorize fish and other seafood. It is frequently used in the hot dishes of the western part of China as an important flavoring agent in its own spicy right. A tropical plant, it is used less in the north.

A light brown rhizome with horizontal ridges, it can be found in Oriental stores, some supermarkets, and in Spanish stores where it is called *jengibre*. The gingerroot should not look withered and the smoothest skinned pieces should be chosen. If only a slice is needed for a stir-fry dish, the ginger need not be peeled. If it is to be shredded, then it should be peeled.

There is no substitute for fresh gingerroot. However, there are a number of ways of keeping it over a long period of time. It will keep for more than a month in the refrigerator but not in the vegetable crisper where it may become moldy. Peeled sliced gingerroot may also be placed in a jar of dry sherry and refrigerated for several months. Finally, the traditional way is to place it in sand in a covered container. Keep the sand moist but not wet and the gingerroot will keep indefinitely. When you need a piece, just dig up the gingerroot and cut off what you need.

GOLDEN NEEDLES   (GUM JUM)

Sometimes more accurately but less poetically called dried lily buds or flowers, these three- or four-inch-long "needles" need to be soaked for thirty minutes in warm water during which time they will expand in size. They have a delicate musky taste and tend to be found somewhat more in northern cooking than elsewhere in China. They keep indefinitely in a pantry.

GREEN BEANS

We routinely substitute green beans for Chinese long beans which are not always available. Long beans which, indeed, measure a foot in length are most likely to be found in the fall if you wish to experiment with them. They will keep for a week in the vegetable crisper of a refrigerator.

HOISIN SAUCE   (HOI SIN JEUNG)

Sometimes called Peking sauce, hoisin is a dark sweet thick sauce used both as a condiment and as a cooking ingredient. Some brands have a touch of chili added while others do not. Which one to buy is a matter of personal preference. This sauce comes in both cans and jars. After a can is opened, the contents should be transferred to a glass jar and stored in the refrigerator where it will keep for months.

HOT BEAN SAUCE   (LOT MEIN SEE)

Sold in six-ounce cans in Oriental groceries, this sauce should be transferred to a glass jar and stored in the refrigerator after opening. Brown bean sauce (MEIN SEE) combined with a touch of hot oil may be substituted.

HOT OIL   (LOT YOW)

Used as a condiment for Chinese food although sometimes used as an ingredient in cooking. Hot oil is available in Chinese markets or you can easily make your own by heating 1 cup peanut oil almost to the point of smoking, then removing the pot from the heat and adding ¼ cup crushed red pepper. The oil should turn red almost immediately. If not, return the pan to medium heat and cook until it does. When the oil has cooled, drain through cheesecloth to remove the flakes. Hot oil will keep indefinitely on the pantry shelf.

KETCHUP

Curiously enough, the word ketchup is derived from the Chinese words meaning "brine of pickled fish." The tomato-based condiment we associate with the word ketchup, however, did not originate in China but has nonetheless found its way into Chinese cooking, often in combination with another import, Worcestershire sauce.

KOSHER SALT

See Salt.

LACE FAT

The name of this lovely-looking fat is indeed descriptive. It is in fact the peritoneum or abdominal lining of a pig. It is somewhat difficult to find, but can usually be special-ordered from a sympathetic butcher who may also know it as caul fat. An excellent wrapper for fried food, it pretty much disappears in the cooking but leaves a delicate crackling taste. No substitute unfortunately.

LEEKS   (DAI GOW CHOY)

This gentle member of the onion family is most commonly used in northern cooking. Leeks are about one and one-half feet with broad leaves that merge into a white bulb at the base. Only the white part is used for cooking and care must be taken to wash out all the grit that has accumulated at the base of the leaves. Half the amount of scallions may be substituted for leeks. Leeks will keep for at least a week in the crisper of the refrigerator.

LIGHT SOY SAUCE   (SANG CHAU)

See Soy Sauces.

MINIATURE CORN   (SEEL SOOK MEI)

These tender, miniature ears of corn come canned and are found in Chinese markets. Corn, while not native to China, was introduced there by the Portuguese almost five centuries ago. Once a can is opened, its contents should be transferred to a jar where it will keep in the refrigerator for a week or more.

MONOSODIUM GLUTAMATE   (MEE JING)

This white crystalline powder is often found in Chinese recipes. It has no flavor of its own but is said to enhance the flavor of other ingredients. We do not ordinarily use M.S.G. in our cooking, for if the ingredients are fresh and reasonable skill is shown in the cooking, it is not needed. Also if too much is used, flavors are no longer enhanced. In fact they all merge together with each dish tasting not unlike the one before it.

If you wish to use M.S.G. you can do so in the knowledge that this substance was first synthesized in either Japan or China and has been widely used there for centuries. In any event, it should be added with the liquids in the recipe and in only very small amounts of no more than ¼ to ½ teaspoon for for each dish. Also keep in mind that if you double a recipe, the M.S.G. as well as the salt should not be doubled.

ONION   (CHOONG TOW)

When we speak of one medium onion, we are speaking of a common yellow onion approximately three inches in diameter.

OYSTER SAUCE   (HO YOW)

Made from the "essence" of oysters, this sauce is used both as a condiment and for cooking. It will keep indefinitely in the pantry. There is no substitute for oyster sauce. The flavor is definitely not fishy and even oyster haters find it unoffensive.

PEANUT BUTTER

See Sesame Paste.

PEANUT OIL   (FAR SUNG YOW)

Lard is the principal cooking medium in China. It has the advantage of giving a clear color and a rich flavor to whatever is cooked in it. It unfortunately has disadvantages as well: for example, dishes cooked in lard cannot be reheated; it can be used only for hot dishes or else the lard will congeal; and finally there is a general wariness about using animal fats as a result of recent medical research.

Peanut oil, on the other hand, tastes very much the same as the best Chinese lards and has none of lard's disadvantages. Other vegetable oils may be used for cooking, but the taste of peanut oil is preferred. The only exception comes in deep-frying where corn oil is preferred because of its slightly higher smoking point. Deep-frying oil can be reused until it has darkened.

PEPPER

Unless otherwise specified, finely ground black pepper should be used. White pepper is occasionally called for in light-colored dishes for purely aesthetic reasons. It is sometimes preferred because of its slightly different flavor. In any recipe black pepper can be substituted for white.

PRESERVED TURNIP   (CHUNG CHOY)

Used frequently in soups and steamed dishes, *chung choy* is sold in plastic bags in two forms, either in sheets or rolled into balls. We use a ball of *chung choy* as our basic measure in this book, but if you have the sheet variety already, use 1½ ounces for each ball stipulated. Before using *chung choy*, unwrap the ball and rinse it well under running water to remove the excess salt. *Chung choy* will keep indefinitely on the pantry shelf in a closed plastic bag or jar.

PRESSED BEAN CURD (DOW FOO GON)

This variety of bean curd is sold fresh in some Oriental markets. It is much tougher and less prone to crumble than regular bean curd. If your store does not carry pressed bean curd, the pressing is easily done at home by placing the bean curds on a shallow tray, placing another some-what smaller tray on top, and slowly stacking books on top to provide pressure. After several hours, the bean curds will be only half as thick as when you started and they will be ready to use.

RENDERED CHICKEN FAT

Chicken fat can be obtained either from a butcher or by collecting it a bit at a time from the cavity of whole chickens and freezing it until you are ready to render it. To render the fat, place it in a saucepan over medi-um heat. When the fat has melted and the residue has turned dry and brown, remove from heat and let the fat cool. Strain the fat through cheesecloth into a glass jar, cover, and store in the refrigerator. The fat keeps for a month or two but eventually becomes rancid.

Chicken fat is often used as a sauce enrichment in much the same way that the French often will stir a tablespoon of butter into their sauces just before they are served. Particularly in the south of China it is used as a cooking oil in some dishes although care must be taken to avoid burning the fat.

RED BEAN CURD   (NOM YU)

Sold in cans in Chinese markets, red bean curd is frequently labeled bean curd, but the picture on the can will show the red sauce (once again the language problem). The bean curd has been preserved, so leftovers can be stored in a covered container in the refrigerator for several months although eventually it will lose its punch.

RED RICE WINE VINEGAR

See Vinegars.

RED WINE SEDIMENT PASTE

An important ingredient in Fukienese cooking, the sauce is almost impossible to find even in the largest Chinatowns. A homemade substitute is given on page 83.

RICE FLOUR   (DONG MEIN FAN)

This flour is simply fairly coarse-ground raw rice. It is sold in Oriental groceries in one-pound bags. If you have a fairly sturdy blender, you can grind your own at home.

ROASTED PEANUTS

We are talking about the kind you buy in the supermarket in tins, which we find much easier to use than the raw unroasted variety found in a Chinese market. However, if you want to be authentic, here's how: First soak the nuts in very hot water for two minutes. Rinse them under cold water, slip off the dark skins, and then pat them dry with a towel. Heat a cup of oil in a skillet or wok. Just before the oil begins to smoke, add the blanched peanuts and turn off the heat. The peanuts should brown of their own accord. If not, turn the heat on briefly to medium. Remove the peanuts when they are a light golden brown. They will continue to cook on retained heat. If you roast your own peanuts, remember you may wish to increase the salt in the recipe slightly.

ROCK SUGAR

See Sugar.

SALT

Use regular salt in all of our recipes. Occasionally kosher salt may be specified for its greater sweetness, but an equal amount of regular salt may be substituted.

SCALLIONS   (CHOONG)

Sometimes called spring onions or green onions, scallions are sold by the bunch in most supermarkets and are used throughout China as a garnish and as a seasoning. The northern Chinese prefer the larger ones which they sometimes eat raw with bean sauce or hoisin sauce. For garnishing dishes and for use in stir-fried dishes the smaller variety is preferred. Unless noted otherwise in the recipe, use both the green and white parts of the scallion. Scallions will keep in the vegetable section of the refrigerator for more than a week.

SESAME OIL   (MA YAU)

This should be bought only in a Chinese or Japanese market. The Middle Eastern variety and the sesame oil that occasionally show up in supermarkets are not acceptable. Since sesame oil burns easily, it is added in small quantities just after the dish is removed from the heat. A little goes a long way. After a number of months it will begin to turn rancid; thus it is best to buy sesame oil in small quantities. Sesame oil does not need to be refrigerated.

SESAME PASTE   (JEE MA JEUNG)
  May be found in small jars in Chinese groceries. Substitute creamy peanut butter thinned slightly with sesame oil. Refrigerated after opening, sesame paste will keep for several months.

SESAME SEEDS   (JEE MA)
  These seeds can be bought in little tins in your supermarket or more inexpensively in Oriental, Middle Eastern, and Italian markets. There are white sesame seeds and black sesame seeds. The white variety looks more attractive in most dishes and is therefore recommended. To toast sesame seeds simply place the seeds in an ungreased pan over medium heat and shake the pan until they are golden and fragrant. Lower the heat if they appear to be burning. When they are done, remove the pan from the heat but keep shaking the pan until they stop cooking on residual heat.

SHARK'S FIN   (YU CHEE)
  Along with caviar and truffles, shark's fin is one of the most expensive foods on this earth. Fortunately, a little goes a long way. Shark's fin is sold either whole or shredded. In our recipes we call for the whole variety which means a bit more bother in preparing it, but it gives definitely superior results. Choose the palest fin available. Shark's fin is dried and will keep indefinitely in the pantry.

SMITHFIELD HAM
  Unless otherwise specified in a recipe, assume that we are talking about the cooked sliced Smithfield ham that one finds in delicatessens and some supermarkets. Smithfield ham is the closest equivalent we have in this country to Chinese ham. It is frequently used as a garnish as well as a main ingredient in Chinese dishes. Westphalian ham and prosciutto are also satisfactory substitutes. Boiled ham is not recommended but it is better than nothing.

SNOW PEAS   (SOOT DOW)
  These flat wide pea pods which are eaten whole are one of the joys of Chinese food. Sweet and succulent, they are best bought fresh in Chinese markets. Since they are not readily available in the winter, the frozen va-

riety that can be found in many supermarkets may be substituted although they are only about half as good as the fresh peas. Before using, the frozen pods should be completely defrosted and as much of the moisture as possible gently pressed from them with paper towels. If you can't get frozen snow peas, substitute regular or green peas.

SOY SAUCES

Soy sauce is certainly the most frequently used ingredient in Chinese cooking. It is also one of the most variable, ranging from light to dark, from thin to rich, from salty to almost sweet. Most important, it must be of the highest quality or else the food will suffer as a result. For this reason we urge you not to buy your soy sauce at the supermarket. American soy sauces have been artificially fermented using a chemical process and are very salty and bitter. Frequently a Japanese brand can be found at the supermarket, but this too is very thin and very salty with almost no soy flavor. Instead, go to a Chinese market to buy your soy sauce and if you live some distance away, buy several bottles, for it keeps indefinitely.

Throughout this book, we specify either light soy sauce (SANG CHAU), dark soy sauce (SEE AU), sometimes called black soy sauce, or a combination of the two. The reason for this is that the flavors are quite different. The light soy sauce is lighter in body and color than dark soy sauce, and is somewhat saltier. It is widely used in southern Chinese cooking, in light-colored dishes, soups, and as a dip. The dark soy sauce is darker in color richer in body and color, and has a slightly caramelized, less salty taste. Dark soy sauce should not be used for soups. As long as you are in a Chinese market, buy one of each and if you are confused about which is which ask the shopkeeper.

SPRING ROLL SKINS   (CHEUN GUEN PAY)

Superficially similar to egg roll skins, these skins are thinner, much more delicate in flavor, and not as widely available. Sometimes shopkeepers confuse the two in translation, for the Cantonese name for egg rolls is translated spring roll. In any event, if you can find the *real* Shanghai spring roll skins by all means try them. Besides their lack of availability, their only drawback is that they do not freeze well. A recipe may be found on p. 82.

STAR ANISE   (BOT GOK)

An important spice, *bot gok* resembles an eight-pointed star about three-fourths inch in diameter. Its licorice flavor blends well with soy sauce and also with other aromatic spices such as cinnamon and fennel. Store as you would any spice in a tightly closed container in pantry. Anise extract may sometimes be used very, very sparingly as a substitute, but in general it is best avoided entirely.

STRAW MUSHROOMS   (CHAO GOO)
These mushrooms can be found in eight-ounce cans in Chinese markets. They have a crisp texture and a light pleasant taste. Supermarket canned mushrooms can be substituted in a pinch.

SUGAR
Sugar is used with surprising frequency in Chinese cooking, but generally in small amoungs of ¼ to ½ teaspoon. The sugar, which can hardly be detected, serves to blend and harmonize the various flavors in a dish. It serves to offset slightly the saltiness of the soy sauce and it has a great ability to bring out the flavor of vegetables. Use regular granulated sugar for this purpose.

From time to time, light or dark brown sugar will be specified. Brown sugar has more body and flavor and it is usually used in greater quantity than white sugar as a major flavoring agent.

Rock sugar is favored in the Shanghai area for long-simmering dishes cooked with large quantities of soy sauce. The rock sugar is supposed to impart a deep glaze to the meat. Chinese rock sugar differs from rock candy in that it is made from less refined sugar and has a pale brown color. It may be be bought at Chinese markets but is relatively expensive. Granulated sugar is an adequate substitute.

SWEET POTATOES   (TIEM SHEE)
Introduced from South America by Portuguese traders in the sixteenth or seventeenth century, the sweet potato has a rather lowly reputation in China where it is raised principally on steep hillsides as fodder for animals and only the poorest of the poor who cannot afford rice would consider it as a food for themselves. Nonetheless, a few dishes have been developed which capitalize on its genuine culinary virtues.

SZECHWAN PEPPERCORNS   (HWA JO)
Aromatic and only mildly hot, these black peppercorns release their almost flowery scent when toasted in a dry skillet over medium heat, shaking the pan constantly to keep the peppercorns from burning. When the peppercorns have reached their peak of fragrance, remove the pan from the heat but keep shaking the pan back and forth since the peppercorns continute to cook on retained heat. At this point, they are coarsely ground with a mortar and pestle or in a blender. The peppercorns should be stored as you would any other spice in an airtight container in the pantry.

TAPIOCA FLOUR   (LING FAN)

This flour is sold by the pound in Oriental and health food stores. It should be stored like any other flour. Unfortunately there is no substitute.

TEA MELON   (CHA QUA)

Sometimes this pickled melon is sold in one-pound cans labeled sweet white cucumber even though tea melon is the literal translation of its original Chinese name. Tea melon's flavor is hard to describe, rather like a very delicate sweet pickle. It goes very nicely with steamed dishes and adds a nice zest to any sweet-and-sour recipe.

TOASTED SALT AND PEPPER

In an ungreased pan, over medium heat, toast ¼ cup salt, 3 tablespoons Szechwan peppercorns, and 1 teaspoon black peppercorns for 4 minutes, shaking the pan from time to time. When the peppercorns are fragrant and the salt slightly browned, remove the mixture from the heat and grind the peppercorns using a mortar and pestle.

TOMATO   (FON CARE)

First introduced to China about two hundred years ago and thus a relative newcomer to Chinese cooking, tomatoes are now naturalized there and are grown in many places.

VINEGARS

In this book we use a variety of vinegars, both grape wine vinegars and rice wine vinegars. All of them are rather similar and can generally be used interchangeably, keeping in mind that red rice wine vinegar is basically a dipping vinegar and thus milder than its white counterpart that is used for cooking. The white rice wine vinegar stands midway between the red and white grape wine vinegars.

WATER CHESTNUTS   (MAR TAI)

Sold in cans in Chinese markets and some supermarkets, water chestnuts are grown in water fields like rice. Occasionally, fresh water chestnuts can be found in Chinese markets. They have a dark brownish purplish skin and do resemble a chestnut. This skin must be peeled off before using. The fresh variety will keep in a jar of water in the refrigerator for about a week. The canned variety will last a month if similarly stored and if the water in the jar is changed every few days.

WATERCRESS   (SEE YONG CHOY)

The Chinese have the same appreciation as the French of the subtle tang of watercress. It is used in soups, as a garnish and as a very tenderly cooked vegetable.

WHEAT STARCH
Sold in one-pound bags in Chinese markets. No substitute.

WHITE PEPPER
See Pepper.

WHITE RICE WINE VINEGAR   (BOK CHO)
See Vinegar.

WINTER MELON   (DUNG QUA)
A handsome melon the size of a pumpkin, *dung qua* has a green skin that looks rather frosted, hence the name. It is available in Chinese markets through most of the year and is sold by the slice or by weight. The tough rind and the seeds must be removed from the white flesh before cooking. It will keep for a week or more in the vegetable crisper covered with plastic wrap.

WONTON SKINS
A recipe for Wonton and Egg Roll Skins may be found on page 253, however, it is much simpler to buy them from a Chinese grocery. They keep three or four days in the refrigerator if tightly wrapped to keep them from drying out. They also freeze very well. When you use the skins, cover them with a moist towel, for they dry out noticeably even in a few minutes. If you do not want to have both wonton and egg roll skins on hand, buy just the egg roll skins and cut them down to 3- or 4-inch squares for use as wonton skins.

WORCESTERSHIRE SAUCE
Introduced to China by its British inventors, Worcestershire sauce has found a permanent home in the Chinese cuisine, which is hardly surprising since its two main ingredients are soy sauce and vinegar.

CHINESE GROCERIES THAT ACCEPT MAIL ORDERS

Gim Fat Company, 953 Grant Avenue
San Francisco, California 94108

Wo Kee & Co., 949 Grant Avenue
San Francisco, California 94108

Kwong On Lung Co., 686 N. Spring Street
Los Angeles, California 90012

Joyce Chen, P.O. Box 3
Cambridge, Massachussets 02138

See Sun Co., 36 Harrison Avenue
Boston, Massachusetts 02111

Sun Sun Company, 34a Oxford Street
Boston, Massachusetts 02138

Wing Fat Co., 35 Mott Street
New York, New York 10013

Sam Wah Yick Kee, 2146 Rockwell Avenue
Cleveland, Ohio 44114

Adler's Fine Foods, 2014 Broadway
San Antonio, Texas 78215

Wah Young Co., 717 South King
Seattle, Washington 98104

Mee Wah Lung Co., 608 H St. N.W.
Washington, D.C. 20001

General Index

Recipe Index

Regions are indicated by (n), (s), (e), (w).

313

Index

Meatballs
  for Lion's Head (e), 47
Melon. *See* Bitter Melon; Fuzzy Melon; Tea
  Melon; Winter Melon
Minced Chicken with Lettuce Soup (s), 241
Mock Duck with Snow Peas (s), 235
Mock Szechwan Fish (w), 148
Mongolian Hot Pot (n), 119
Moo Goo Gai Peen (s), 183
Moo Shu Roo (n), 103
Mushrooms. *See* Chinese Black Mushroom;
  Chinese Mushrooms; Straw Mushrooms;
  Braised Three Mushrooms (s), 233
Mustard Cabbage Soup (s), 242

Nanking Salt Duck (e), 45
Ningpo Fried Fish Roll with Bean Curd
  Sheets (e), 59
Noodles
  Brown Bean Sauce (n), 121
  Cellophane, Beef with (s), 213
  with Chinese Chives and Roast Pork (s),
    251
  Cold Mandarin (n), 123
  Roast Pork Lo Mein (s), 251
  Soupy, Braised Beef with (w), 173
  Szechwan Sesame-Flavored (w), 172
  Three-Flavored (s), 252
  Two Sides Brown (n), 122

Onions, Beef with Peppers, Tomatoes and
  (s), 210
Oyster Sauce
  Beef with Bean Curd and (s), 214
  Chicken with (s), 181
  Clams and (s), 231
  Squab with (s), 194

Pancakes
  Mandarin (n), 123
  Moo Shu Roo (n), 103
Pan-Fried Shrimp (s), 223
Paper-Wrapped Chicken (n), 93
Peking Duck (n), 110
Peking Egg Yolks (n), 102
Peking Fried Bean Curd (n), 115
Peking Glazed Apples (n), 128
Peking Pork Rolls (n), 127
Peking Precious Pot (n), 120
Peking Salt-Cured Chicken (n), 94
Pepper, Toasted, 304
Peppers
  Beef with, Tomatoes and Onions (s), 210
  Hot, Stuffed (w), 168
Pepper Sauce. *See* Hot Pepper Sauce
Pickled Cabbage

Beef with (s), 214
Szechwan (w), 171
Pig's Feet, Red-Cooked (e), 49
Poached Fish with Hot Pepper Sauce (w),
  161
Poached Sweet-and-Sour West Lake Carp
  (e), 57
Pon Pon or Hacked Chicken (w), 140
Pork. *See also* Ham; Pig's Feet; Spare-
  ribs
  with Bitter Melon (s), 201
  with Black Beans and Broccoli (s), 199
  Braised, with Bean Curd (e), 51
  with Chinese Broccoli (e), 49
  Curried (s), 202
  Fukienese Steamed, Fish with (e), 63
  Ground, Spicy, and Bean Curd (w), 147
  Ground, Steamed
    with Chinese Sausage (s), 207
    with Ham (s), 207
    with Salted Duck Egg (s), 208
  Lion's Head Casserole (e), 47
  Moo Shu Roo (n), 103
  Roast
    with Bean Sprouts (s), 204
    Chinese (s), 203
    with Chinese Vegetables (s), 205
    Eggs with Chinese Chives and (s), 198
    Lo Mein (s), 251
    Noodles with Chinese Chives and (s),
      251
  with Scallion Sauce (e), 54
  with Sesame Seeds (e), 50
  Shanghai Red-Cooked (e), 51
  Steamed, with Preserved Turnip (s), 208
  Stir-Fried, and Scallions (n), 105
  Sweet and Pungent Fukienese Lychee
    (e), 55
  Sweet-and-Sour Cantonese (s), 200
  Thrice-Cooked (n), 104
  Twice-Cooked (w), 146
  Yu Shiang (w), 149
Pork Cantonese Steamed Dumplings (s), 257
Pork Filling
  Curried, for Buns (s), 262
  for Jao Tze (n), 125
  Roast, for Steamed Buns (s), 260
Pork Kidneys
  Liver and (w), 151
  Stir-Fried Scallops and (e), 71
Pork Liver
  Fukienese (e), 55
  and Kidney (w), 151
Pork Rolls
  Hunan Curried (w), 149
  Peking (n), 127